Germaine de Staël

Ad Feminam: Women and Literature
Edited by Sandra M. Gilbert

Christina Rossetti
The Poetry of Endurance
By Dolores Rosenblum

Lunacy of Light
Emily Dickinson and the Experience of Metaphor
By Wendy Barker

The Literary Existence of Germaine de Staël

Charlotte Hogsett

Foreword by Madelyn Gutwirth

Southern Illinois University Press
Carbondale and Edwardsville

For Sue

Printed in the United States of America

Edited by Heidi Langner
Designed by Joyce Kachergis
Production supervised by Natalia Nadraga

Library of Congress Cataloging-in-Publication Data
Hogsett, Charlotte, 1938–
The literary existence of Germaine de Staël.
(Ad feminam)
Bibliography: p.
Includes index.
1. Staël, Madame de (Anne-Louise-Germaine), 1766–1817—Criticism and interpretation. 2. Women and literature—France. I. Title. II. Series.
PQ 2431.Z5H58 1987 848'.609 87-4295
ISBN 0-8093-1387-1

Contents

Foreword

Madelyn Gutwirth

"Women," Germaine de Staël would declare in one of her plainer characterizations of their plight, "have the means neither to make the truth plain, nor to improve their lot." Aware as she was of their disbarment from discourse and from action, she yet chose to become a writer so as to effect both these ends. But the very times in which she lived and wrote—revolutionary France—had mitigated the impact of discourse, as she commented, through its inflation of vehemence in litanies of sloganeering as well as its sophistries in defense of the Terror. "Once we are constrained to abstain from the truth, we cannot be eloquent" (*Litt., II, VIII*), she claimed. Thus both the repressive political climate and the malevolence of public opinion toward women who dared to break the established social code played their part in the formulation of her writing posture.

The Revolutionary *fin de siècle*, in fact, proved an extraordinarily inauspicious moment for a woman to endeavor to carry out a writing project like hers. Three interrelated factors external to personal biography impinged upon it, forcing it into deviations, strategic withdrawals, sullen or ringing rebellions—conflicts expressed overtly or covertly or simply repressed. The first of these was an increase in open hostility to the role of women in culture. It was Rousseau who proved to be most influential in fuelling this incipient resentment. His ambivalent anxiety toward the women of Paris appears in his *Nouvelle Héloïse*, in which Saint-Preux writes to Julie that "all depends upon them: nothing is done except through or for them." He does point out at the same time that the mode of French courtship tends to denigrate women rather than to serve them. For all his praise of the intelligence and grace of the Parisiennes, Saint-Preux confides to his beloved that he "finds their overtures shocking, their flirtation repulsive, their manners devoid of modesty" (*NH*, II, XXI). Although Rousseau cannot help but admire these women for their "common sense, reason, humanity and goodness of nature," he yet concludes that none of these qualities could make them lovable, for they are nothing but meritorious honorary men, lacking in what were for him the ultimate feminine qualities of sweetness and gentleness.

The social and cultural roles of women continued to be debated, sometimes cordially, sometime viciously, through the Revolution itself, finally leading Staël to report, in 1800, that "since the revolution, men have thought it politically and morally useful to reduce women to the most absurd mediocrity." We must recall that the Revolution had been a heady moment of rising hopes for many women, as it was for all other classes of the dispossessed and unenfranchised. Women in groups and as individuals had, in numerous *cahiers*, set forth their grievances against their conditions of work, their lack of property rights or of education. Whereas some of their pleas were heard in the early expansive years of the Revolution, others went unheeded; and by the turn of the century, a number of gains, like divorce, had been attenuated or lost, especially with the institution of the Napoleonic Code in 1804.

The misogynist publicist and pamphleteer Sylvain Maréchal had reflected in his 1801 satire, *Project for a law prohibiting women from learning to read*, the final emergence into dominance of a maternal female ideal.

> If the tree of knowledge is forbidden to you
> In the gentlest of ignorance you'll dwell without rue,
> As guardians of virtue and mothers of pleasure;
> You'll live, with your innocent pasttimes, at leisure.[1]

This tendency to substitute models of motherhood for those of grace and charm, a tendency which long antedates the Revolution and is visible in such paintings as Greuze's "Well-Beloved Mother," achieved true primacy in precisely the period of Staël's maturity. Spurning the Old Regime's adulation of the women of the court and the salons, the new dispensation concerning women's nature and portion placed Staël in a posture of maximum stress as she continued to write as well as to cultivate and maintain an intellectual circle.

A concomitant development at this time was the masculine idealization in the bourgeois society of Napoleonic France of the military, technocratic, adult male.[2] The martial spirit that dominated Bonaparte's empire buttressed a huge expansion of concern with engineering, architectural, and administrative technologies. The arts, which had enjoyed a sometimes embattled position of primacy under the monarchy, were in this control-minded period relegated to the margins, and the pursuit of an artistic career lost caste in consequence as a heroic masculine calling.

Yet in this same period the romantic revolution, in full sway in England and Germany, would extoll the poet's role, conceived—as in the case of a Goethe or a Wordsworth—as a male existence lived in and through works of literature. Germaine de Staël would feel authorized by the relative abandonment of Frenchmen of the poetic vocation to appropriate for her own female uses the romantic conception of a life in art.

The tensions generated for Staël by these contemporary issues, combined with the pressures of her personal and psychic evolution, make it imperative to read her texts in the context of the problematics of her womanhood. As Virginia Woolf held, while engaging in that heresy, that it was (is?) "fatal for a woman . . . to speak consciously as a woman,"[3] it cannot be denied that Staël not infrequently did just that: in her plea for the life of Marie Antoinette, in her novels *Delphine* and *Corinne*, and in her ambitious studies *De la littérature* and *De l'Allemagne*, she often speaks openly as a woman, sometimes especially addressing women. Evidently she could not prevent herself, in her inner dividedness, from breaking out into such attempts at candor. This feature of open questing as a woman is the more arresting in an author on the rack, pulled by the divergent but passionately embraced projects of being a "man of letters" in the French or romantic mode, a nonwriting conversationalist and *salonnière*, or a beloved daughter, mother, mistress.

Yet Staël's overt statements, wrested from her ultimate project of finding a rationale for her pain, are less fascinating, revealing, and enriching than the subject of Charlotte Hogsett's scrutiny: the *démarche*, or progress, of Staël's tergiversations of style, her psychic twists and turns from assertion to apprehension, from revolt to conformity as she seeks, even as she shrouds them, to reveal her truths. As a woman and the woman she was, Staël could only speak in pain and semiconcealment, and so her texts exhibit that deep duplicity that Sandra Gilbert and Susan Gubar have uncovered in other women's texts.

Hogsett, taking the works as a whole and thus rendering Staël's intellectual and artistic range better than other extant criticism in English, shows them as coterminous with her life, largely lived in exile from Bonaparte's France. The works exhibit Staël's huge energies, ambitions, and frustrations; her searching, openness, and vulnerability. At first, in reading Hogsett, I mentally compared her method to the reading of a palimpsest for its ability to see behind the text to its impulses at revelation or concealment, its subtexts. Perhaps it is better to sustain the metaphor of sound that Hogsett quotes from Staël—the noise of words and the voice of conscience. One might then think of a skillful musical analysis of a quartet which one has previously heard only as a unity but which is now shown in all the complexity of its inner voices—alternately tender, protesting, pompous, evasive, confiding, vital, exhausted. Through Hogsett's exegesis, one comes away with an entirely altered sense of what Staël's works are about. What they turn out to be about, primarily but far from exclusively, is the struggle for authority of voice as a woman and a writer. This quest is expressed in a multiplicity of guises, which Hogsett assesses in a wide array of texts. Staël's search, then, no matter how occult a form it may take, is shadowed by Hogsett's, so that this study of a literary style often takes on the allure of a good detective story. Hogsett's close textual analysis remains throughout free of jargon and readily accessible, even in its subtleties, making no pretense to a secret incommunicable congress with Staël's words.

Living to only her fifty-first year, Germaine de Staël crowded into her privileged but painful existence political, literary, and social lives any of which would have made her a figure to be reckoned with. Yet those who have made the study of women and literature so exciting a study during the last fifteen years have, with the exception of the dismissive Ellen Moers, not chosen to take either her work or her life into serious account. One reason for the few critical accounts on Staël is the inaccessibility of her work to English readers—now to be rectified by the appearance in English of both *Corinne* and a general Staël reader. But there are other reasons.

Except for George Sand, Staël is virtually the only French female author of the nineteenth century who has always remained in the *male* canon. Never mind that her place there was always secondary and limited, inferior to those of Chateaubriand and Constant, her contemporaries, or that she remained the butt of sexual innuendo or implications that her works were dictated by men. Her grudging acceptance into the male canon has simply made her suspect to modern scholars of women and literature.

The second reason that modern feminist literary study has excluded her is that she wrote as a woman of privilege and sought from literature reputation and power akin to that achieved by men. We are not at all attracted, in the 1980s, to ambitious heiresses as modern heroes. We dislike their acceptance of wealth and status and regard their aspirations to genius and fame as capitulations to a "timeless" patriarchal model of achievement. Charlotte Hogsett's cogent, patient, and fruitful probing of Staël's texts should help dissipate the cloud of anachronism that our justifiably more egalitarian beliefs may interpose between ourselves and the texts of women from another era. Staël's words are testimony to her generous and searching mind and to her tormented spirit—tormented by a lucidity and a wish for acceptance that, because of the preconceptions about her, could never take on a form consonant with her self-conception. This enlightening study comes close to answering that need unassuaged by her contemporaries or by her posterity.

Preface

Germaine de Staël referred to her writing career as her "literary existence."[1] The phrase implies an analogy between life and writing, between a life story and a literary career. It suggests that at the same time as one's ordinary existence is running its course, a second existence is also being led, not in the realm of everyday or of extraordinary events, but in that of words. While one goes about one's business, that other life is constantly or at least intermittently on one's mind. One has one's being both in a world of acts and in a world of words. The verbal existence takes place, of course, between the beginning and the ending of the life story, but the two are not entirely parallel. A "literary existence" will be influenced by events, but it will not be limited to them or even necessarily reflect them in any direct way. It develops as much according to its own internal dynamics as in response to external activity. In order to tell the story of a literary existence, one may refer to the author's life story as a framework and indeed as a force: Literature is not written, after all, in a historical void. But the major pieces of evidence in the elaboration of such a story are the texts themselves. This book is a study of the writings of Germaine de Staël, a biography of her literary existence.

Like ordinary life, a literary existence does not always develop in ways which are foreseen or even desired, stubbornly resisting our efforts to control it entirely and yet forever responding to our initiatives, albeit not necessarily in ways we envisioned. Germaine de Staël herself was keenly aware of these perversities. Her view of history, a subject in which she was passionately interested, was double. She wanted to believe it proceeds rationally and progressively, but suspected, because of her observation of her own life, literary and otherwise, that it is characterized instead by interruption and discontinuity. One's literary existence is no less subject than one's ordinary life to those directions and changes of direction, shapings and misshapings, doings and undoings that transform our projections and expectations into unanticipated configurations. Such is the story to be recounted in this book.

If a life story can usefully serve as a metaphor for a literary existence, many of the same elements will be treated in each one. Before any words of this book could be written, one of those elements had to be dealt with: name. Probably the first question we ask, in order to begin to know another person, is that person's name, which then becomes more than just a label but a part of the identity of the person for us. Names are rather problematic in the case of women, who typically, or at least traditionally, pass from the name of the father to the name of the husband.

Germaine de Staël's position on this point is quite interesting. She was proud of her father's name because it was the name of a father she respected, indeed, almost worshipped. For a different reason she was pleased with her married name, not because she loved Eric-Magnus de Staël (she did not) but because it contained the prestigious aristocratic particle. In her adult life she typically signed her name "Necker de Staël," following in this a pattern other women of her time also used. The name by which she has traditionally been known, even during her own lifetime, is "Madame de Staël."

This is rather odd. After all, in French, male writers are not referred to as "Monsieur So-and-So" or "Monsieur de So-and-So." We do know, though, that men and women are differentially named. As Sandra Gilbert and Susan Gubar point out, it is not uncommon to hear Austen called "Jane" or Dickinson "Emily," but one would not call Milton "John" or Whitman "Walt."[2] Not wishing to continue the tradition of differential naming, believing that it has the effect of belittling the author, I had to ask myself what I would call "Madame de Staël." I decided to avoid the gender-marking title and call her, simply, "Staël."

"Nominal" matters, common usage notwithstanding, are seldom trivial. The difference in our naming of male and female writers signals other discrepancies between the circumstances in which men and women carry out literary existences. Parents, for instance, are a second element one would discuss in a biography. The parents of a writer are not only those persons who play the nurturant role in the life of the child, but also those writers whom she chooses as her models. In Staël's case, there is some overlap between the two types of parents, since her biological parents were also writers. As she set out on her writing career, what difference did it make to her that her mother (who, despite Staël's refusal to credit her, influenced her deeply) had given up writing, for publication at least, upon the request of her husband and Staël's greatly admired father, Jacques Necker? What did it mean to her that the overwhelming majority of those after whom she planned to pattern her own career were men? How Staël dealt with her male and female models at the beginning and throughout her career played an important part in molding her literary existence.

This asymmetry between her own female identity and the male identity of those whom she wished to emulate caused Staël to experience a great deal of difficulty in establishing and acting upon a stable and satisfying writing identity of her own. Like Madelyn Gutwirth,[3] I do not believe that the writing person somehow becomes an androgyne, but rather that one writes as a man or woman and, within those excessively broad categories, as the particularly gendered being one has become and is becoming. This identity is a fiction, perhaps, but one in which we do indeed stand as we work out our lives. The attempts of Germain de Staël to establish, make her peace with, and write from the standpoint of her own identity marked her choices of forms and genres in which to work. They had an impact as well on her search for a rhetoric, a language if you will, that would allow her to feel she was speaking authentically, with her own words and in her own voice.

This book, then, attempts to trace the story of Staël's literary existence from her struggles to be born as a writer, through her conflicts concerning "parents" and writing identity, with their impact on her choices of subjects, forms, and rhetoric. It focuses not so much on how her career as a writer was affected by what happened to her in public or private life, but on how its elaboration was molded by the conflicting energies and impediments within her regarding the enterprise of writing. Each work she composed or tried to compose presented particular problems to her. How she solved, partially solved, or failed to solve them generated the new openings and new obstacles of the works she undertook thereafter. To follow the dynamics of that process and to narrate it is to tell the history of a literary existence.

The solutions Germaine de Staël worked out are not those of everywoman, nor do the problems present themselves to every woman writer in the same terms. Yet the forces she encountered were not only those of her age; they are, unfortunately, those which to some degree we still have with us. Her answers to them are marked by movements of courage which we might all try to emulate, and shot through with reactions of cowardice with which most of us can identify all too well. We have much to learn from her—about her, about others, and about ourselves.

The original edition of the complete works of Germaine de Staël is *Oeuvres Complètes de Madame la Baronne de Staël, publiées par son fils* (Paris: Treuttel et Wurtz, 1820–1821). Page numbers in this book, however, refer to the 1861 edition of the complete works, published in Paris by Firmin Didot, and reprinted in 1966 by Slatkin Reprints of Geneva. It is this edition to which most readers are likely to have access. In order to facilitate the finding of quotations in other editions, I have given, when appropriate, references to the part, section, or chapter numbers of works. I also point out critical editions and modern translations into English.

All translations in this book are my own.

Acknowledgments

Nearly ten years ago, after I had written initial drafts of two chapters of this book, I learned that another scholar had written a book on what seemed to be a subject dangerously like my own and which was about to appear in print. I summoned my courage and wrote to her. That act, as it turned out, did not result in my abandoning my own project, as I had feared. Quite to the contrary, it established a relationship that has provided the inspiration I needed to continue it. I am glad to have the opportunity now to pay tribute to Madelyn Gutwirth.

I would also like to express my warm appreciation to Elaine Marks, another colleague and friend who read my work in early and late stages, and, over the years, encouraged me to complete it. Simone Balayé made me feel like a member of the community of Staëlian scholars by welcoming me into her home in Paris. A College-Teacher-in-Residence Fellowship from the National Endowment for the Humanities enabled me to spend the academic year 1976–1977 at Yale University in a seminar under the direction of the late Paul de Man. The time, the library, the new ideas provided by this experience were valuable indeed.

People associated with Southern Illinois University Press have of course played an essential role in seeing this project through to its end. Sandra Gilbert, editor of the *ad feminam* series, took notice of my book as a potential volume for it. Robert S. Phillips, Editorial Director of the Press, transformed from an invisible presence in letters, into a telephone personality, into a real person standing before me unexpectedly one day at a professional meeting—at every stage providing support all the more helpful for not being uncritical.

Heidi Langner, the Editorial Assistant who served as copy editor of my manuscript, represents to me all those people, most of whose names I do not even know, who have worked to get this book into your hands.

Sue V. Rosser has shared with me the wisdom which comes from her wide and deep knowledge of Women's Studies and given me her daily support, while her daughters, Meagan and Caitie, cheered me on with their robust renditions of Springsteen's line "I'm just sittin' around here writin' this book."

Germaine de Staël

1. *Introduction*

The readings that are the substance of this book, the claims based on them, and the structures into which they are organized have been elaborated in the context of the feminist literary theory and criticism of the last twenty years. The work of those involved in that endeavor has resulted in impressive accomplishments: fresh readings of works in the traditional and predominantly male canon; forgotten or little-studied women writers brought to light; many of those already well-known examined anew; work on the establishment of a female literary tradition linked by echoing intertextualities; provocative inquiries into the interrelation of language, psyche and gender.[1] At the same time, this body of work does not provide an easy and stable background against which to work, since theoretical underpinnings have by no means been agreed upon and definitively established. Like anyone engaged in an undertaking that raises essential issues and moves into territory as poorly known and as threatening to contemplate as gender-related matters, feminist critics find that we have to rework our foundations while we are building our house.

Even an essentially critical project, like the one that generated this book, inevitably involves "prises de position" on a number of theoretical issues. The critical text becomes both the evidence of how the author has resolved them and a demonstration of the process by which she arrived at her stance. Standing prior to and underlying all these issues is one basic question: Is it, or is it not, valid to speak of "women's literature" or of the "woman writer" as a distinct category of writing or writers? This question is perhaps particularly pressing for a critic like myself, an American whose critical instincts align her with that tradition but who professes French literature, for the answer to it has tended to break down along national lines.[2] Critics of Anglo-American inspiration, generally speaking, are interested in establishing a female literary tradition, in defining the nature and demonstrating the value of what women have written, and in revealing the impediments to literary creativity that women have faced.[3] Meanwhile, many of those whose primary influence comes from France question the validity of the very categories "masculine" and "feminine." The claim is that to accept such categories is to take an essentialist view of gender and to position oneself in a humanist perspective that sees literature as a reflection of life. Further, the argument continues, theorists and critics of this persuasion tend to center on the author as a unitary entity, when, in fact, the subject's solidity is by no means established. Toril Moi, who has recently summarized these objections both effectively and sympathetically, claims that Anglo-American assumptions emanate from a fundamentally conservative social stance that can lead only to a repetition of traditional dualisms and thus replicate hierarchical valorizations of the terms of those dualisms.[4]

However a critic of Anglo-American proclivity might wish, in her turn, to counter these remarks, clearly it has to be said that they are not trivial, certainly not to a feminist. By defining issues that are related to the central question, and by raising them in the contexts of Germaine de Staël's literary reputation and of her life story, I hope to demonstrate in a preliminary and preparatory way why her work has proved to be a rich *locus* for meditations on these matters. In so doing, I will be pointing toward the kinds of stances which this book can be expected to take.

A survey of Germaine de Staël's place in literary history suggests that she took part not in one but rather in two histories. An initial issue her case raises, then, is the relationship between the two. In the first place, it is generally agreed that she is a tremendously important figure of the late eighteenth and early nineteenth centuries, a period marked in France by its Revolution, the ensuing political chaos, and finally the order established by Napoleon's empire. Steeped in the literature and philosophy of the Enlightenment, she participated in the creation or development of romanticism, both through her ideas and through her style.[5] She took part also in the great political upheavals of her time, all the while producing a voluminous work in a variety of genres. She introduced the cultures of other countries to France: Germany, Italy, Russia. In short, her role in what we ordinarily think of as history and her place in the traditional literary canon are secure. She is likely to be the only woman or one of the few women included in anthologies of French literature of the eighteenth and nineteenth centuries. She is one of the few women mentioned by René Wellek in his monumental *History of Criticism* and one of the even fewer to whom he devotes more than a sentence.[6] Her work continues to command attention, as the wealth of studies devoted to her yearly attests.[7]

At the same time, feminist critics and historians recognize her place in another literary history, a female tradition. It was Ellen Moers who did the initial, groundbreaking work on this matter.[8] Hélène Borowitz has traced the influence of Mademoiselle de Scudéry on Staël.[9] Madelyn Gutwirth points out her relationship with her contemporaries Madame de Krüdener and Madame de Charrière,[10] and Joanna Kitchen, her acquaintanceship with other contemporaries, Madame Cottin, Madame de Souza, Madame de Genlis.[11] Woman writers as varied as Maria Edgeworth, George Sand, George Eliot, Elizabeth Barrett Browning, Harriet Beecher Stowe, and Margaret Fuller have undergone her influence.[12] The story of that literary tradition has been told only partially and its integration with conventional literary history, barely begun. This book will contribute to such a project only indirectly, by setting forth a detailed reading of the work of Staël herself. Such synchronic studies, while the story they tell is limited, will eventually serve to make a more accurate and inclusive literary history possible.

The book is positioned, however, in such a way as to confront directly a second issue suggested by the status of Germaine de Staël's literary reputation: What assessment may we make of the work of this woman, which has been praised by some, has been subject to the ambiguous admiration of some, and yet has been denigrated, even ridiculed, by others? It is hard to think of a major writer of whom more mock has been made. Rebecca West has remarked, "Year in, year out, she has been tittered at as a funny, and really this is quite absurd."[13] Noreen J. Swallow words very strongly the conclusion to which her study of Staëlian criticism has led her. She found attitudes ranging from the "prophetic sexism of Jacques Necker in 1785, through the patronizing chauvinism of Le Breton in 1901, to the misogynous hysteria of Anthony West in 1975."[14] What may well help to explain the derogatory irreverence which this admittedly great writer has attracted is the lightning rod of her gender. The personal life of a woman writer seems to be easily assimilated into judgments concerning her work. Such, at the very least, has been the case of this writer, leading her major American critic, Madelyn Gutwirth, to state, "Since the novels have been interpreted almost exclusively as fictional projections of self, Mme de Staël's personal reputation has had a decided influence upon that of her novels."[15] A similar conclusion has been reached by Gutwirth's French counterpart, Simone Balayé: "There has too often been a refusal to treat her completely as a writer."[16]

The effect of this sort of criticism has been to skew interpretation, sometimes even grotesquely. Some critics, apparently unable to reconcile her gender with her status as a writer, have concluded that she is "virile."[17] Still others, otherwise excellent critics, have difficulty in seeing her, finally, in other than stereotypically female terms. Georges Poulet imagines a narcissistic Staël when he speaks for her as follows: "I admire therefore I am, that is, I discover myself in the feeling of admiration that I experience."[18] In contrasting Staël's *Corinne* with Benjamin Constant's *Adolphe*, he discovers immanency and immediacy in the former but distance and objectivity in the latter.[19] In like manner, Jean Starobinski sees a writer incapable of that "artistic suicide" which liberates a work from its author and gives it a life of its own.[20] "The major experience is that which carries her toward others," he states in another context. The whole apparatus of the female stereotype is here: narcissism, self-absorption, subjectivity, dependence, limitation. It is little wonder that the vast majority of her critics have not accorded to her writing the kind of serious attention which her male contemporaries have commanded. Instead one finds statements whose dismissiveness precludes detailed analysis. Jean-Albert Bédé's Germaine de Staël is too derivative to merit attention: "Of course we can exhaust quickly the nomenclature of her procedures: these are distinguished neither by newness, nor by variety."[21] That of Paul de Man is capable of shedding new light on a subject she treats, in this case Jean-Jacques Rousseau, but she herself is embarrassingly inept: "The analytical language of Mme de Staël is capable of the worst aberrations: banality, dissimulation, self-serving sentimentality, it's all there."[22]

When a well-known writer is treated in such a manner, one may well be tempted to conclude that one is dealing with a great but flawed writer. In this case, the flaws seem to be related to gender. Staël's talent, which some who knew her called genius, and the advantages that she, unlike most other women, had kept her from falling to the silent fate of Virginia Woolf's Judith Shakespeare. But, at the same time, and again in the words of the mother of feminist criticism, she would apparently belong among those who "did not get their work expressed completely."[23] In such cases, we admire the writer, but with serious reservations. We have cleared the way to treat her accomplishments on the one hand and her failures on the other. But we have not asked what relationship might exist between the two, and certainly we have not questioned the criteria according to which we decide what is accomplishment and what is failure.

It is no coincidence that it has been critics of feminist sensibility who have begun to depict Germaine de Staël with accuracy and nuance, by overtly examining what Madelyn Gutwirth calls the "feminine dimension" of her work rather than allowing it to mold their commentary into stereotype. The work of a number of these critics has been and will be cited in the course of this one. Chief among them are those already mentioned, Madelyn Gutwirth and Simone Balayé.[24] This book is an attempt to continue their work and to make a further contribution. Madelyn Gutwirth treats fictional works of Staël, whereas here I relate the fictional and the nonfictional. Simone Balayé has extraordinary knowledge of the life and times of Staël, of her bibliography, and of her manuscripts and editions. My work centers on critical analysis of texts. Our diversity is as striking as our accord on many points. We would agree, I think, that what she expressed *was* her work, completely, and that it is extraordinarily rich, more so and differently than has been said.

Madelyn Gutwirth states that Staël is being "most herself" when she is living in the "tension generated by the problem of creating what would be in her own eyes an identity both feminine and her own."[25] Indeed, factors which might generate such tension were at work even in Staël's earliest initiation to writing. She was born in 1766, the only child of Jacques Necker, the rich Swiss banker who became finance minister under Louis XVI at the end of his ill-fated reign, and of the Swiss-born, highly educated "salonniere," Suzanne Curchod Necker. The young Germaine, a child prodigy, received a fine education at the hands of her very intelligent but rigid and cool mother, appearing at her mother's side while the most celebrated men of her day, guests of the salon, chatted with her.[26] She became an accomplished conversationalist at a tender age, and began also to write. While her early efforts were no doubt encouraged for educational reasons, the more her vocation for writing declared itself, the more concerned her socially conservative parents became: Women did not commonly become writers; it was considered unseemly for them to do so. Suzanne Curchod Necker, in fact, had shown an interest in writing but gave it up when it became irritating to her husband, who himself had literary ambitions, writing and publishing widely.[27] Toward his daughter, Jacques Necker was doting and indulgent; especially in Germaine's adolescence father and daughter became very close while the mother-daughter relationship became increasingly strained and distant. Yet he mocked her literary ambitions, overtly discouraging her from pursuing them in any public way.

In such a background one sees strong sources of energy coming into conflict with equally strong currents of anti-energy. Staël had the training and the ability to write; she even had the example of adult writers constantly before her. But her mother and father conveyed to her unequivocally what society as a whole had to say about writing: that it was a male prerogative and that she would make herself ridiculous, perhaps unlovable, if she should try to encroach upon it. Germaine de Staël was subject, then, to the "anxiety of authorship" which Sandra Gilbert and Susan Gubar have identified and studied,[28] and which Madelyn Gutwirth calls the "problem which was to become central to her creative life and the core of her novels."[29]

The young Germaine's ambitions were not only literary. A person of intense energy and astonishing intelligence, from an early age she wanted to take part in politics. Because of the position of her father, she was close to sources of power when she was barely beyond adolescence. The husband chosen for her was Swedish ambassador to the French throne, Eric-Magnus de Staël, whom she married in early 1786. As the position of Louis XVI weakened, she saw her father dismissed in 1787; in 1789, called back to his position amidst tremendous popular acclaim, in what was no doubt the greatest moment of triumph in his life; and finally resign in the politically hopeless situation in which the monarchy found itself in 1790. Having once been that close to power, Germaine de Staël naturally enough never wished to lose touch with it. She took an active part in the doings and undoings of politics during the confused early revolutionary years. But then, a series of reversals in her political fortunes began. First, in 1792, she barely escaped from Paris with her life, and spent the troubled years of the Terror, beginning in 1793, in exile, first in England and later at Coppet, her family home in Switzerland, returning to Paris only in 1795. Still participating in political maneuvers, she became disillusioned as it became increasingly evident that the high promise of a new order of things (she had basically envisioned a constitutional monarchy akin to that of England) was falling into chaos and cruelty. Initially hopeful concerning the order Napoleon might bring to this morass, she eventually fell out of favor with him, and he with her, so irremediably that she gradually found herself exiled farther and farther from her beloved Paris, the center of existence for her.

Her political vicissitudes had an impact on her writing career. In the first place, she always had to act by proxy; it was her father, her husband, and later her friends, often also lovers of this unhappily married woman, who occupied public positions. Her part had to be played behind the scenes because of course women could not advance to center stage and act unmediatedly for the audience. This action by indirection is disappointing enough for an active woman when she is on the winning side but quite thwarting when she is losing.

Moreover, involvement in the public world signaled and was related to another of her ambitions: to write not only novels—a genre in which women had indeed traditionally written—but also expository works about politics and other subjects, both concrete and abstract, which had not commonly been topics of female authorship. It is quite likely that if she had restricted herself to novels, she would not have attracted the disapproval that her parents were the first to express. Nor would she have felt, throughout her career, that her topics might provoke widespread wrath. This fear was not unfounded: it seems clear that a part of Napoleon's distaste for her was that her aspirations went beyond the boundary of home and family, a boundary he strongly believed should be drawn around women. Here was a woman who wished to write as only men were expected to write. Thus, her writing is the scene of a crisis concerning sexual writing identity.

In reading Germaine de Staël in the light of this concept, I take a potentially controversial stand on the already controversial question posed at the beginning of this introduction. That people write out of sexual identity is far from being an established fact. Many women writers today articulate very clearly their denial of it. For example, in the December 16, 1984, edition of the *New York Times Book Review*, Elaine Showalter quotes several of these women: Joan Didion, maintaining that her heroines do not have "specifically women's" but instead "more general problems;" Cynthia Ozick, avowing that she "wiped the 'woman'" out of her female narrator; Margaret Drabble, exclaiming that she is "bloody sick of bloody women." As if to add to Showalter's list, Joyce Carol Oates wrote in response to the article, "We are [woman] writers who aspire to the conditon not of maleness, still less of androgyny, but of being simply writers." (December 30, 1984).

Despite such aspirations on the part of writers, as Judith Kegan Gardiner documents,[30] Anglo-American critics, directly or indirectly influenced by such psychologists as Erik Erikson and Heinz Lichtenstein especially as interpreted by such literary figures as Norman N. Holland, commonly speak of the woman writer's search for identity, at once assuming and studying its existence. "Gender identity," Gardiner summarizes, "means knowing to which sex one is socially assigned" (p. 183). How the qualities associated with the two sexes are formed and valorized has been examined by Nancy Chodorow,

Carol Gilligan,[31] and others. Feminist literary critics like Gardiner take concepts elaborated in these contexts and ask how women function differently as readers and as writers because of gender, or sex as socially defined.

Whereas American-style psychology undergirds and validates such endeavors, French psychoanalytic theory questions them radically. To be sure, some French writers, especially Hélène Cixous and Luce Irigaray, have in at least part of their writing veered perhaps dangerously close to implying a biological determinism in the quest for an "écriture féminine," to use Cixous' phrase. More typically, "masculine" and "feminine" are seen as an excessively schematized, stereotypical, and simplistic way of looking at what should be viewed rather, in the words of Jacques Derrida, as "the multiplicity of sexually marked voices."[32] Julia Kristeva argues that access to what Jacques Lacan calls "pre-symbolic language" is not limited to males or females, but is rather a matter of finding a way of standing prior to the Law of the Father. For her, such a stance also involves questioning the existence of the speaking subject itself as an entity with a stable identity.[33] In this light, one would be in error not only to speak of a sexual identity but indeed of any definable identity at all. Caught between these conflicting theoretical stances, the critic may feel stymied: How can she proceed with a discourse about women's writing which is based on the assumption that it exists as something about which one may write, in the face of objections that this is not the case?

The answer to the question on which this book is based is practical rather than theoretical. Mary Jacobus points to the necessity of postulating "women's writing" as such, "if only to remind us of the social conditions under which women wrote and still write," because such a labeling "makes vividly legible what the critical institution has either ignored or acknowledged only under the sign of inferiority."[34] "We need it, so we invent it," she boldly states. Nancy K. Miller's stance, as formulated in 1982, is similar. "Let us retain," she suggests, "a 'modern' post-humanistic reading of 'literature' that has indeed begun to rethink the very locations of the center and the periphery, and within that fragile topology, the stability of the subject. But at the same time, we must live out . . . a practical politics . . . . This is to call for, then, a decentered vision (theory) but a centered perspective that will not result in renewed invisibility."[35] These moves make it possible to avoid the pitfalls of humanism, essentialism, and biological determinism at least long enough to proceed to an inquiry on the basis of a working hypothesis our very research may eventually undermine.

Germaine de Staël's writing career was deeply influenced by her search for a sexual writing identity which could authorize her to write without putting her sexual identity itself in danger. Beyond that, she was at least dimly aware that a "decentered vision" might provide an escape from the male/female dualism within which she struggled.

Her insights into this and many other matters were made possible and sharpened by what was for her the tragedy of exile from Paris. She was to spend the years 1802 through 1814 in exile, at Coppet and in long trips that took her most lengthily to Italy and to Germany, but also to Russia, the Scandinavian countries, and England. Involved as she was in finding her way into satisfying writing rather than losing her way either in the currents of ambition and discouragement or in the maze of writing identity, she made discoveries there that enabled her to work out a quite individual rhetoric while she was writing the books on which her fame has largely depended. One must take into account that, in the words of Simone Balayé, "There is a contradiction between what Madame de Staël is, how she sees and analyzes herself, and the appearance, the spectacle that she involuntarily offers to strangers and to posterity. This woman, active *par excellence*, is a passive one forced to activity."[36] This is to point out that whereas Staël is most commonly associated with aggressiveness and energy, she was acutely and painfully aware of her own weakness. It would be presumptuous to pretend to explain such timidity entirely, but it was doubtless related not only to her very real political powerlessness but also to her consciousness of the secondary status of women in her society. As Barbara Watson rightly states, if one wishes to understand the thought of those whose situation with respect to power is weakness, one must not look at overt manifestoes. "We begin instead to look at such techniques as ambiguity, equivocation, and expressive symbolic structure."[37]

It is from this perspective that a study of Germaine de Staël's writing must be made. The crosscurrents and the dilemmas in which she found herself form and deform her work into the quite individual performance it is, both standing in the way of her accomplishing all that she might have and yet also generating insights and discoveries for which a less troubled crucible might not have been propitious. They caused her to develop an indirect way of expressing herself, a language which is, in the phrase of Gilbert and Gubar, "magnificently duplicitous."[38] The effort of her critic must be, in the striking image created by Staël herself, to hear, through the noise of her words, the voice of her conscience, in which she speaks, perhaps unwittingly at times, about herself as a woman trying to write in the face of interdictions against her doing so.[39]

The term *voice* connotes for Germaine de Staël an authentic self-expression. When we use it we should remember that in her own time Staël was known as a brilliant conversationalist. We are told that she would introduce the subject of the chapter she was working on into the conversation of her guests the night before she planned to compose. Then she would begin to talk out her ideas on the topic and to encourage others to do the same. Those who heard the conversations claimed that the written result was never as exciting as her oral remarks. But traces of their oral origin are discernible in the texts. Marie-Claire Vallois, in her very perceptive study of Staël, states that despite the fact that she rarely uses the word *I*, critics commonly speak of "hearing" her. As Vallois also demonstrates in her analyses of Staël's fiction, this voice—or rather these voices, for Vallois discerns more than one—is not a simple one because it has been "alienated from the right to the word, unable to speak in the name of woman."[40]

This book is an attempt to hear the voice, or voices. I share with Madelyn Gutwirth the "sense that Staël has a voice better heard in certain parts of her works than others,"[41] and endeavor to determine of which texts this is true, and why, and what they have to say. It is a work of textual analysis that tries to watch the text unfold as if one were standing at the moment of its creation. From that vantage point, each passage becomes a dynamic piece of work one observes in the making. The text is what remains of the thoughts the author had while she was writing. To be sure, there is a moment before the composition itself, a moment always ephemeral, disappearing as quickly as it happens. One cannot remember these moments for oneself, much less recreate them in the cases of others. But formulation of that moment exists in the text. The vestiges of its making are there, bearing witness to the labor involved in those fleeting moments of creation.

This is a particularly interesting endeavor in the case of what Germaine de Staël wrote. Like Sandra Gilbert and Susan Gubar's Jane Austen, she had a "cover story."[42] For concealing her traces, for assuring that she was proving her willingness to remain in the bounds set for women writers, she had strategies which are perceptible in the texts. The task of her critic is to discover the ruses and to uncover the voice which they both express and muffle. As Marie-Claire Vallois says of Staël's fiction, "Her novelistic writing is doubled with the autobiographical, which it camouflages immediately."[43]

There is some reason to believe that Germaine de Staël was at least to some extent conscious of her subterfuges. She reflected: "A book is always made according to some system or other, which places the author at some distance from the reader. One can guess at the character of the writer but his talent must put a kind of fiction between him and us."[44] The relationship between subject and subjectivity is complex, in part intentionally so, so that in order to understand either or both, one must discover what "system," what "kind of fiction," Germaine de Staël is placing between herself and the reader. Unraveling this relationship promises to make a very interesting kind of sense of her apparently aberrant, shifting style and to tell us about matters that are not overtly discussed. The texts are multi-layered, the voice of the author sometimes near the surface, sometimes diving beneath to various levels, appearing and disappearing only to appear again. Once we have learned to read the texts we may be able to describe them not as "brilliant but flawed" but as something in themselves, of value and interest without reservation.

When the final fall of Napoleon in 1815 made it possible for Germaine de Staël to return to Paris, she was still writing and planning for writing, but as it happened her career was virtually over. She traveled once more to Italy and sojourned on two more occasions at Coppet. By the time she got back to Paris, in late 1816, her health was poor. She had a stroke in early 1817 and died on July 14 of that year. In her own mind her career was unfinished. For us it takes on a specific shape formed by what retrospectively looks like a traceable development.

A writer of Germaine de Staël's time looked back on the "philosophes" of the French Enlightenment for models. This is not to say that Staël did not belong to a tradition of woman writers. But because she consciously intended not to limit herself to genres and topics to which women, in general, had limited themselves, some of her most important models were men. She most explicitly speaks of Rousseau in this respect, but obviously Montesquieu and Voltaire were equally important.[45] Those literary careers typically, though not always, included work in a variety of genres, both fictional and expository, treating many topics, especially philosophy, ethics or "moral philosophy," politics, literature, history, and sometimes science. Rousseau's work caused confession to be added to the array.

Staël's male contemporaries conformed rather faithfully to the example set before them, with allowances made for the differences in interests that were coming about at this time. Benjamin Constant and René de Chateaubriand, for example, show a fascination with religion which has replaced interest in science. But if we look for a moment at the literary career of Constant, we see that his production indeed includes confession (the *Journals*), fiction (*Adolphe, Cecile*), politics (*On the Spirit of Conquest and Usurpation* and *Principles of Politics*.)

To identify the genre or even topic to which Staël's works belong is not quite so easy. *Corinne*, for example, is a novel, but it is also an introduction to Italian culture. *Ten Years of Exile* is autobiographical, but it is not confessional. As early as the mid–1790s Staël planned a major statement on political theory, but never wrote such a work. Her *Considerations on the French Revolution* is narrative rather than theoretical and includes biographical material about herself and especially her father. The comparison is complicated still further by the quite different rhetoric of this male and this female writer.

Constant was clear about what kind of work he was writing and adhered to the conventions of that kind. In his fictional work there is fiction, and little overt reference to the political scene. His expository work centers on the topic and is free from reference to personal life. Germaine de Staël's rhetoric is not nearly so neatly compartmentalized into the public and the private. Instead the two domains are continually interwoven, distinctions between them blurred. In short, her works do not fit into existing categories and her rhetoric is, according to ordinary standards, inappropriate.

It is the kind of work Constant did, in genre and in rhetoric, that criticism has sanctified and valorized, the shape of his career that seems to have form rather than to exist in chaos. Because Staël's work differs, it seems defective, and will continue to seem so as long as the assumption is that in literature there is a mark, a "point of perfection," as the neoclassics put it, one either hits or misses. The effort here is to avoid making that assumption; it is to concentrate rather on watching in detail what Staël did and on looking for explanatory clues. The endeavor has convinced me that "women's literature" and "the woman writer" do indeed exist as valid, indeed as essential, categories of analysis. As long as woman has different status and experience from that of man (she does now; she did two hundred years ago) her creativity will be marked by that status and experience. Her performance will have, like his, the virtues of its faults and the faults of its virtues; it will be, in other words, itself. This book is an attempt to manifest one such performance.

2. *The Threat of Silence*

Germaine de Staël had reason to have ambivalent feelings about writing from her earliest years. On the one hand, writing was an important part of her education: her mother saw to it that she acquired the habit of writing. The young girl took to it easily and enthusiastically, thus revealing her native talent. She seemed destined from childhood to a literary career. Her first friend, Catherine Rilliet Huber, recounts how she met the eleven-year-old Germaine in this early scene from her life. Her first words to her new friend bespeak a fascination with writing.

> We did not play like children; she asked me immediately what subjects I was studying, whether I knew any languages? I told her that I did. If I went to the theater often? I told her that I had gone three times in my life; she protested, promised me that we would go often; but that upon our return we would have to write the subjects of the plays we had seen; and what had struck us, that her mother required it . . . (she said) "Oh, what a good time we will have! How happy we will be! We will have to write each other every morning!"[1]

The first question the child thinks to ask of her friend is whether she knows a language; the first activity she projects, that of writing; the first sign of friendship, a correspondence. Writing filled the days of the young Germaine: panegyrics and portraits, after the fashion of the famous men who attended the "salon"; a rewriting into prose of the *Seasons* of Saint Lambert; the composing and presenting of plays.[2] Even at this early stage of her life, writing is sparked by tremendous enthusiasm and channelled into habitual activity.

The young Germaine Necker also had examples of adult writers constantly before her, not only in the guests of the house but perhaps more importantly in her mother and father. Yet from the outset, there is a troublesome factor in the girl's introduction to the world of writing. Her mother, she tells in an early diary, sacrificed a promising writing career to her husband's disapproval of writing women. Indeed, her father made mock of her own nascent career.

> If mama had written I am sure that she would have acquired a very great reputation for wit; but my father cannot stand a woman writer and just in the last four days when he has been watching me write his portrait, he has already gotten worried and calls me in his jokes "Mister Holy Writing Desk." He wants to put me on guard against this weakness of self-love. Mama liked very much to compose, she sacrified it to him. "Imagine," he said to me often, "how worried I was, I didn't dare go into her room for fear of tearing her away from an occupation that was more pleasant to her than my presence. I watched her, in my arms, still pursuing an idea." Ah! How right he is! How little made women are to follow the same career as men, to struggle against them, to excite in them a jealousy so different from the one which love inspires. A woman should have nothing of her own and should find all her enjoyment in the one she loves! . . . Sorrow upon us when we reverse the order of nature.[3]

In docility, more than that, in a single-minded burst of heart-felt agreement, Germaine de Staël at least apparently accepts the example of her mother and the attitude of her father. Writing is a male prerogative. She is both encouraged to write and discouraged from it. She wants to write and practices writing; yet she appears receptive to the idea that women should not do so.[4]

The young Germaine Necker was, then, no stranger to writing. But from the scribblings of a child to the publishable writings of an adult there is a considerable distance to be traveled. Rarely, I suppose, is it traveled easily, but surely special difficulties lay in wait for a woman writer who had heard such ominous warnings about what would happen if she should write for the public. The pieces Staël wrote in her late teens would make the female reader wonder quite seriously, if she did not already know the rest of the story, whether this young woman was ever to be born as a writer. To be sure, she was already writing in a public way by producing plays that were presented to family and friends. Notably, she wrote and mounted *Sophie or Secret Feelings* in 1784, and later, in 1786 was working on another play, *Jane Gray*. These plays were not to be published until 1790. In private, showing what she wrote to none or to few, she was writing pieces which tell us that the threat of, perhaps the temptation to, silence was very real. I want to look here at two early works that open for us a view into the question this writer was asking herself, this writer who might very well never have become one had she remained trapped by the literary dead ends to which her early experimentation led. We witness a woman trying to emerge from the chaos that precedes those insights that finally permit a writing performance to get underway and to proceed. It is precisely working through such confusions and feeling one's way around such obstacles that make eventual breakthroughs possible.

Like many budding authors, Germaine Necker kept a journal, which she began in 1785. In some cases, initial works are autobiographical, the groundwork for them having been prepared by journals. In the case of Staël, autobiography was not a form with which she felt comfortable at the beginning of her career, nor was it ever to be so. One can learn why it was not and what kinds of obstacles the young writer was encountering by analyzing this early journal.

Here, as throughout the career of Staël, a parental figure plays a key role. Even as she works her way toward a literary existence, the parents are there, watching over and, in this case, impeding the birthing process while, of course, at the same time making it possible. The journal begins with an epigraph from her father and an apostrophe addressed to him.

> The heart of man is a painting one must see from the distance at which the organizer of the universe has placed it.
>
> (On the Administration of Finances, Second Volume)

> Turn the page, papa, if you dare, after having read this epigraph; ah! I have placed you so close to my heart that you must not envy this small degree of more intimacy I keep with myself.[5]

At issue here are distance and intimacy. In her initial remark, Staël insists on her right to be distant from her father, in the sense of having with herself a closer relationship than she has with him. The writing of her journal is the establishment of that distance, and she uses the quotation from her father to justify it. But it is a troubled separation. Her apostrophe reveals a fantasy: that her father might accidentally come upon and begin to read her journal. She assumes he would resent her writing it, using the word *envy*. One feels envy when someone else has what one wants oneself; in this case Necker is supposed to want a total intimacy with his daughter that her distancing herself from him by this writing would destroy. Her journal begins in uneasiness and guilt, which she tries to diminish by quoting him, by telling him how close they are, by addressing herself to him. But it begins also in defiance; she knows she is doing something he would not like, but she is doing it, in spite of his menacing and disapproving shadow.

The troubled feelings do not go away. The journal we are to read, it turns out, is not the one she originally wrote. "I wanted to write completely the journal of my heart, I have torn up some pages."[6] We will not, of course, find out what these torn pages contained, but the reasons she gives for having destroyed them hint at their content. The first has to do with how feelings look when put down in written form. "There are movements which lose their naturalness as soon as one remembers them, as soon as one thinks that one will remember them; it seems that one would be like kings, they live for history, and one would feel for history."[7] The act of formulating one's feelings into written form, whether for oneself or for someone else, is inevitably to distort them from their natural state into a presentation. To reread this artificial account of originally strong emotions is unendurable. "Sorrow to the one who can express everything, sorrow to the one who can endure the reading of his weakened feelings."[8] But a more fundamental reason emerges as Staël, in the continuation of the sentence just quoted, indicates another reaction to the reading of written-down feelings: "To him will come still greater sorrow [than] to the one who, having enough eloquence to inflame his paper with the same fire that was devouring his heart would yet tear up his pages, and would turn his eyes away from his image."[9]

Staël has just said that she tore up her own pages. Since one of the actions she describes is the one she in fact performed, the other with which she surrounds it may well stand as an explanation, albeit indirectly and impersonally expressed. If so, she is describing a painful moment in which, rereading what she had written, she was shocked to the point of averting her eyes and destroying. What had she written? Or what, at the very least, did she fear to write?

Apparently, judging from the phrase "to inflame his paper with the same fire which was devouring his heart," the subject was strong passion. The act of averting suggests shame or embarrassment. The introductory passage ends with a protest that she is not embarrassed, does not feel passion, feels, in fact, only the noblest of sentiments. "For me, however, I do not blush over my heart, and alone in the silence of passions, I feel it still beating beneath my hand for honor and virtue."[10] She turns her back on the moment when she viewed on paper the expression of feelings she judged to be unacceptable, preferring an idealization of herself that gives the lie to any untoward emotions the pages might have captured. They must be suppressed. One must give a better account of oneself than that. She seems to reestablish the distance that she began by denying; that is, she will keep a distance between her true feelings and her words. As her mother put it, speaking of Rousseau, she will cast a veil over those feelings. She will express herself only in the form of an idealized image, couched in lofty and admirable terms.

The journal itself proceeded fitfully. There are ten entries over a period of about six weeks. Many of the pages are filled with commentary about conversations she had with her father, portraits of friends who came to call. Personal remarks are not lacking: admiration for her father, fear of his death and hers, feelings toward her husband-to-be and toward the fact that her mother had preferred a different match for her. There is interesting biographical material here, but the discussion is generalized. Certainly there is no more said about passions one might blush to describe. Then twenty more torn pages. Then nothing.

It seems that we are dealing with a writer who, if she will express feelings at all in her work, will do so in an indirect and covert way. She is not at all predisposed to confessional literature, despite her great admiration (examined in chapter 3), for Jean-Jacques Rousseau, who had established a masterful archetype of that genre. The very idea that her parents might see what she had written and thus look into her heart frightens her terribly. Throughout her career Staël will reveal her feelings about many matters, but one may be certain that the version one is seeing is a highly censored and transformed one. If she is to express herself about herself, she will need to find some way of doing so which will at once reveal and conceal, some "fiction" or "system," to borrow her own phrases, by which she may present herself safely.

Around this same time, Staël was trying her hand at fiction as well as at dramatic pieces and confession. The three short stories she wrote were, like her plays, to be published only later, in the case of the stories, in 1785. One of them, *Histoire de Pauline* (Story of Pauline),[11] is particularly significant for our efforts to explore her struggle toward writing. It reveals that the obstacles she was encountering went beyond matters of discovering that a given form is not congenial. Here she writes a deeply skeptical piece about woman's ability to write, indeed to handle language at all. If one is to become a writer, it is of course essential that one's relationship with the written word be enabling, that it permit and encourage the creation of verbal structures. Perhaps artists, generally, experience their various media as stubborn, recalcitrant, resistant to being molded into the desired and imagined forms. Nonetheless, it becomes necessary to make peace with one's medium in some way, however uneasy, that allows performance to get underway and to continue. Because of her early experiences with writing, Staël might be expected to be relatively at ease with words. Yet she was in fact suspicious and skeptical of them from the beginning. The *Story of Pauline* is about the relationship of writing to the feminine condition and the adequacy of words to self-expression.[12] It tells us that Staël was far from sure that a woman can become a writer.

The book may be divided into four parts. The first part takes place in the French colony of Santo Domingo, depicted as a physical and moral inferno: "These burning climates where men, occupied only by barbarous trade and profit, seem, for the most part, to have lost the ideas and feelings which could inspire horror for those activities in them."[13] Pauline, married off at age thirteen, is an orphan with no parental figures to guide her and without moral education of any kind. Her soul is untutored, unformed, unstructured by ethical principles. The wicked Monsieur de Meltin decides to corrupt her by maneuvering his young cousin Théodore into seducing her. Théodore does indeed do so, drawing on his knowledge of the language of novels for technique: "He had read a few novels; he spoke their language to her."[14] In this unprincipled world the language of love is factitious and fictitious. People are manipulated by the lies and insinuations of others, so that one may not count on a solid relationship between words and reality. Words are grounded in nothing and thus become toys played with by those of bad faith. When Pauline yields to Theodore's borrowed charms, her own language is also tainted by bad faith, by a posing not only before Théodore but also before herself: "This child had become a passionate lover; her young language was that of the noblest eloquence. Perhaps one could perceive that she was exaggerating her feeling to herself in order to diminish her fault in her own eyes; but the most elevated, romantic things that love can imagine—these she developed for Theodore."[15] The guilty act, itself brought about by verbal trickery, unleashes in its turn a language of dissimulation, again described as eloquent and novelistic.

To make matters worse, the narrator herself seems uncertain about the nature of the world she intended to evoke here. Pauline, as we have just seen, was capable of a language of dissimulation used to engage her lover further and to hide the sordidness of her act from herself. Yet at the same moment in the story, an opposite claim is made for her: "No artificial feeling had entered her soul, none of these movements that one stirs up in oneself in to be able in good conscience to show them to others."[16] Moreover, she had received no moral upbringing and thus theoretically should be amoral. But her reaction to her seduction implies some conception of the difference between right and wrong. She feels "a state of turmoil and despair whose violence surpassed both the strength and the reflexions of her age."[17] Meltin reproaches her for having "the prejudices of her childhood." She has a horror of becoming a fallen woman, characterized by her as "these vile creatures."

In short, the narrator seems confused concerning whether or not to depict Pauline as guilty. She indicates that at least in part Pauline cooperated in her downfall, while at the same time she is at pains to exculpate her entirely, to show that she is fundamentally innocent, incapable of wrongdoing. If she is innocent, then guilt must belong to someone else; if another person is indeed responsible for her troubles, then it would seem appropriate to become angry and to express the anger in some form. But anger is not a feeling that comes easily to Pauline or one with which the narrator herself knows how to deal. For this reason the guidance the narrator gives the reader is not clearly delineated.

For this moment in the story, in any event, the confusions about guilt and innocence find their resolution in a conflict that is fundamental to this Staëlian hell: Pauline has an instinct for virtue to which nothing in the world outside her corresponds and which nothing confirms. In her confusion one single word, the word "virtue," resounds clearly amid the noise of borrowed and ungrounded language. It is a substantive but devoid of meaning for Pauline: "this virtue which I do not know well but whose name was dear to me."[18] Linguistically, in fact, this first part of the story may be characterized as suffering from a discrepancy between signifier and signified. Words do not express feelings; one has feelings for which there are no words.

In the second part of the story, the virtuous and well-intentioned Madame de Verseuil comes to Santo Domingo to deliver Pauline from the inferno. She speaks to the nearly crazed young girl a new language.

> Madame de Verseuil spoke for a long time to Pauline: She [Pauline] felt, while listening to her, an impression impossible to render; her soul was developing, feelings up to then uncertain, confused, were becoming clear and fixed; she was hearing the language that she had desired without knowing it; she saw open before her the way for which she had searched; she found in Madame de Verseuil the character that she had imagined like an illusion, of which she had conceived the idea without having encountered it.[19]

Now the word virtue, which had resounded in Pauline's mind without context, devoid of meaning, takes its place in a continuous discourse within which it makes sense. What had existed before only confusedly is now elaborated into a comprehensible system that structures the unformed soul, grounds an appropriate manner of speaking, charts a path for life, and provides an example to be emulated. A new world is made possible by the invitation of Madame de Verseuil: "Come, follow me into another country; put the immensity of the seas, put a virtuous education between your childhood and your youth."[20] One more act of dissimulation, to keep Meltin from interfering with her departure, and Pauline follows her mentor to France, where civilization and morality replace spiritual chaos. She finds a mother figure in Madame de Verseuil and sees the portrait of the father she had never known. With formative parental influence in place, the word virtue is filled with meaning through an extensive moral education. Signifier and signified are now united. Madame de Verseuil has thus played in Pauline's life the role of Staël's own mother, who provided her education and was particularly attentive to the moral development of her daughter. Up to this point, that maternal role is seen in a positive light. As for the father, he occupies a more distant position, that of a picture rather than of a presence, as did the Necker of Staël's own childhood.

But to live in a world of meaning exacts a price, in that Pauline can now experience a feeling which was as obfuscated as the word virtue in the old world, the feeling of remorse, guilt. Along with meaning comes reflexivity: one looks in at oneself with the knowledge of good and evil and is shocked at what one sees. The positive contribution of a significantly worded world is a reassured focusing of one's life. But its dark side is the guilt which takes form as Pauline compares her own history to the values she now understands. She condemns herself to solitude, cuts herself off from the world outside the safe, secluded cottage of Madame de Verseuil, particularly shunning the company of men. It is precisely at the point where language takes on meaning that Pauline settles into a life of silence.

She is not allowed to remain there. In the third part of the story, Staël maneuvers her heroine into a situation where she marries a virtuous young man without telling him of her past. Now she must dissimulate again; language, once more, is troubled. She is torn between telling and not telling, so that her utterances are enigmatic, truncated, vitiated, deformed into half-truth and innuendo. The idyllic existence her happy marriage and her new-found virtue should have created is unstable. The characters are not as voluble in Staël's false paradise as those of her inferno, but their halting speech is no less dissimulating.

By chance, Edouard, the righteous husband, learns of his wife's past from Meltin, briefly sojourning in Le Havre near their home. In the story's final section, Pauline's tongue is freed and she tells the truth. Not unrealistically, she fears losing Edouard by this revelation. He had always said that he could not bear to be married to a woman whose past was not pure, even if in the meantime she had repented and reformed. However, in an effort to overcome his own prejudices, Edouard promises to continue to love Pauline and urges her to believe in his love. Finally, words and deeds are brought into full relationship with each other. A new story may begin, in which dissimulation disappears, in which the past may be integrated into the present, and in which language is finally liberated.

But that is not what happens. Pauline falls ill from a fever that for three days plunges her into semimadness. When her reason returns, she announces her imminent death. She is not a moral fanatic, she claims. She believes she has expiated her past sins. But she will die. "The errors of my youth, the greater wrong of having hid them from you, have forever stained felicity that, by its very perfection, could not endure any change. By dying, I believe myself worthy of you; the excess of my passion is proved to you . . . . See, Edouard, if I am not happy to annihilate thus all the barriers that separated your soul from mine. We will be united in heaven, and until that moment my image will remain in your heart, as it was before."[21] Pauline here demonstrates the same ambiguity about guilt and innocence we have noted before. She insists that she is not obsessed by a feeling of guilt, yet she will behave as if she is so obsessed, by dying. For the second time in the story, once meaning is bestowed on or restored to language, words are cut off and silence sets in. At the moment when the lovers might have begun to speak together a new language and form from it a new life, Pauline makes one final statement and dies, preferring wordless union in heaven to spoken union on earth. Apparently any language at all, however honest and free, is basically an obstacle between people. The story has carefully worked itself to the point where authentic language seems possible and then radically rejected it. Any linguistic mediation, even one that would seem ideal, is finally undesirable, unsatisfactory.

Pauline cannot deal with language because what her parental figures had conveyed to her about how she should speak was ambiguous. In this, she revealingly figures the young Germaine Necker, caught in contradictions about her literary career. The narrator presents the mother figure as one who, having begun positively by introducing the world of meaning to her daughter, then takes on a more disquieting role, that of advising her to curtail her activities in that world, not to tell what she knows about it, to give a different public account of herself than that which is actually true in private. It is the mother who traditionally has the task of representing the voice of society to her daughter on most matters, particularly that of woman's appropriate manner of behaving. Many daughters particularly resent, as Staël apparently did, their mother's communication of this message, even more than their father's role in the matter. The mother, after all, is a woman too. Could she not feel solidarity with the daughter rather than with society? Apparently she does not, playing rather the role of the moralist, the one who transmits the normative message.

As for the father, he goes from the passive position of a mere portrait to that, embodied in another male character, of an active legislator. It is he who determines the laws which regulate the entire system in which all people must function, the "Law of the Father," to borrow the Lacanian phrase. Not surprisingly, he reserves the finest role for himself and dictates a subordinate one for woman. Edouard's conception of female morality specifically condemns any dissimulation whatever on the part of woman. "The heart of a woman is totally perfect only when it has no knowledge of itself; and the impressions she recognizes, the emotions she remembers never have the same energy."[22] The purity and perfection demanded of woman here is not compatible with meaningful language, which entails reflexivity on the part of the speaker, as Staël demonstrated in the second part of her story. Man wants woman to be a simple creature who neither looks in upon herself nor back upon the past. Woman's energy depends on her living in an eternal present, with her gaze directed forever outward. Her truth must be devoid of knowledge and meaning. This masculine attitude causes Pauline to feel, when her deception is revealed, that she must annihilate all her speaking. A relationship between the two characters may take place only in a supramoral, supralinguistic world, since neither the truth nor the lie will do. There, in that timeless beyond, no story can be told.

Each linguistic possibility that presents itself is less satisfactory than the others. Man insists that woman tell the truth but also stipulates that he will specify what the truth is. If it is not the woman's truth, then she must decide whether she will lie by speaking his "truth," risk his wrath and rejection by voicing her own truth, or remain silent. Yet silence is death. She who does not speak becomes an incorporeal image in the mind of someone else—the Pauline whom Edouard will remember. It is an image which one can only leave behind, not act out or inform with words.

Language will always be an inadequate instrument for the woman. She is a secondary being who depends on the male mind for her existence. Every word she speaks travels out of her contingent place, its route to the listener inevitably indirect, distorted. The primary, fundamental role belongs to man. It is he who substantiates, who defines, who decides on and imposes meanings. He insists that she function in his world, where he has established the links between signifier and signified. At the same time, he confers upon her a definition which makes it impossible for her to function; even as she awakens into consciousness she realizes that she has already fallen from the pure and unreflective state which he has defined for her. When Pauline speaks to Edouard of the perfection of their felicity, she is depicting their life together from his standpoint and not from hers. Happy though she was in the early period of their marriage, before the revelation of her past, she was always haunted and hampered by the thought of her guilt. In one sense, it can be said that the revelation caused a fall from bliss, a banishment from an idyllic existence. But it is more nearly accurate to state that the fall had already taken place. As in the Biblical archetype, one has already committed the guilty act before acquiring knowledge of good and evil. One is guilty before one knows of the possibility of innocence and guilt.[23] There is no return to a state of innocence, since she has never occupied it originally. Neither is there any way to work satisfactorily within the state in which she finds herself. That is why the acquisition of reflectiveness and the bestowal of meaning always undercut her speaking and why the only ending for Pauline is eternal silence.

The picture of Germaine de Staël that emerges from these early, embryonic works is strikingly different from the one we commonly have of her. We see her in contact with kings and queens, princes, emperors, the highest ranking and most brilliant people of her day. Then she seems somehow larger than life, bold, extraordinary even in her weaknesses and sufferings, exercising even stereotypically female wiles with a broader palette than an ordinary mortal. But here we glimpse the roots of the feelings her most perspicacious readers have seen, the "reticence and bashfulness" as an author to which Madelyn Gutwirth has referred,[24] which meant that "every time she took up the pen it was with trepidation."[25] When it came to writing, she fearfully shrank from a task she had set for herself. She was deeply intimidated, potentially crippled with guilt, cowed by threatening voices and disapproving looks.

And yet, from a different point of view, perhaps the truest measure of her courage is that she was to continue to write, and next, for the public, despite her fears. Perhaps the best measure of her talent is the self-pitiless lucidity with which she faces, exposes, writes out in detail those very forces that bid fair to silence her. She learns through this early writing that she will not feel free to speak openly and directly about herself. A woman who writes may fear the worst, for she works within a society where prohibitions, even taboos, against her are deeply rooted and fiercely defended. But she wills herself to write, and write she will. She has opened the way out of this chaos and confusion not by avoidance but by confrontation. She has acknowledged opposing forces and presented them to herself in their most virulent form. Now she is free to feel her way toward a literary existence, to give birth to herself as a writer, despite these forces.

3. *The Pedestal and the Statue*

The first task of the would-be writer, to launch her career—this was a matter very much on the mind of Germaine de Staël in 1786, her twentieth year and the year of her marriage to Eric-Magnus de Staël, Swedish ambassador to the French throne. She was full of desire to appear in print, to turn her private literary acts into public ones, capable of drawing recognition and, she naturally hoped, praise to her.

Her first published works are of particular interest for an inquiry about the literary existence of the writer. They recount her literary birth. One's birth, to be sure, does not determine one's life. Having been brought into the world under certain circumstances, having begun life with a specific set of situations do not mean that it is those situations, those circumstances that will always dominate. But one's birth is not a matter of indifference, either. It sets the stage, establishes certain expectations, hints at patterns which are likely to recur later, though frequently in changed forms. In the case of a literary birth, what counts is not so much those parents as historical figures but rather the way parents and literary models are experienced and imagined in the creative mind. What Staël's "parents" had to say to her through word and through example entered the life of her imagination and played a major role, for good and ill, in her birthing experience.[1]

She broke into print first in the *Correspondance Littéraire*, a newsletter prepared in Paris and sent abroad in order to keep friends of the Enlightenment informed of what was going on there. The editor introduces Staël's first little essay by identifying it as belonging to an ephemeral genre in vogue at that time, the "synonym." "A few conversations about the way to write synonyms, which the book of abbé Roubaud had inspired, gave the ambassadress of Sweden the idea of trying herself out in this genre. This essay appeared to be a model."[2] This indication is all we know about the circumstances behind the composition of Staël's synonyms. Apparently she was in the vanguard of the fashion. Further, it would seem that she was looking for, or at the very least sensitive to, ways of "trying herself out" as a writer. Finally, the editor suggests that she succeeded immediately in writing a piece which was judged to be a model in its genre. In this brief incident one can see a paradigm of what is to come. We perceive her ambition and her will to write in the rapidity and assertiveness with which she seizes upon and illustrates the suggested genre, while at the same time sensing her timidity and hesitation in her choice of such a small genre and one the idea for which came from someone else.

The chosen genre resembles closely the kind of writing done by Suzanne Necker. Among her works, published posthumously by her husband, are numerous maxims—pithy, wise statements focusing on a limited subject. At times these maxims involve close definitions of words, like the one whose beginning reads: "Nobility of character is a different quality from generosity: one can be noble without being generous, or generous without being noble; one can also unite these two merits at once."[3] How similar is this excerpt to the first of the two "synonyms" which were eventually published in the *Correspondance Littéraire*: "One is frank by character, one is true by principle; one is frank in spite of oneself, one is true because one wishes to be. When frankness is questioned often it cannot keep a secret; but since truth is a virtue, it also yields to a virtue of a higher order when it meets one."[4] The preoccupation with morality as well as a structure based on the distinguishing of similars are hallmarks of the mother's and of the daughter's work here. It is safe to speculate that Germaine de Staël learned to write pieces like synonyms with her mother, since Suzanne Necker provided her early and formative education. Thus, Staël is doing more than following or initiating a literary fashion when she writes synonyms: she is walking in the footsteps of her mother, regarding her mother as a model to be emulated, a sturdy place on which to stand in order to launch, however modestly, a career. At the same time, it might be argued, she is acting rebelliously, writing like her mother, but, unlike her, in defiance of her example, actually allowing—even encouraging, no doubt—what she writes to be published. Use of a model as point of departure, defiance of the model in order to depart: These are not unusual attitudes on the part of a budding author. In the case of Staël, they bespeak a complex relationship with the mother, in particular. The body of the mother nourishes, but it must be left behind, in a violent act of severance, if one is to move into self-nourishment. The mother, here, underlies but also undermines.

This double movement is very much in evidence as Staël proceeded to her next brief publication, again in the *Correspondance Littéraire* and again illustrative of a literary fashion of the moment, this time the writing of "folles," or "madwomen," described by the editor as "the depiction of a feeling exalted to madness."[5] The editor claims that the "folle" of the Swedish ambassadress was given to him under the seal of secrecy, but that he does not believe that his promise will be broken by publishing the piece—a way of indicating that the author has conveyed to her editor an attitude of false diffidence, letting him know that she wanted to be published while coyly claiming that she did not have such a wish. This is a fairly comfortable position for an ambitious yet unsure writer, in that she can both be published and yet not feel responsible for the publication. She has what she wants, but the parental figures can be answered, should they criticize.

That this genre was in vogue at the same time Staël was occupied with setting up her writing career is, of course, coincidental, but her attraction to it is surely not. Gilbert and Gubar put the theme of the literary madwoman at the forefront of their study of nineteenth-century women writers.[6] Staël seems here to be a prophetic precursor. In her piece, a gentleman, while passing through the forest of Sénart, is accosted by a talkative and yet mute crazed woman, who shoots through his sane world like an unpredictable comet. The feelings she expresses reveal what must have been preoccupations of her creator at this time, and, as the definition of the genre suggests, exalts them to madness. I distinguish three major affective areas. The first is the feeling of being rejected by a man. While the story, as we know it, of Staël's marriage would not seem to indicate that rejection came entirely from the masculine side, or indeed even chiefly, it does seem likely that Staël interpreted her husband's reaction to her as indifference (referred to as "horror") because of expectations she had, based on her father's adoration of her during her adolescence. She proudly recounts that once when she was dancing with her husband-to-be, her father intervened, saying, "Here, sir, I will show you how to dance with the girl you love."[7]

A second feeling is that of having left, practically abandoned, mother and father. Many children, perhaps especially daughters, are haunted by such thoughts when they leave the family to establish a home of their own. The problem was probably exacerbated in Staël's case by the fact that her husband was not the first choice of her parents for her. Suzanne Necker in particular had preferred the Englishman William Pitt the Younger. Staël's resistance obliged the family to find another suitable match for her, not an entirely easy task for this Protestant family in heavily Catholic France. The mother took the daughter's refusal all the harder because she herself had wished to marry an Englishman, Edward Gibbon, but been rejected by him.[8] While Staël apparently was not sorry that she had turned down Pitt, she did have reason to regret the marriage to the Swedish ambassador, since that marriage turned out to be unhappy virtually from the outset. Further, Staël was keenly aware, as we have already discussed, of going against parental wishes through her literary ambitions. Her madwoman feels lost, unable to turn back, miserable in her present circumstances.

These haunting feelings take the form, and this is the third principal affectivity of the text, of an inability to express herself. Marie-Claire Vallois, the only critic who has paid serious attention to this early composition, and who has done so with much acuity, identifies the woman's malady as aphasia, the total or partial loss of verbal function, and points out that the alienation of woman from the word is the theme here.[9] The narrator repeatedly asks her to explain her quite enigmatically expressed sentiments. She is never able to do so, giving evidence of a derangement of language which corresponds to her mental lapse. The narrator remarks "The movements of her eyes expressed the return of her ideas, but words were lacking. She moved her lips; a supernatural power seemed to bind her tongue; she made useless efforts and all her traits depicted impatience and pain."[10] The madwoman herself comments, "You see . . . I think, I cry, but I can no longer speak."[11]

To unbind one's tongue, to speak—this is what the writer must somehow do. Certainly Staël's madwoman is a hyperbole of her predicament, but hyperbole bears the shape of that which it exaggerates. The parents have been deserted. That is, Staël is setting out on her own way with acute misgivings. The madwoman says that she left them for their own good, which implies that they had reason to be disapproving of her, or would have had reason had they known her completely. Thus, also the male figure in her life-after-parents has experienced horror upon looking at her. No doubt we cannot entirely know to what fundamental feeling or feelings such statements refer. But the fact that speechlessness results suggests that at least one part of whatever cluster is functioning here has to do with the production of words. The disapproving faces cut off her words, lay low her ability to explain, to come to another (an outsider, a stranger, the public) with a verbal performance.

To publish in the *Correspondance Littéraire* was to publish timidly and to a very limited audience. Such a move is a useful one, for it unties the tongue (an especially important action when one's tongue threatens to remain bound) in a relatively safe, restricted environment. But because one is read only by the few and because, in this case, Staël was writing within quite restrictive conventional boundaries, such writing could not prove to be satisfying for long, not for an ambitious writer. Her next essay was to be published more openly and for a wider distribution, though, as Madelyn Gutwirth points out in her study of the two prefaces to the work, still anonymously with "everyone calculatedly informed of the author's identity."[12] It was the *Lettres sur les écrits et sur le caractère de Jean-Jacques Rousseau* (Letters on the writings and on the character of Jean-Jacques Rousseau), published in 1788.

This is a choice of subject matter as interesting as the choice of the form in which Staël first wrote. In the first place, Rousseau was a writer whom Suzanne Necker, née Curchod, particularly admired. Her protector, Paul-Claude Moulton, for whose children she served as teacher in order to support herself after the death of her parents, was a friend of Rousseau. Later, while in Paris, she corresponded with a friend, in admiring terms, about Rousseau's novel *La Nouvelle Héloïse*. She was to write to Moulton: "As long as *Héloïse, Emile*, all these divine and essential portions of Rousseau are in my hands, I can only regard the life of their author as a weak accessory and it seems that one should cast a veil over the faults of this father of virtue."[13] These are the very works the daughter will admire most and terms quite similar to those in which the young woman, once facetiously referred to as "the little Curchod" ("la Curchodine"), will express herself regarding Rousseau's life.

If the presence of the mother is palpable in the choice of subject matter and in certain attitudes and critical judgments, that of the father makes itself felt in two ways. First, Jacques Necker, unlike his wife, was not an admirer of Rousseau. In choosing to write about him, then, Staël has gone against the father's literary and philosophical preferences. James Hamilton observes that Staël's own preferences did not always put Rousseau first; he claims that her work should be viewed as "a point of departure rather than as a lifelong commitment to one model."[14] Indeed, the influence of another of the major "philosophes" of the Enlightenment is suggested in Staël's use of "letters" which are actually essays, reminding one of Voltaire's early *Philosophical Letters*. But as we examine the work, we will be able to observe how she handled this small act of infidelity to Necker's opinions, this choice of Rousseau as a "point of departure."

Her father's presence makes itself felt in the choice of the genre of this book. Staël identifies it as belonging to the extensive if minor genre called the "éloge," or panegyric. In the Necker salon, where Staël grew up, there were many who practiced the genre. Most particularly the abbé Thomas was known as especially proficient.[15] This Thomas, author of a 1772 work entitled *The character, the mores, and the spirit of women*, had been attending the meetings of the salon for a number of years. He is said to have helped Jacques Necker in the writing of his "Eloge de Colbert"(In Praise of Colbert), which won the prize of the Academy in the 1773 competition for the best work in that genre.[16] The work marked Necker's debut as a serious writer. Further, the choice of Colbert for his subject was not gratuitous. Aspiring already at that time to a ministerial position, Necker thought it expedient to associate his name publicly not only with laudable writing but also with the name of a great minister of the past. By choosing to write a panegyric Staël is thus closely patterning herself after her father, who had used such a work to launch his career, while at the same time she is affirming her independence from him by choosing Rousseau as her subject. In this decision she is perhaps giving herself more room to develop as a writer independent of her father than her contemporary Maria Edgeworth, who "wrote stories illustrating [her father's] theories."[17]

However, Jacques Necker was not the only member of the family who wrote in this genre. Staël's mother composed a number of "éloges." In her early journal, Staël mentions one of these in particular, a portrait of Necker the mother wrote at the same time the daughter was herself writing a portrait of her father. These—not coincidentally contemporaneous—projects set up, the young Germaine Necker says, a competition between them. Necker, she reports, did not pronounce a winner (wisely enough), but she makes a lengthy comparison between the two pieces, favoring her own subtly but unmistakably.[18]

Since both parents are present in this choice of subject matter and genre, it is important to note the particular nature of the Necker family drama and its impact on her literary birth. Whereas Staël and her mother had been quite close during her childhood—the mother provided the girl's education personally—in early adolescence a rift between the two women developed that was only to widen over the years. At the same time, though, a special closeness grew between daughter and father.

In her work and in her correspondence Staël speaks frequently of her father, rarely of her mother. Thus, it is not surprising that father and mother are quite differently present in this first published work. One must infer the mother's presence, whereas that of the father is overtly proclaimed. On several occasions Staël veers from speaking about Rousseau's writings to discussing those of her father, sometimes identifying him by name, sometimes not. At other times she merges the two father figures into one, transforming them tacitly into a paternal cluster. Meanwhile, the mother's presence is never acknowledged: one must be informed about her and about their relationship in order to sense it at all.

To pass over the mother in silence, especially when even the silences speak loudly of her, bespeaks self-deprecation on the part of the daughter and reveals negative feelings about herself as a woman. Staël is trying to show that she is one with her father, that she does not identify with her mother. To refuse one's identity in this way is not an action performed with impunity, as the continuation of Staël's literary life will show. Yet, at the same time it may have been necessary at the point of birth, in that Staël had to refuse the example of her mother's silence if she was to speak publicly. But presences not overtly recognized have a way of asserting themselves surreptitiously, insinuating themselves into the intentionality of a text and changing it in certain ways. The rejected and yet internalized presence of the mother, along with the openly discussed presence of the father, mold this text into a certain shape that gives considerable information about Staël's state of mind as she began to plot out a course for her career. Moreover, if it can be said of writers generally, as Staël says of Rousseau in the first of her letters, that their first work bears already the seed of those to follow, then one may expect to find in this inaugural piece some of the questions the young writer was asking herself, hints as to which subjects would energize or enervate her writing, and what plans she was making for her unfolding career.

As she saw it twenty-six years later, the essays on Rousseau appeared along with her "entrance into the world" and marked the beginning of her writing career. She viewed her debut rather ambivalently: "These letters on the writings and on the character of J. J. Rousseau were composed in the first year of my entrance into the world; they were published without my consent, and this chance happening involved me in a literary career. I will not say that I regret that, because the cultivation of letters has brought me more enjoyment than sorrow."[19] That the Staël of 1814 would have mixed feelings as she looked back on her literary life is entirely believable, since her writings did draw both praise and blame. Less plausible, though, are the claim that she had not wanted to publish this first work (Madelyn Gutwirth says that she was in "bad faith" in so stating)[20] and the concomitant implication that she was not at that time really planning a writing career, that she was by chance plunged into it by someone else. Both the enthusiasm of the *Letters* themselves and certain assertions in them strongly suggest that, to the contrary, this is the work of a young person who had every intention of becoming a writer, who had a life's work in mind, and who was with this short book announcing and setting out on that work. Apparently the tentativeness we have been observing in the young woman of twenty-two still existed in the mature woman of forty-eight, a telling comment on the powerful forces against which this woman must have struggled to become, to be, and to remain a writer.

That Staël fully expected this book to foreshadow her work and that she envisioned a close relationship between her writing and Rousseau's is made clear by the comments with which she concludes her work: "Who is the great man who would be able to disdain assuring the glory of a great man? How fine it would be to see in all ages this league of genius against envy! What a sublime example for their successors would be given by superior men who would take up the defense of superior men who preceded them! The monuments that they would raise would serve one day as a pedestal for their statue."[21] This passage illustrates the ambivalence which we will keep seeing throughout the work. The language is not quite direct. Staël uses all masculine words—"the great man . . . superior men"—when in fact she is speaking of and including herself, although in an oblique and indirect manner. She does not specify who belongs to this "league of genius," although it is not difficult to guess that she is a member of it, protecting one who is now dead, giving an inspiring example to those who will follow. Nor is the expression entirely free of grammatical ambiguity—to whom does the "their" of the last lines refer? The choice of the conditional and conditional perfect tenses weakens the effect that a future or a present would have and makes the tone appear guarded. Lucia Omacini documents Staël's frequent use of the conditional perfect tense, remarking that it "constitute(s) . . . a restriction of validity."[22] Such language creates uncertainty about the attitude being expressed, a diffidence that prevents the author from saying how ambitious she is, combined with an unmistakable expression of that ambition—to be one in that communion across the ages of the great, to forge her own link in the chain that provides continuity among them. Moreover, although the exclamatory form communicates excitement and enthusiasm, the affect here is partly negative, characterized by a defensiveness born of the feeling of being attacked, or vulnerable to potential attack. Yet despite the hesitancies in the passage, the central idea is clear and conveyed through a striking image: Staël compares her *Letters* to a pedestal which will support what will one day become the statue of her work.

The image is rich in implication. It indicates that Staël did indeed, in the late 1780s, have a "statue," a life's worth of writing, in mind, that she was consciously planning a literary career. Her planning, though surely not molded in advance, did appear to her as having a shape and a size. One does not ordinarily prepare a pedestal for a statue before the statue has been carved out, but presumably if one did so, as Staël's image says she did, one would make the foundation appropriate to that which it is to sustain, or, conversely, gradually form one's statue to fit the foundation. The image implies the need for a base, a grounding for one's planned work. One does not begin writing out of nothingness. There must be a point for the departure, a point of leverage upon which to lean at the beginning. What is announced through this image is a career of certain hoped-for proportions, grounded in the work of Rousseau. Clearly, then, a second subject of this book, and one as important as its most obvious subject, the works of Rousseau, is the work-to-be of Germaine de Staël. As Simone Balayé puts it, "this study on Rousseau . . . is indeed a way of reflecting about herself."[23]

The first question one would wish to ask about a foundation is whether or not it is a solid one. Not only the proportions but indeed the very existence of the statue to be built upon it would surely depend on its relative firmness. The passage in which the image of the statue is introduced suffices to indicate in a preliminary way that this grounding may be rather shaky. The tone gives witness to fear and eagerness, which mutually belie each other. The 1788 preface to the entire work, too, conveys uncertainty, built up as it is by a series of developments which tend to alternate in succeeding series each of which undercuts the previous one. It begins positively, "no panegyric of Rousseau yet exists: I felt the need to see my admiration expressed.[24] It draws back immediately, "I would have no doubt wished that another had depicted what I feel."[25] But then moves ahead, "but I experienced some pleasure in recalling the memory and the impression of my enthusiasm."[26] However, a bit later, Staël imagines a critical judgment upon her enterprise: "Perhaps those whose indulgence deigns to foresee some talent in me will reproach me for having hastened to treat a subject beyond even the strength that I would hope one day to have."[27] But she justifies herself in the face of this potential attack, saying, "how can one accept waiting for oneself."[28] The shiftings of this introductory passage suggest the ambivalence of an ambitious yet self-questioning writer. Rousseau inspires her to write; but his very greatness makes her both recoil in self-doubt and search for self-justification. He is both the reason to write and the threat against doing so. It is a strange and undependable foundation which constantly rumbles menacingly beneath one's very feet. These rumblings originate not only in the writer/model Rousseau but also, and more importantly, in those parents who stand over the birth of this new writer. They hover over this work as they will continue to do throughout Staël's career, suggesting some ideas, censoring others, enabling and undercutting, forming and deforming, unleashing and repressing.

These movements determine the conformation of the book itself. It consists of five "letters" on the writings of Rousseau, as follows: one, on the two discourses (arts and sciences, and inequality) and the letter to d'Alembert on the theater; two, on the novel *La Nouvelle Héloïse*; three, on *Emile*, Rousseau's treatise on education; four, on his political thought; and five, on his taste for music and botany. In the sixth and final essay she discusses his "character," using the *Confessions* as her material. The book's shape gives us a vivid image of the author's ambivalence.

The letters describe an irregular arc which begins at a low point, in doubt. A fragility of feeling about her own inspiration and talent mark the preface and continue throughout the first letter, dedicated to a discussion of the two discourses and the letter to d'Alembert. Concerning the first discourse, *Discourse on Arts and Sciences*, Staël expresses herself in a very hesitant way. Clearly she has criticisms to make about this work, but, apparently reluctant to speak against the great man here, she begins each of them with a timid "perhaps." The section ends with a veiled reference to her father, to whom are attributed intellectual and rhetorical gifts superior to those of Rousseau in his initial discourse. Rousseau bends his mind to a system; Necker wrote according to "reason."

The passage gives witness to considerable confusion about just what the author should think about the discourse, a confusion which may well arise from a conflict of models. In her letter on Rousseau's political writings (letter four), Staël will valorize practical experience and action, like that of her father, over abstract thinking. If her father's example puts into question the validity of general constructs, how can she praise Rousseau's creation of just that? Yet to attack Rousseau must have seemed equally prohibitive. She is faced with a difficult choice. Self-doubt clouds clear and original judgment here and obscures the language and the thought.

The self-questioning becomes all the more acute in the discussion of Rousseau's next two works, still in the first letter. Staël interprets Rousseau's second discourse, *Discourse on the Origin of Inequality*, as an opposition to ambition, understood as the desire of one person to distinguish herself/himself from and over others. This reproval seems to her to discourage achievement. As the text moves ahead, it will appear incoherent unless one remembers that the subject is not the discourse itself but Staël's struggle with the personalized idea that she read into it: that she should not have high aspirations and that, if she does, she will suffer loss of happiness.

> It is remarkable that one of the men who is most sensitive and distinguished by knowledge and genius wished to reduce the human mind and heart to a state almost like brutishness; but it is that he had felt more than others all the sorrows which these advantages, carried to excess, can cause one to experience. It is perhaps at the expense of happiness that one obtains this extraordinary success which is due to sublime talent. Nature, exhausted by these proud gifts, often refuses to great men those qualities which can make one happy. How cruel it is to give to them with such difficulty, to envy them with so much fury this glory, the only enjoyment that is, perhaps, in their power to taste.[29]

Staël is objecting to what she has decided Rousseau is saying, finding a reason for his having said it, pitying him for the unhappiness she supposes explains it, and finally defending him, and through him, herself, perhaps also her father. Her own ambitions are threatened in advance by this discourse: she wishes to distinguish herself, to rise above others, to obtain extraordinary success. It is disturbing to find that one of the "stones" of the pedestal upon which she is building that success opposes it in advance and warns of a painful sacrifice which she will be called upon to make.

Considerably more threatening is the message she saw in the *Letter to d'Alembert on Spectacles*, that women should not play an active part in society. Since to do so, by her actions as well as by her writings, is Staël's most definite intention, it was necessary for her to deal with this contention. She uses two strategies. The first is a reasoned argument: she accepts the idea that women should have an inactive role in a republic, while demonstrating that such a role is inappropriate for them in a monarchy. This is an idea to which Staël will return many times and which signals the presence of still another "philosophe" whose work was to continue to influence her: Montesquieu. The second is a so-called "feminine" technique: an exaggerated coquetry which claims to accept denigration. We have already seen this attitude in what she had to say about her father's disapproval of writing women, and her embracing of that disapproval. In this, she was following the example of her mother, who wrote a not dissimilar account of her own decision to act according to her husband's wishes regarding writing. In her most exclamatory and gestural style, she defends Rousseau for having attacked women by claiming that he loved them and that, for women, being loved is all that matters: "Anyway, he believes in love, his grace is obtained."[30] But finally, as the passage ends, she abandons both her reasoning and her posturing, and overtly objects to one remark of Rousseau on women. In a footnote of the letter to d'Alembert, she recounts, Rousseau had said that women are not capable of depicting passion. In her objection she concedes to Rousseau the point that there are sorts of writing women should not do: "These vain literary talents which, far from causing them to be loved by men, put them into conflict with them . . . . This powerful mental strength, this profound capacity for attention with which great geniuses are endowed."[31] This is to give up a great deal, but clearly Staël is giving up only in order to be able to make her more limited argument more pointedly: that in fact women are particularly well-suited to describe highly emotional states. "This sublime abandon, this melancholy sorrow, these all-powerful feelings, which make them live and die, would take emotion perhaps further into the heart of the readers than raptures born of the exalted imagination of poets."[32]

Again, a whole element of her foundation not only lacks the support one might well need; where there should be solidity there is not only shakiness, not only emptiness, but an actively undermining voice which conveys the idea that she cannot do what she aspires to do, that she should not aspire at all, in fact, and certainly not to write about the very subject which interests her most. And yet, it is in that very negative force that Staël begins to find inspiration to write, and that, not despite the lack of support beneath her, but against it, to prove that what Rousseau said was wrong. In that sense, her writing is an act of rebellion, however covert, however clothed in apparent obsequiousness, however undermined by her own inability to shake off self-doubt. The next letter in the essay shows further how this interaction of admiration and revolt works.

As the second letter, on *La Nouvelle Héloïse*, begins, the arc which began at a low point rises with abrupt energy, generated both by the argument with which the preceding letter ends and by this fourth work of Rousseau. His novel provides positive inspiration which sets the aspiring writer off not only in this lively letter, relatively free from the hesitancies and gestures of the previous one, but also in three works upon which she will embark after finishing her first piece. The *Essai sur les fictions* (Essay on Fictions), 1794, is prefigured when Staël, at the beginning of her discussion of Rousseau's novel, divides the genre into three subdivisions, as she will do in the later piece, albeit changing somewhat the content of the three. The criticism that Rousseau's treatment of love had evoked leads Staël to speculate here, as she will in the *Essay*, about whether other passions may effectively be the subject matter of novels, passions such as ambition and love of glory. She goes on to treat those passions and others in her *De l'influence des passions* (On the Influence of the

Passions), 1796. The beginnings of both lines of interest and inquiry are visible in this second letter.

Equally clear is her initial planning of her own epistolary novel, *Delphine* (1802). By means of examining criticisms which have been leveled against various moments of Rousseau's plot, Staël speculates on how else it might have been formed; in doing so she is in fact replaying, reformulating, and potentially rewriting that plot into another quite different one, which will be hers. The situations of the two are rather similar in broad outline, with sex roles reversed. In both cases a passionate young couple is separated by the marriage of one of them; the plot deals with their handling of their now impossible love. But Staël is already imagining how she will do things differently (her "Julie" will not be guilty of premarital sexual relations with the beloved) and at the same time revealing how she will profit from Rousseau's example. (Her novel will contain set pieces on various topics such as divorce and suicide.)

A comparison of these first two letters, the first, on the *Discourse on the Arts and Sciences*, poorly written, unclear, shifting abruptly among subjects, tortuously arguing and posturing, the second, on *La Nouvelle Héloïse*, flowing, specific in its references, centered on its subject, the one choked and bound, the other energetic and freed, presents the two sides of the evidence in this book regarding Staël's literary inspiration. Some of it seems positive and direct—admiring a work makes one desire to emulate it and evokes ideas for one's own endeavors. But a great deal of the energy behind her work is the negative or indirect force so evident at the ending of the first letter, the desire not so much to rewrite as to undo the predecessor's work and to put her own in its place.

The most obvious subject matter of the *Essay on Fictions* for example, is to be seen in the second letter, when Staël evaluates various kinds of fictional writing. But the generating energy behind it is more nearly explained in the first, where Staël objects to Rousseau's attitude toward women writers. In fact, the *Essay* is a response to Rousseau's *Letter to d'Alembert*. That book attacked theatrical spectacles as harmful to moral and political life within a state and presented, in passing, a misogynistic position toward women in general, woman writers in particular. Staël indirectly disproves all that in her book, in which she forms an argument which aims at carving out a useful place for fictions and which, by its very existence, gives the lie to Rousseau's negative contentions about women's capacity for writing. The *Essay* ends with praise of Rousseau's own novel: by this praise, Staël may well be attempting to turn away from herself the anger which she imagines the paternal force will direct against her for her act of rebellion. But the fact that her book contradicts Rousseau's arguments remains.

On the Influence of the Passions emanates from a similar motivation. Rousseau had said that a woman cannot write well about the passions. Well, here is a book in which one does. In this case the sacrificial offering to the supposedly angry gods is in the form of the thesis of the work, that only the suppression of the passions can lead to happiness. Yet still the rebellion, the act of describing them, is there. Several works of the next ten years of Staël's career, then, are in fact efforts to rewrite Rousseau in such a way as to negate and destroy those very threatening factors which she found in his writings and which, perhaps, echoed or were echoed by the parental powers in her psychic life. In this way it seems that Staël's image of the pedestal and the statue works in two ways. One compliments and defers to those who have been influential by claiming to have founded one's work on theirs. At the same time, the gesture toward the precursors is an aggressive and hostile one, which involves placing one's own work on top of theirs, substituting one's own work for theirs, replacing, erasing. By incorporating Rousseau into her own pedestal, Staël both perpetuates and consumes him.

The next movement of the arc one can trace through the book is an abrupt, downward motion. It is as if the mounting energy of the work, the build-up of inspiration, the excitement about making her own creation lead out into a dangerous area where her own rebellious pride invites punishment which must somehow be warded off. If the threatening parental cluster is relatively absent in the second letter, it is very much present in the third, on *Emile*. It is not, however, present from the beginning, not in any evident way; nor does this letter apparently have any particular interest for the present inquiry: Staël did not, after all, ever write a major work on education.[33] *Emile* has less echo in the Staëlian canon than many other works of Rousseau. The letter praises *Emile* as the first great triumph in Rousseau's career, defends it from potential criticism, and praises most aspects of it unstintingly. She is critical, to be sure, of the supplement to *Emile* which treats the education of the woman, Sophie, who is to be educated uniquely to serve and give pleasure to man, and certainly not to harbor ambitions of her own, literary or otherwise. Here she is tackling the double, Rousseau/Necker, father figure. Simone Balayé states that as she does so she is thinking of Rousseau to some extent, "but also [of] her father, who was equally opposed to the attempts in this area [i.e., that of writing] of his wife and of his daughter, and a whole society which accepts only grudgingly that a woman write."[34] Yet even here the confused strategies with which she confronts Rousseau's misogyny elsewhere are lacking. In short, the letter seems to proceed as easily as the previous one, on *La Nouvelle Héloïse*. No particular threats are apparent, so that the obscurity, shiftings, and gesturing which signal problem areas for Staël in Rousseau are at a minimum.

But certain aspects of the letter are strange and revealing. Staël speaks favorably here of two matters of which she had spoken unfavorably in her quite unsuccessful little piece on the first discourse, in her first letter. Formerly, she had vaunted her father's approach to thinking over Rousseau's. Here, though, she is better disposed toward "systematic" thought, calling Rousseau's approach a "sublime effort" (p. 10). Moreover, the basic movement of the two works, the first discourse and *Emile*, is similar, each involving imaginative retrogression to a point of origin and then moving forward through time to the present. While Staël was quite interested in history and in tracing causes for social phenomena, she was never able to be interested in speculating on origins which cannot be known for certain.[35] Certainly she considered that effort chimerical on Rousseau's part as far as society as a whole is concerned, but she finds it useful and fascinating in the case of the hypothetical individual Emile. Perhaps it is particularly significant that here Staël praises Rousseau's efforts to think back to origins. One's parents and the education they provide are one's origins, of course. It seems, then, that as Staël discusses this work, inevitably she will be thinking of her own beginnings. Moreover, she seems to have changed her mind on this issue as she wrote in a way which gives witness to a more positive attitude toward Rousseau at, potentially, the expense of her father.

These remarks may lead toward an explanation of why this letter, so full of the praise of Rousseau, ends with praise of Necker. Rousseau's *Profession de foi du vicaire savoyard* (Profession of Faith of the Savoyard Vicar) is inferior to her father's *De l'importance des opinions religieuses* (On the Importance of Religious Opinions), she states. She speaks of the latter in terms not only superlatively laudatory, but even tinged with mystical veneration. Necker is the guardian angel of the earth; she vows a cult to him; she dares not speak his name, so greatly does he inspire respect in her when she contemplates him. One may wonder how the praise of Rousseau, itself poised and thoughtful, modulates suddenly into such rhetorically and sentimentally inflated exaltation of Necker. It is as if the praise of Rousseau has been an act of impiety which needs to be expiated by making a linguistic sacrifice to the perhaps displeased first object of her worship.

The imagined displeasure might well have been exacerbated in this chapter by the subject matter, leading Staël as it did to praise Rousseau's system of education. She paraphrases some of Rousseau's central ideas and praises his approach to education, in the following terms:

> The child whose mind is not at the level of his memory will retain what he does not understand, and this habit disposes one to error.[36]
>
> How I love this education without ruse and without despotism, that treats the child like a weak man and not like a dependent being![37]
>
> With what care does he forbid these motivations of emulation and of rivalry that prepare the passions of youth in advance.[38]
>
> It is the eloquence of Rousseau that revived maternal feeling is a certain class of society . . . The happiness of the child depends on its mother: alas! one day perhaps she will press him in vain against her breast; her caresses will no longer cause calm to be renewed in her soul.[39]

Particularly admirable in his system are natural rather than artificially rapid intellectual development, honesty on the part of the educators, relative freedom for the child, motivation by need rather than by emulation and rivalry, closeness of mother and child.[40]

What we know of Staël's upbringing puts the particular points she chooses to raise about *Emile* in rather poignant light. Her education was apparently characterized by emphasis on mental rather than physical or emotional development, to such an extent that the latter were neglected and the adolescent Staël came close to a psychic breakdown. Her rather unloving mother conveyed, apparently, a repressive attitude as well as expectations the child felt at a loss to fulfill. We know also that Jacques Necker gave control of their daughter's education to his wife, as was customary at this time.[41] Perhaps it is valid to read the letter on *Emile* as implicit criticism of her own education and therefore of both of her parents, her mother who planned it and carried it out, her father who consented to it. That is the first step of rebellion, so that in the ending of the letter one can see a strategy to which the writer Staël frequently has recourse: exaggerated language used to hide real feelings or to compensate for having dared to suggest them, however covertly.

Another strategy is perhaps also at work here. Every child knows that parental authority is weakened if she plays one parent off against the other. Staël defuses parental authority in this letter by criticizing her mother, the parent principally responsible for her education, while praising her father, thus exonerating him for his part, removing him from the focus of her resentment. The letters on Rousseau as a whole use this same tactic. While one might say that Staël's parental figure is triply strong in that it contains both Rousseau and the Neckers, in fact, their combined voice is not thrice as powerful. Staël provides for herself the opportunity of finding her own writing space by undercutting each one with the others.

In this letter also one finds an initial explanation for still another striking phenomenon in Staël's career as a writer, the peculiar presence of the unwritten. Education was, for example, a subject frequently treated in the works of the eighteenth-century writers who, along with Rousseau, served as her models. She was quite interested in the topic, as this lengthy letter indicates. But she never treated it extensively. If one compares the shape of Staël's work to that of Rousseau, probably her single most important model, one finds missing pieces like this one in hers. To be sure, any writer may decide to treat or not to treat a given topic without the critic's being obliged, for all that, to view the omission as significant. Yet the pattern of omissions, especially in the case of a career which begins with such an obvious foundation in another writer, can suggest that a meaning is to be found. Moreover, the unwritten is so often in the case of Staël oddly present; that is, she constantly mentions subjects about which more could be said, even gives the impression she would like to go into them further, in some instances goes so far as to announce that she intends to treat them—but then the projected work never appears. This creates almost tangible, palpable voids which give a certain shape to the work, a shape characterized not only by what is there but, like all shapes, by what is not there as well. The suggestion in the third letter is that education is a dangerous subject, one which might lead too much in the direction of unfavorable reflection upon parental authority, one which the writer would do better to leave alone, or for which, if she treated it, she would have to redeem herself by some ingenious tactic.

The phenomenon of the unwritten is central to the fourth letter, on the political writings of Rousseau. The arc created by energy and atrophy in the book is now distinctly descending, perhaps because of the dynamics of the previous letter, so that now politics, a subject in which Staël had passionate lifelong interest, both theoretical and practical, which she discusses in many of her works, a major concern of countless letters, politics, then, inspires the second shortest letter in the work. It is only slightly more lengthy than the fifth letter on two subjects which interested her rather little at this time in her life, music and botany. This peculiar lack of expansiveness does not prevent the letter from containing the evidence the reader needs to interpret its very brevity; on the contrary, it is rich and revealing, suggesting why in Staël's whole canon no great work on politics exists (here again she deviates tellingly from her model) and containing a brief rehearsal of a technique she actually does use time and again in her writings. It consists of two movements, the first of which reveals what conflicts undercut her ambition to write about politics, the second of which involves the rehearsal for what she will write.

The first part of the letter is a meditation on what an ideal political work would be like. The first model is that offered by Rousseau in his *Social Contract* which Staël sees as a work of pure speculation and intense enthusiasm. It presents "a plan which is faultless as far as the imagination is concerned,"[42] worthy of the high praise due to "one who has made known to us everything which one can obtain by meditation."[43] He elaborates that plan according to what Staël calls the method of the geometers, that is, Rousseau takes a great central idea and follows it step by step in all its implications tracing it to its ultimate source. This method and its result are abstract and metaphysical; they are useful and admirable, and yet finally, she thinks, inadequate. For example, enthusiasm leads Rousseau to be consistent with his own theory to the point of insisting on a government run by general assembly of all individuals. This seems unrealistic to her, refusing as it does the representative form of government. In this instance, Rousseau fails to accept a political system which may actually be put into effect because of an idealistic ideological purity. This is the weakness as well as the beauty of Rousseau's approach to political thinking.

A second model is provided by Montesquieu, whose *Esprit des Lois* (Spirit of the Laws) examines specific laws in detail while placing them in the context of general ideas. This more practical approach, based not on speculation about how things might be but on study of how they are, has its own usefulness in leading toward a system less perfect than that of Rousseau but more nearly possible. The conflict between the abstract and the concrete, the metaphysical and the empirical, is not simply a conflict between the two models, Rousseau and Montesquieu. As the first part of the letter continues, it becomes clear that Staël is thinking not just of them but also of her father. Rousseau's limitation, one from which neither Montesquieu nor Necker suffered, was lack of actual administrative experience. "Let us place above the work of Rousseau that of the statesman whose observations have preceded theories, who has arrived at general ideas by the knowledge of specific facts, and who expresses himself less as an artist who designs the plans of a regular building than as a man capable of repairing the one which he finds already constructed."[44] In the final analysis, then, Staël opts for the second model, despite her admiration for the first.

But if these are the two models to follow, what kind of political work might this young author aspire to write herself? If she attempts to follow that of Rousseau, she will be hounded by the criticism she imagines from the Montesquieu/Necker figure, that she is wasting her time in idle and finally inapplicable speculation. At the same time, the other route will be equally closed to her by the simple fact that a woman cannot realistically hope to acquire practical experience in the actual administration of government programs and policies. She will then find herself unable to travel either of the roads which have been opened by her precursors. If she is to write at all, she must find some other way. Staël's work will be affected sharply by this impossibility and this search. Simone Balayé has described the conflict in this way: "Rousseau and her father, the writer and the statesman, these two faces of genius, will always remain two poles of the thought of this woman tortured by the desire to aid in furthering the happiness of humanity and limited to the role of writer."[45] But one must add that the role of the writer was itself limited by the conflict. Fewer than ten years after her letters on Rousseau she will announce, in the preface to her work on the passions, a yet-to-be-written work on the influence of the passions on government. She must have felt that this approach would enable her to elaborate a work on politics which could be neither speculative nor dependent on practical political experience. Yet she did not write even this book. The part of the statue which should treat politics if it is to conform to the contours of that of Rousseau is missing, and this brief letter tells why.

But it tells also what Staël is beginning to discover that she can do, in what sort of writing activity, related to politics, she can engage without confronting unresolvable conflicts. Its second movement begins in praise of Rousseau's eloquence, which does more than simply present a perfectly formed edifice of thought to the reader, which in addition evokes adherence and enthusiasm. When swept up by the exaltation Rousseau inspires, the reader ceases to examine the theories rationally but moves to another plane of experience entirely, wherein one does not reason, but feels, believes, adopts. What remains after such a reading is a state beyond intellectual acceptance of a theory; it is belief in the noble idea of freedom. The tone of this second movement is characterized by an increasing emotionality which culminates in two passionate apostrophes, the first to the French nation on the eve of the assembly of the States-General, the second to Rousseau, who is called upon to aid and inspire the French, and particularly the Frenchman whom Staël considered the key to the whole process, Necker himself.

The second of these two apostrophes contains some apparently rather strange sentences, if it is indeed addressed to the dead Rousseau. "Ah! Rousseau, what happiness for you, if your eloquence were to make itself heard in this august assembly! What inspiration for talent, the hope of being useful! What a different emotion, when thought, ceasing to fall back upon itself, can see in front of it an aim that it can attain, an action it can produce! The sorrows of the heart would be suspended in such great circumstances."[46] It seems peculiar to wish for Rousseau, whose work lies finished as a monument to his memory, inspiration for his talent. Surely the hope of being useful comes nearer to being a likely aspiration of the ambitious young writer, as does the desire for a "different emotion" which shall be inspired by the prospect of attaining a goal, producing an action. Staël is sketching out her own feelings here, the haunting thought that she cannot be useful, the depression which comes from fearing that she may not be able to act, the recoiling from the possibility of being radically banished to the world of her own inner life, incapable of coming outside of herself into the world of action. Staël is not exhorting Rousseau here; she is exhorting herself. Further she is trying out a form of writing which does seem available to her (unlike speculative or practical politics): rhetoric, a writing which will inspire those who can act to do so well. From this example of rhetorical flourish are to come, in the work of Staël, countless other such passages, which also emanate from her search for how to write and what to write about, and from her not-to-be-denied desire to turn the words which are at her disposal into the actions which are not. Here she is not just imagining herself rewriting, undoing, and redoing; she is actually trying herself out, practicing for what is to come. She foresees a way to write in the domain of politics without arousing threatening criticisms and encountering frustrating impossibilities.

The fifth letter, on music and botany, leads logically into the lengthy sixth letter, as both treat not Rousseau the writer but Rousseau the man. The driving energy behind this letter does not come, as did that of the letter on Rousseau's novels *La Nouvelle Héloïse*, from Staël's plan to emulate and rival the *Confessions*. With respect to autobiographical writing, Staël plans both to follow and not to follow the example of Rousseau. She finds appropriate the fact that he waited until his other writings had firmly established him before writing directly about himself. In like manner her most overtly autobiographical works come late, the *Dix Années d'Exil* (Ten Years of Exile) and *Considérations sur la Révolution Française*, (Considerations on the French Revolution). But neither of those works is truly confessional, nor indeed entirely autobiographical. Staël already knows in 1788 that she will not do such writing because of her own early autobiographical experimentation in her journal.

She does not even entirely admire Rousseau's book in that genre. "This work does not, no doubt, have that character of elevation one would like in the man who speaks of himself . . . ; but it seems that it is difficult to doubt his sincerity; one hides rather than invents the avowals *Confessions* contain."[47] Elevation apparently means omission of confessional statements of base actions, the purging of one's narrated life of the less than noble. The counter-example to that of Rousseau is her father's, as she revealed in her journal. "Elevation of the soul is of all qualities the rarest; my father is almost the only man who possesses it to its entire extent."[48] This is another instance in which Staël confronts a conflict of models. Out of her own experience, itself no doubt deeply influenced by her father's example and by her acute sensitivity to his watchful eye, she rejects for herself the path carved out by Rousseau. A lofty and idealized style is generated by just such thought.

This decision explains why this last letter is set apart from the rest. The book as a whole is entitled, we recall, *Letters on the Writings and on the Character of J. J. Rousseau*. When Staël calls this chapter "On the Character of Rousseau," it is clear from the outset that she will treat the *Confessions*, not as a piece of writing, but as a dependable and accurate transcription of his character. She does not ask to what extent the filter of perception through which Rousseau's memories passed has altered events; she takes the confessional statements at face value, sometimes justifying the traits they reveal but not stepping behind to question. Yet, what is written here is only briefly dispassionate description, only at first as Staël discusses physical appearance and qualities of personality. Then each development is introduced by some accusation generally or sometimes made of Rousseau, followed by a justification or explanation of each action or quality. Staël takes up each reproach in its turn: Rousseau abandoned his children, he was crazy, hypocritical, proud, base, ungrateful, wanted to distinguish himself, played a role, pretended unhappiness. The justifications are themselves fascinating, at times objective and shrewd, at other times mixing defense of Rousseau with self-defense, finally maudlin with sentimentality. Certainly tinged with self-defense, for example, are Staël's remarks on Rousseau as tainted with excessive desire to distinguish himself from others, the very point on which Rousseau's own criticism had evoked, in the first letter, strong reaction from Staël, who took the criticism personally. Sentimental without a doubt are those passages where she imagines that what Rousseau needed was a good woman to love him and indulges herself in the obviously futile fantasy of having been able to be that woman. It is just this close identification of self with Rousseau, whether confusing him with her or with an idealized imagined lover for him, that is interesting, especially in a letter whose beginning is critical and objective. The identification becomes stronger and stronger as the letter progresses, to the point that Staël herself recognizes it and exclaims, "Ah! now a useless tenderness is mingled with the enthusiasm which he inspires."[49] By the end of the letter, clearly Staël has identified sufficiently with Rousseau to see her defense of him as an advance defense of herself. "If calumny dared to attack them also [that is, those who have defended great men], they would have inspired mistrust against it in advance, blunted its odious traits."[50]

It is, moreover, from this self-defense that the letter's considerable energy comes. The sense of need for self-justification is itself rather peculiar. As Staël herself says at the outset of the *Letters*, it was her first book and appeared along with her entrance into the world. One wonders why at such an early date the young writer feels vulnerable to attack. Presumably no one has attacked her yet, either as a writer or as a person, yet the fear of that is palpable. The experience of stepping into the world of writing is tinged with danger. Writing is an active movement outside oneself toward others; it is an action fraught with danger. Certainly one would not, with such an attitude, speak of oneself overtly, confessionally, freely, directly; any self-revelation would have to take some sort of self-protective detour. It is in this sense that the ending of the letter explains the negative attitude toward confessional writing with which it began and, moreover, suggests a motivation for the obliqueness and indirectness of her style.

The ending of the letter is also the ending of the work, over which it casts, retrospectively, the shadow of its defensive posture, a posture present in its pages from the beginning. The very strategy of the work is aimed at advance justification. The author is saying to these parental figures who embody and echo so accurately and powerfully eighteenth-century society's judgment of the woman writer, they should not look askance at her enterprise for any reason, nor for her youth, not for her womanness, not for any unworthiness, because she is grounding her work solidly in theirs. Theirs is the authority behind her "author-ity." Their work, which she describes here, is the pedestal of her statue. She presents herself as defending and exalting them. That, however, is only part of the information which the book gives. She is pointing to places where there will be emptiness in her own work, compared with that of Rousseau, and providing suggestions as to how her parental models were speaking to her about what she should and should not write. But more importantly, Staël is, although covering her traces with hedges, maybes, flatteries, indicating where she disagrees with her parents, where she will deviate, rewrite, disprove, find a new way of her own.

The work on Rousseau is a paradigm of the canon that it so appropriately and accurately announces. It approaches and avoids its subject matter, in shifts occurring not only from paragraph to paragraph but from sentence to sentence and even within sentences. Its language and developments dart nervously to and fro, spinning out from an overflowing energy source of ambition and optimism at the outset of a literary career, yet encountering spiritual obstacles and therefore dodging, turning this way and that, using verbal strategies which permit the flow to continue, though sometimes compromising its course and its strength. The book sets the author off on a career to be characterized by an energy not to be stifled and yet by specters and threats never to be entirely overcome.

The letters on Rousseau are the first episode in the elaboration of a literary career. I have made certain suggestions already about the directions it is taking. In the next chapters, I follow up those suggestions in more detail by examining her continuing search for the subject matter about which she may both usefully and comfortably write and for the form, whether fictional or nonfictional, in which she may most effectively work. As the initial piece of writing indicates, her elaboration will be successful to the degree that she is able to marshal positively the forces present for her in her models without being overcome by the obstacles they set up nor discouraged by their threats. This is not to imply that she remains always the same person she was at the beginning of her career; on the contrary, hers is a dynamic and ever-changing story which involves the making of discoveries, the ferreting out of new avenues of exploration, the opening of subjects and means of expression which allow a continuing flow of writing. Yet the entire journey bears the imprint of its excited and uneasy point of departure.

4 *The Moralist and the Legislator*

Masculine Writing/Feminine Writing

A writer birthing herself with as much energy as misgiving, Staël moves out into the world of writing and yet fearfully glances backward as if she might at any moment flee into silence. Signs both of her determination to write and of continuing impediments are clear in her literary behavior of the early and middle 1790s. A period of intense political activity, it was not a propitious time for writing. It did, to be sure, provide occasions for Staël to do the kind of inspirational political writing she had projected in the *Letters on Rousseau*. She published a number of newspaper articles, "Réflexions sur le procès de la Reine" (Reflections on the Queen's Trial), 1793, and "Réflexions sur la paix" (Reflections on Peace), 1794. But it was also a forbidding time for such political writing. Two of her pieces, "Réflexions sur la paix intérieure" (Reflections on Peace at Home), 1795, and "Des Circonstances actuelles qui peuvent terminer la révolution et des principes qui doivent fonder la republique en France" (On Current Circumstances Which Can End the Revolution and on the Principles Which Must Found the Republic in France), 1798, were to be published only posthumously; apparently she felt that they were too dangerous to publish at the time when they were written.[1] It is not very satisfying for a writer to produce works that are to remain in a drawer.

However, Staël was getting a number of pieces into print. In 1790 she published her "Eloge de M. Guibert" (In Praise of M. Guibert) and the two verse dramas she had written in the late 1780s, *Sophie ou les sentiments secrets*, and *Jane Gray*. And in 1795 there appeared a little volume of works entitled simply *Recueil de pièces détachés* (Collection of Detached Pieces). The first of the works to appear here is a piece she had apparently written fairly recently, *Essai sur les Fictions* (Essay on Fictions), but included also were short tales which she says she composed before she was twenty years old, before the Revolution. (They included the *Story of Pauline*, discussed in chapter 2.) These works have never been dated with any accuracy, though it does seem likely that her claim to have written them earlier is correct. If so, perhaps Staël is satisfying her somewhat frustrated desire to publish ("Reflections on Peace at Home" was too dangerous, the *Influence*, still unfinished) by resurrecting some works from the past, writing a new introduction, and getting them into print, lest the reading public fail to notice that she is still a writer.

But political writing and the publishing of previously written pieces were not the only literary activities of Staël during these troubled years. Occupied as she was with the turmoil around her, she was very much thinking of her career, "forging a vocation," in the words of Madelyn Gutwirth.[2] In 1793 she began what was to be her major long-term project of the early and mid-1790s, *De l'Influence des Passions sur le bonheur des individus et des nations* (On the Influence of the Passions on the Happiness of Individuals and of Nations). She was to spend three years on this work and to publish it only in September of 1796. At that point, she preceded it with these words: "People will think, perhaps, that there is haste on part of an author who publishes the first part of a book when the second is not yet done."[3] This book, so long in the making already, was still unfinished. The author seems to be in a hurry to get it into print, but at the same time encountering difficulty in completing the project. Why was she having trouble with this work, so much so that half of it not only did not appear in 1796 but in fact was never to appear? It seems that while Staël obviously wanted to write and to publish, she was running up against some obstacle in doing so. Her difficulties are to be explained not only by reference to the distractions of her personal and public life, but, more interestingly, by their connection with those same kinds of conflicting feelings about writing which we have already seen in the *Letters on Rousseau*.

Specifically, what was giving Staël trouble at this stage of her career was her search for what I call her sexual writing identity. The conflict for her over this issue was acute. Here was an individual who personally identified quite clearly as a woman but who wished to perform the act of writing, ordinarily a male prerogative. Does one suspend one's femaleness while writing? Does a man suspend his maleness? Does each become some *tertium quid*, the writer, devoid of sexual identity? If not, if one, quite to the contrary, writes out of one's sexuality, then presumably a male can proceed without troubling himself about sexual identity. Since writing is traditionally a male act, he will feel at home as he moves into that world, however many other difficulties may beset his project, difficulties which, of course, I would not wish to minimize. But a woman—will she be obliged to leave her sexuality at the gates, whether of horn or of ivory? If she does not do so, will either her sexuality or her writing suffer harm or danger? Will she turn, as Gilbert and Gubar show many women writers do, to "male mimicry" or "some kind of metaphorical male impersonation"?[4] These are questions fundamental to an understanding of whether there is such a creature as a "woman writer," whether one writes out of or without one's sexual identity. For Germaine de Staël these were questions to which she had to find answers for herself, under penalty of falling forever silent. Two works which she wrote in the mid-1790s tell of her search for a sexual writing identity.

In the first of these, the *Essay on Fictions*,[5] Staël makes a number of distinctions among kinds of writing which, when we study them, reveal what types of literary performance and what qualities she associated with maleness and femaleness. In order to understand her struggle toward her own sexual writing identity, it seems useful to look closely at how she conceptualized male and female writing.

The structure of the *Essay* is differential. Staël distinguishes between modern or "natural" fictions and other fictional forms, between life and fiction, between reason and imagination, between moral philosophy and fiction, between virtue and happiness, between speculative philosophy and fiction, between history and fiction, between modern fiction and historical novels. Her mind is functioning on a base of two, proceeding by a series of binary contrasts. The basic distinction which underlies all of the others is that of "supplementarity" and "alterneity." Fiction is said to provide a supplement to life which by itself is characterized as unsatisfactory because those who are sensitive and intellectually superior have needs beyond that which reality can supply. Fiction can fill the gap between desire and fulfillment with at least temporary happiness and plenitude. In order to fit into the empty places it is intended to supplement, it must keep a basic consonance with experience. To form a fiction, then, one imaginatively selects certain moments from experience and recombines them into a more satisfying whole.

There is little new in this conception of fiction. *Imitatio naturae*, literature as imitation of nature or life, had been the fixed phrase and central idea of literary theory since Aristotle and, with few exceptions, certainly dominated French thought from the Renaissance until well into the nineteenth century. What is typically Staëlian here is the insistence on life as inadequate and full of sorrow, in need of some supplemental entity in order to enable one to carry on.

The other types of writing Staël discusses—moral philosophy or ethics, speculative philosophy or metaphysics, and history—do not function by supplementarity but rather by alterneity. Virtue, the product of moral philosophy, is set aside early in the essay into an untouchable and separate domain of its own. It is "positive," that is, definable, certain, settled once for all. Its realm is delimited and complete within itself. Its limitation appears only when it is brought to bear upon the world of feelings, where its results are devoid of application, so different are they from emotion. Moral philosophy utters wise and inapplicable dictums. Virtue dictates; it does not supplement, though its precepts must be followed by the individual.

When Staël speaks of moral philosophy, the words of her parents are echoing in her mind. It was her mother whose (posthumously) published works consisted of maxims—those wise and inapplicable dictums—and a work on divorce rather obviously directed toward her daughter, who, Suzanne Necker thought, was insufficiently devoted to the institution of marriage.[6] Staël's way of handling the matter here consists of two movements. In the one she pays respect to the requirements of virtue by claiming that one must conform to them. In the other she shows her rebellion against them by claiming that, imperative as they are, they do not really apply to life and by setting them aside in a revered but ignorable other place.

Speculative philosophy is alternate in a different way. Metaphysics is not "positive." It does not posit but rather supposes (surposits). Its domain is "abstract regions" and anything which is said within them is hypothetical. This kind of philosophy has its own rules, but they are not the rules of life. It involves a more free and nonverifiable way of thinking than fiction, which must conform to reality in order to be effective. Staël calls allegorical fictions, which express philosophical hypotheses in fictional terms, "fictions within a fiction." These hypotheses, then, are invented or created like fiction but at the same time more so. That is, they are more fictional (in its etymological sense of being made up) than fiction, in that the latter is subject to something tangible and immediately knowable. Fiction, then, does not take us away from experience; if it did so it would not play its role as supplement. Speculative philosophy, in obeying its own internal rules, belongs to the structure of alterneity, that is, it opens the way into an alternative world.

Staël makes a similar distinction between historical and fictional writing. History is more similar to fiction than speculative philosophy in that it selects some events and some lives from the past (everything that has happened). However, its principles of selection are not the same. It does not concern itself with the "life of private men," being interested only in that which resulted in "public events." Thus the narration of history contains "immenses intervalles" (large empty spaces) where most private destinies are played out. History omits the private and concentrates on the public. In that sense it is abstract, exclusive, even though it does recount events which actually happened. Staël's thought joins that of Jane Austen, as described thus by Gilbert and Gubar: "Austen implies that history may very well be a uniform drama of masculine posturing that is no less a fiction (and a potentially pernicious one) than gothic romance. She suggests, too, that this fiction of history is finally a matter of indifference to women, who never participate in it and who are almost completely absent from its pages."[7] In short, both history and speculative philosophy are abstractions (literally: that which has been taken out) which, though precise in their manner of elaboration (speculative philosophy must be faithful to its inner laws; history must recount what really happened), exist in realms whose connections with experienced life have been cut, which depend on a process of leaving aside. History, thus, like speculative philosophy, is alternative, not supplemental. The difference between philosophy and history on the one hand and fiction on the other seems paradoxical in that the latter is finally presented as less imaginary, less "fictional," than any form of theoretical writing, where there is truly an alternative universe. In the final analysis, Staël, who began her essay from the banal perspective of the classical *imitatio*, sees all forms of writing as fictional but fiction as fictional least of all.

These associations take on an unmistakable logic when one analyzes how Staël conceptualizes literary maleness and literary femaleness. In the first place, in setting up her distinctions binarily, she is certainly demonstrating that she "thinks like a man." The history of thought is characterized by dualisms and struggles with dualisms. Staël has very much internalized this way of thinking here and throughout her entire work. Things are this or that, spiritual or physical, concrete or abstract, and so on. Furthermore, Staël shows that she has completely internalized concepts of what is stereotypically male and that which is stereotypically female. Her distinctions can be spelled out in this way: on the one hand, speculative philosophy and history, the abstract, the invented, and the public represent maleness; on the other, imaginative fiction, the concrete, the imitative, and the private reflect femaleness. For Staël, the public domain was the more attractive: it was the "theater" in which she wished to play out her life. She suffered profoundly from the fact that as a woman she was barred from doing that in a direct way. At the same time, it seems to have had a certain unreality for her because she was excluded from it. It seemed abstract, fictional, made up, an alternate universe. The private domain was in most ways not as attractive as a stage for a life, but it was more real to her as a woman. If male and female are so clearly distinct that they function in different literary worlds, then must a woman not limit herself to the world associated with her sex? But if she does not wish to do so, how, then, can she proceed? Unlike Jane Austen in this respect, Staël does not show a "willingness to inhabit a house of fiction not of her own making."[8]

Rather she is trying to find a way to work outside "houses" built for women in her next work, *On the Influence of the Passions*, 1796.

In her introduction to the work Staël spends a great deal of energy expounding the plan of her work. She was, as we know, publishing only half of the work at this time. Regarding its two parts she makes conflicting claims. The first is that the two are connected; the second, that they may be considered separate works. Which of these claims seems more nearly to fit the case? Staël does stoutly maintain their connection. She says: "Two works are found in a single work: the one studies man in his relationship with himself; the other, in the social relation of all individuals among themselves."[9] There is, she says, an analogy between these two conceptions. The strength of government acts over a nation as reason over an individual. Moreover, the whole, she claims, is depicted in each of its parts: "What is big is found in that which is small, with the same exactness of proportions. The whole universe is depicted in each of its parts, and the more it seems to be the work of a single idea, the more admiration it inspires."[10]

To this extent, then, it is appropriate to accept Staël's claim that these "two" works are a single unified whole. The first consists of three parts: one, an examination of major human passions: love of glory, ambition, romantic love, vanity, gambling, avarice, drunkenness, factionalism, crime; two, "feelings which are between passions and resources one finds in oneself," friendship, filial, paternal, and conjugal tenderness, religion; three, "resources which one finds within oneself," philosophy, study, beneficence.[11] The aim of the piece is to demonstrate the disadvantages each of the passions, no matter how attractive, has when viewed in conjunction with the happiness of the person undergoing the passion and to find ways to comfort the wounded, passionate soul. As Staël readily admits, she is preaching to herself as well as to others.

What she has written here belongs to the female series of the duality described in her *Essay*. She is depicting private life. Though her work is not fictional, fictional forms do play an important part in its developments. The chapter on love is, in the completed work, an expository piece, and thus a work of moral philosophy in the terms of the *Essay*. However, originally Staël intended to insert in the place of that chapter a short story written especially for that purpose, as in fact her contemporary Chateaubriand later did when he intercalated the fictional piece "René" into his *Le Génie du Christianisme*. She decided against using this story, entitled *Zulma*, and published it separately. But the fact that she contemplated using it indicates how much fiction was in her mind as she wrote the *Passions*. Two chapters, the one on ambition and the one on vanity, incorporate a fictional form, the "portrait," in the manner of La Bruyère.[12] Moreover, the parent she most associated with the "book on morality" was her mother, from whom she learned the classical French writers, such as La Bruyère, and who, as we have seen, wrote moralistic maxims and treatises. This is a work that concerns the private sphere, a woman's work, in which she fulfills the same role as the mother figure in the *Story of Pauline*, that of the moralist. By placing herself in the position previously occupied by the mother, she is displacing her mother, acting in a covertly aggressive way, substituting her own work, her own thought, her own approach to morality, for that of her mother. She rejects the kind of morality which resides in wise and inapplicable dictums, such as "one can always conquer oneself, one is always master of oneself." Such maxims are of no use to the passionate person. Her book shall be different. "Among so many books on morality, [I hope that] this one can be useful."[13] This, then, is the book of the woman, the moralist.

This act of replacing the mother's writing with her own is bold indeed, but her boldest move is this: She planned to combine a feminine with a masculine work, thereby showing that she could function in either mode, according to the associations of either side of the dichotomy set out in the *Essay*. In writing the masculine and the feminine together, she would demonstrate, she apparently felt, that she was more than a woman writer, rendering inapplicable the accusations ordinarily hurled at woman writers, the dilemmas "they" face. It will not be necessary for her to remain silent or to lie as "they" do because she is not one of them. She is a woman and writes as a woman does, as she demonstrates in part 1 of this work. But part 2 is the work of a masculine mind, the work of a legislator, clearly associated with the male series built up in the *Essay*: historical, abstract, public, dependent on invention in that it is the mind which is to build up the structures of interpretation.

The second part that she announces in her introduction is to treat various types of government with respect to the question of how much freedom they leave to individual passions. It is to consist of three parts: one, those governments which are too repressive; two, those governments which are too permissive; three, the inadequacy of small states for the development of the individual; and, finally (apparently a sort of coda), representative governments as the kind most likely to avoid the excesses of the first two types. She makes the claim that the first part of the work leads necessarily to the second because of the analogy between the individual and the nation stated above. To establish such an analogy would be to suggest that the masculine and feminine, the legislator and the moralist, are alike or at least commensurate. One person might, therefore, play both roles or write a book that includes both. If Staël can indeed set up the analogy, she will be working toward realization of her dual sexual writing identity. But in the development of these analogies, several disquieting inconsistencies appear. She defines happiness in the case of individuals and of nations as being alike, but her definitions are in fact not at all alike. She wants to show that in both cases happiness involves a union of opposites, as it does in the case of nations, which find it in the conciliation of the freedom of republics and the calm of monarchies. However, she describes individual happiness as "hope without fear, activity without worry, glory without calumny, love without inconstancy."[14] Such a process is not one of rendering opposite things compatible but of excluding some elements from others. There is something wrong with these claimed analogies. Again, she states that the aim of individuals in dealing with passions can be to make themselves morally independent of them, that is, to be able to conquer and rule over them entirely. In the case of governments, total rule over individual passions is not the aim but rather a calculation of how much freedom can be allowed and how much governing can be tolerated without interfering with it. Moreover, in speaking of individual passions one observes oneself and others; analysis of governments, Staël claims, will eventually become a science—political science, as we call it today; it will attain mathematical certitude in its projections and descriptions. Part 1 of the work, then, is subjective and inexact. Part 2 is to be exact and objective. Finally, the attitude that will characterize each part with respect to individual happiness will be different. "As much as the moralist must reject this hope [i.e., the hope of happiness], so much must the legislator endeavor to approach it."[15] Apparently the two "analogous" parts are not so much alike. The moralist and the legislator do not proceed in parallel fashion.

Neither here nor later in her career did Staël write a political work of the amplitude and level of abstraction that she envisions in this introduction. In fact, the reader has the impression that, even as she wrote her fairly lengthy description of the complete work, she knew that she would never finish it. Madelyn Gutwirth states in fact that the *Passions* is "a political act in that it was intended to prove that she was *not* a political animal."[16] Staël says that she has scarcely begun the political part and that it is obviously going to take a long time to do the research behind such a work. But, she goes on, "if the accidents of life or the sorrows of the heart were to limit the course of my destiny, I would like another to finish the plan which I have proposed for myself."[17] Later she repeats the idea that perhaps someone else will have to write the work she has in mind, "this work, which I will do or which I would want someone else to do."[18]

It has been suggested that Staël did, after all, write her political work in the unpublished "On the circumstances which can end the revolution . . ."[19] Indeed, this unfinished work contain discussions of the kind of constitution Staël wanted to see adopted in France. To that extent it is the work of a would-be legislator, although, while its author puts forth her ideas, she is very careful to point out on several occasions that she allows herself to make suggestions along these lines only because, precisely because, she, as a woman, cannot possibly foresee playing any role in the actual political arena. The argument is that this inability to act gives her the vantage point of a disinterested outsider. Further, she states that she lacks the ability to play a political role, even if her sex were to permit her to do so. She speaks of her wit, which enables her to perform brilliantly in conversation, but claims that she lacks *adresse*, the skill which politicians must have. But even having so carefully built defenses around her political statements, she still could not publish this work. In fact, it was not among those unfinished works found in her papers when she died and published within a few years thereafter. It had been confided to her friend Madame Récamier and was to be published only many years later.

The moralist has carried out her plan; as for the legislator "he" is silenced. She has wanted to compose a woman's work and a man's work in one. In this way she is apparently trying to combine her own female identity with what she perceives as man's world, in which she so much wants to participate. But her analogies simply do not work, not even at the theoretical level at which she discusses them in her introduction. The bringing together of the masculine and the feminine is a potential solution to her dilemma. If she can, as writer, be both, then she can escape the limitations to which patriarchal society assigns her. Perhaps her ambition to do a great political work was sharpened by the fact that not only her male models, such as Rousseau and Montesquieu, but even the men around her, Benjamin Constant and her own father, did this kind of writing. But her approach to sexual writing identity here is flawed in the very definitions she assigns to male and female, so polarized and incommensurate does she make them appear. The masculine and feminine provinces of writing seem too removed from each other. To write them together, with analogies and connections in place, is impossible. Perhaps Staël is perceiving that a woman cannot serve both as the legislator, who sets up the laws which exclude her, and the moralist, who indicates to herself and others what the appropriate behaviors within them are. Certainly she is chafing at the restrictions placed on woman writers, tapping along the walls in search of a way out.

Moreover, that in Staël's view the woman cannot serve as legislator is emphasized in her discussion of woman in the *Passions*. Like Pauline, she lives always after the fall. "Nature and society have disinherited half of humankind; strength, courage, genius, independence, everything belongs to men; and if they surround the years of our youth with hommage, it is to give themselves the amusement of overturning a throne, as one permits children to command, certain that they cannot force one to obey."[20] Issues of power, those dealt with, precisely, by a legislator, are prominent here. Women are always in the position of children, humored for a time by men who give them the illusion of power. But these same men are always laughing secretly at women. They know the real rules, for it is they, the true legislators, who have made them.

A Rhetoric of One's Own

To note the failure of Staël to produce the second part of the *Passions* is not to say that she has reached a dead end in her work of the 1790s. After all, she did write the quite extensive first part of that work, as well as a number of other pieces. If she has not solved the dilemma of writing in a male and female fashion, she has successfully addressed another problem. Here is a writer who wanted to write about herself and yet who had, early on, decided that she would never write confessionally. The problem became, then, how do you write about yourself without writing about yourself? Staël's male model, Rousseau, and many of her contemporaries, Constant and Chateaubriand, to mention two prominent examples, did not struggle with such a question. They wrote about themselves in the form of confessions, memoirs, or journals, or in fictional forms, transforming their own stories into veiled and artistic form; or they composed expository works on such subjects as politics and religion. When they did each kind of work, they knew, in general, what kind of work they were in the process of writing. By and large they remained faithful to the conventions and expectations of that kind. This sort of rhetoric, which defines its genre and behaves appropriately within it, has been consecrated in the annals of good taste as good writing. Perhaps one reason why the writing of many women has not been adequately appreciated, why not as many works by women find their way into those canonized as the great classics, is that in many cases woman writers do not work according to that kind of rhetorical rule.

Staël is an excellent example of such a writer. She said she was not going to talk about herself, and yet she seems to do little else.[21] A criticism made of her even by her most astute readers is that she failed to commit what Jean Starobinski has called that "literary suicide" that gives characters their "plenitude of literary existence."[22] Taking up this same phrase, Simone Balayé speculates that "perhaps this personality is too strong, too sensitive, too disquiet, to forget itself, to commit 'literary suicide,' the total sacrifice which gives birth to the masterpiece."[23] Martine de Rougement, speaking of her plays, joins in, stating that she "transported her characters into herself rather than transporting herself into her characters," and thus failed to commit "the suicide of the artist."[24]

To make matters worse, it seems that she talks about herself at the most inappropriate times. Does she not know that if one is writing a book on morality, for example, one does so in abstract terms and that in such works it is inappropriate to gesture to the reader for such effects as pity, sympathy, and even love? We have to assume that Staël did know that. She had read many books and was quite familiar with what had been deemed appropriate to say in them. If she chose to write differently, it must have been because her writing was formed by her ways of resolving the conflicts and of meeting the demands that she experienced as she wrote. If one wishes to understand writing rather than simply to judge it by ready-made, time-consecrated values, it is necessary to determine what went into the making of it. At that point, what appears is not simply a "failed masterpiece," albeit "teeming with riches,"[25] but a piece with its own particular value, to be judged by its own standard.

If a woman writer wishes to talk about herself without doing so, clearly she is going to be inventing her own rhetoric. This observations seems all the more true when one considers the dilemma Staël sketches in her story of Pauline. She will need to find a way of speaking that is neither a statement of her truth nor a bland repetition of the "truth" of others. Staël is obviously thinking out this question in the *Passions*. "General ideas would cease to have universal application if one mixed in the detailed impression of specific situations. In order to go to the source of man's affections, one must enlarge one's reflections by separating them from personal circumstances: they have given birth to the thought, but the thought is stronger than they; and the true moralist is he who, speaking neither by invention nor by reminiscence, depicts man and never himself."[26] Where is that most effective rhetorical ground, she seems to be asking herself, that is determined neither by invention (which is too abstract, too removed from experience) nor by memory (which is excessively attached to one's own particular situations)? As she searches for it in this book and in her subsequent writing, she is looking for ways of incorporating confessional materials into the text.

She does so at several levels. The first is simple and direct: she tells us how she feels in the first person. At the end of her chapter on love of glory, she refers specifically and in personal detail to her own father. The chapter on love is different from the others, she specifies, in that, whereas the others are based on observation of people, this one is based on her own experience: "I dreamed rather than observed: may those who are alike understand each other."[27]

At a second level, she refers to details of her own life but obscures them slightly. Speaking of objections and criticisms that people may make of her work, she begins to speak in very general terms of the fact that one is very naïve when one is young. "But at twenty-five, at this very time when life ceases to grow, a cruel change in your existence comes about: people begin to judge your situation; all is no longer future in your destiny; in many ways your fate is fixed and men wonder then whether it is appropriate for them to link themselves to it."[28] No one would be able to mistake Staël's rather self-pitying depiction of the fall from innocence, but she has not, admittedly, "spoken of herself." Many times, though, the echoes of herself are more distant. Hearing them requires knowledge of her recurring preoccupations. Her feeling of guilt, for example, resounds when she asks, regarding celebrated persons who are victims of public calomny, what if the person in question has real faults, has committed real wrongs, "which, however, so often are found united with the most eminent qualities,"[29] Or again, the reader familiar with Staël's frustrated will to power recognizes the cry of her own voice when she speaks of what love does to woman, love that "like the burning wind of Africa, dries up in the flower, beats down in its maturity, and finally bends toward the earth the stem which was to grow and dominate."[30]

At a third level, the one at which she increasingly is to function as her career progresses, the personal element is completely merged into the texture of the text itself. It is only by noting structural and semantic similarities that exist between an apparently "objective" situation she is describing and her own story as she saw and described it that the reader understands that Staël is talking about herself. Because this is the safest level at which to function (one can say one's own truth without seeming to do so, thus avoiding the double dangers of dissimulation and silence) her most interesting and self-revealing confession comes precisely in this way. For example, in the chapter on love of glory, Staël sets out to discuss the impact different kinds of governments have on the development of this passion in individuals. She talks first of those governments in which "hereditary distinctions are established," that is, monarchies. She immediately thinks about difficulties individuals encounter who are filled with a desire for glory but who are not born into a royal or aristocratic family. Those of higher birth take umbrage at one's ambition, thinking that it is scornful on the part of seekers of glory to wish to raise themselves to a higher level by talent. "Individuals of the same class as oneself who have resigned themselves not to leave it, attributing this resolution to their wisdom rather than to their mediocrity, call a different type of conduct from theirs folly."[31] One is reminded instantly of Jacques Necker, the banker turned minister, the man of the middle class who, because of his wealth and political position, came to associate with the aristocracy. But beyond that, since Staël herself was seeking literary glory at this very time, a glory to which her birth as woman did not entitle her, she was encountering a similar reaction. Men, who comprise the class of those who have the prerogative to write, look with disapproval on women who are trying to occupy that same position by talent rather than by birthright. Meanwhile, women who have resigned themselves not to seek such glory (Staël's own mother, for example) also disapprove, in the name of their own mediocrity. This text involves, then, a covert criticism of both men's and women's attitudes toward writing women that Staël probably would have been unwilling to express in any more overt way, not only because she did not want to write confessionally, but also because this topic was too potentially dangerous to treat openly. Again and again, the driving energy behind texts on topics apparently unrelated to Staël's personal situation, or related in some way having little to do with writing, is that they treat situations which, because they are structurally parallel to her own, engage her most passionate interest and unleash powerful writing.

The coexistence of these confessional levels in all of Staël's texts gives them their particular rhetorical status that does indeed occupy a middle ground between invention and memory. Such texts are not better or worse than those based on the principles of male rhetoric that Staël's models and friends exemplified. They are simply other. To appreciate such writing, it is necessary not only to describe it but also to understand the forces that made it. In Staël's case, and perhaps in the case of woman writers generally, the forces have to do with the struggle to function in a world one loves and to which one aspires but to which one is not born.

In her explorations and experimentations of the 1790s Staël was making significant and useful discoveries. She found that she could indeed write about a variety of subjects and that, while doing so, she could talk about herself in a covert way, at several different levels. She will be able to put this skill to good use in the remainder of her career, and indeed to probe further into the potentialities of her personal rhetoric. During the 1790s Staël determined that she could not proceed on the basis upon which she had tried to build in the *Passions*, namely the assumption that she could write a single work with both masculine and feminine qualities. Therefore, she had to search further for possibilities regarding the establishment of a sexual writing identity.

5. *History and Story*

Staël published nothing between *Passions* in 1796 and *On Literature* in 1800. Simone Balayé speculates that between 1796 and late 1798, when she began the writing of *On Literature*, she was perhaps working on the second part of the *Passions*.[1] That does indeed seem likely, especially in the light of her failure to complete "On Current Circumstances . . ." whose subject matter was closely related to the *Passions* project. Realizing the impossibility of doing that piece of work, she began to cast about for a potentially more successful project. Her search seems to have taken two forms. In the first place, she apparently decided that part of her problem was the subject matter she had proposed for herself in the *Passions*, namely, the science of government. Our examination of reasons why government did not energize her writing, a fact all the more odd given her intense interest in it, suggested that Staël felt, in spite of herself, that it was not a topic a woman writer could adequately or appropriately treat. If that is so, it is logical to conclude that she would be looking for a viable topic. She found it in literature, a subject with which women had been traditionally associated. At the same time, Staël thought of a way of treating literature that would enable her to incorporate some of the research she had already done on forms of government through the ages and which would at least partly satisfy her desire to talk about politics. The full title of her work reveals this approach: *De la littérature considérée dans ses rapports avec les institutions sociales* (On Literature Considered in Its Relationship with Social Institutions).[2] One of the "social institutions" that she will treat insofar as it impinged on literary production is, of course, political organization. In little over a year she had written and published her work, so that it seems that she had indeed rethought her topic in a way that allowed her writing to move ahead rather than to remain stymied.

The second reason why the work on the *Passions* presented obstacles to the flow of writing was her plan to include both masculine and feminine ways of thinking and writing in the same book and to present them as "analogous." In her work of the turn of the century, Staël has found a new way of approaching that problem. During this time she writes not only *On Literature* but also *Delphine*, an epistolary novel, her next literary project after the work on literature.[3] These two works are a pair, the first belonging to the "male" series laid out in the *Essay on Fiction* and the second to the "female" series. The first is a work of history that recounts public events and arranges them according to a theory of history. The second is a fictional work that reveals the happenings and feelings of private life, inspired by events actually observed or lived by the author. Rather than trying to write the masculine and the feminine together, as she had attempted in the *Passions*, Staël is now separating them into two distinct works, not claiming any particular relationship between them, making no attempt to show their "analogies." She must have felt that this was a successful approach. Between 1803 and 1810 she wrote another pair of works, one expository, the other one fictional. Toward the end of her career she can be shown to have been projecting still another such pair.

In composing books by pairs, Germaine de Staël has found a most interesting solution to the problem of sexual writing identity. Members of a pair are both associated and dissociated. The latter effect—dissociation—is, I claim, the one actually sought by Staël herself. The androgyny of a male/female work, like the *Passions*, of which she dreamed but which she did not complete, made her uncomfortable. Perceiving maleness and femaleness to be a dichotomy, she could more easily deal with creating works that she could think of as adhering to its parts rather than questioning them by the act of establishing analogies. Writing works in pairs thus satisfied this need to keep the dichotomy intact. Meanwhile, however, it is the associative quality of pairs that is the more interesting and critically useful phenomenon here. If it can be shown that the male and female members of a pair are in fact "analogous" after all, we may conclude that, like it or not, Staël had a single identity that insistently manifested itself whenever she wrote, no matter how different the types of works she created may seem. These assessments differ from that of Simone Balayé who, in comparing the fictional and nonfictional works of Staël has written, "The critical and political work of Madame de Staël proposes, constructs, comforts, while the novelistic work destroys, expressing the anguish of the author."[4] While evidence to support this claim can certainly be gathered in the overt themes of the works in question, their deep structure constantly asserts unity rather than duality.

That *Delphine* and *On Literature* are a pair can be demonstrated by reference to both their tonal and their structural affinities. A major tone struck by both works is that of nostalgia. As *On Literature* ends Staël thinks back to the period ten years earlier, depicting herself as "entrant dans le monde" (entering the world). This is the same phrase by which the Staël of the 1814 preface to the Rousseau letters was to use to characterize her status in the late 1780s and early 1790s. She contrasts the hopeful and confident young woman she was then with the guarded person she has become. The action of the novel *Delphine* takes place in the same time period. Her central character describes herself at that time with this same phrase: "I am entering the world . . ." This nostalgic note is emphasized by the presence of parental figures in both books, *Delphine* being the book of the mother, *On Literature*, the book of the father.[5]

The epigraph of *Delphine* is "A man must be able to defy opinion, a woman, to submit to it."[6] This aphorism was written by Staël's mother. The novel comments on it by featuring a man who submits to public opinion and a woman who defies it. Thus, the qualities that should be associated, according to Suzanne Necker, with a man are exhibited by a woman who permits herself masculine behavior. The appropriate quality has been transferred to the inappropriate sex, so that a crossing, or a chiasmus, has resulted. Staël has crossed or gone against the values of her mother, but in the same ambivalent way that we have already observed, for example, in her attitude toward moral philosophy in the *Essay*. She has indeed created a plot in which the female character fails to act in the way prescribed by the maternal aphorism. However, Delphine is severely punished for each failure. At the same time she is without any doubt the heroine of the novel. Her character is exalted, her actions are blameless, her way of being is valorized. Suzanne Necker had been dead since 1794, and yet even now when her daughter crosses her, she must do so in a shifting way, her aggressive moves tempered by attempted appeasements. *Delphine* is in part a response to Suzanne Necker. The memory of her moral lessons, of her interpretation to her daughter of woman's proper place, is present even before the actual beginning of the novel, and, as Madelyn Gutwirth demonstrates, the "complicity in woman's fate" of both good and evil mothers is depicted and analyzed in the book.[7]

The attitude toward the father, however, is quite different. *On Literature* traces the history of literature and thought in their relation to various other social phenomena from the time of the Greeks through the French Revolution in a first part. Its second part is an attempt to project the nature of the literature of the future, a literature she hopes will develop somewhere in the world, perhaps in France, perhaps in America, when an enlightened and free nation comes into being. In her penultimate chapter, entitled "Du Style des Ecrivains et de celui des Magistrats," (On the Style of Writers and of Magistrates), she discusses her father in terms that recall the Rousseau letters. Her father is the best example of a magistrate/writer and stands as one to be emulated in this essential endeavor. If the first part of the book leads up to the French Revolution, the second part leads up to Necker. He has then a significant place in the overall plan of his daughter's book. The father is not crossed; he is apotheosized.

That *Delphine* is conceived as a response to the mother and *On Literature* to the father, suggests the dissociation between the male and the female Staël seems to have wished to bring about in these two works. Yet structurally, the two works are similar in that they share a central preoccupation and organizing principle: both are stories and thus both are arranged diachronically. Narrations are grounded in some fundamental informing conception of temporality and causality. The writer must arrange chosen or invented events in temporal succession and show how they derive from prior events and lead to those that follow. The events will be related in a way that forms a pattern of development in time and of causation. *On Literature*, the book of the father, is man's history, the story of development in the public realm. *Delphine*, the book of the mother, is a novel which depicts the world of a woman in her relation to the man she loves and of that part of the man's life that is carried out in the private arena. The distinctions Staël set up in the *Essay* lead us to expect that we will be dealing with different stories in the two cases. The public story will be abstract, exclusive of certain elements. In telling it, one will be working under some theory of history according to which one will order events and interpretations. The private story will have to conform to the contours of experience. Some of Staël's critics have adopted this dichotomized picture of her performance. Simone Balayé says, "There are for her novels tragic endings, for her philosophical and political works endings which are never closures" and discerns "a fundamental difference of orientation between these two manners of expressing her genius."[8] James Hamilton, however, senses a "structural polarity" in *On Literature*, two levels of reasoning, the one dialectical and the other "unconscious and skeptical."[9] There is indeed a tension in that work, rather than openings into hope. In fact, the stories of the two books bear striking similarities that provide evidence for a certain Staëlian conception of temporal sequence and of causality, which imposed itself on her rendering of both man's and woman's story. That conception comes from her unmistakable female identity.

In the book on literature, Staël's theory of history is a particularly insistent version of perfectibility, an idealized interpretation that she found in a number of sources. Rousseau, one of the first to use the word perfectibility (in his *Second Discourse*, 1755), actually meant by it "capacity for change," a change that can move toward amelioration or degeneration. Condorcet, probably the most immediate influence on her theory, claimed progress in the development of the human mind but saw little advancement for human kind itself in his "Essay on the history of the progress of the human mind," 1793–1794. Staël wishes to adopt a stronger attitude still, to claim progress for humankind as well as progress in thought. She words her initial presentation of the theory in such a way as to underplay the distinction between progress of the mind and improvement in the human lot. "In looking at the revolutions of the world and at the succession of centuries, there is one prime idea which I keep constantly in mind: the perfectibility of ***human kind***. I do not think that this great work of moral nature has ever been abandoned, in periods of enlightenment as in centuries of darkness, the ***gradual march of the human mind*** has not been interrupted." (emphasis added).[10] The shift in terminology (from "human kind" to "human mind") is not brought out and explained but rather slipped in so as to blur the distinction. The implication is that Staël wishes to claim progress for human kind, but because she cannot do so with an entirely clear intellectual conscience, she expresses herself ambiguously on the point. The strong claim she wishes to make is one that finally she cannot entirely bring herself to make even at this initial, introductory stage. Lucia Omacini discovers this same pattern in Staël's very syntax: "The syntactical structure transmits and reflects at once optimism, faith in perfectibility, hope in a better future, but, if one can read between the lines, it hides traps which lie in wait for the irreparable calamities of humanity."[11]

In this same passage Staël posits an agent (moral nature) which has set out on and continually pursues its activity, that of creating a work. The work is a readable, understandable, sensible story. Human kind and the human mind or both gradually march forward under its influence. There is a force at work that somehow moves events along in such a way as to form a pattern of progress. The causal principle behind the movement posited here is a hidden but active intelligence. "Time reveals to us a design, in the sequence of events that seemed to be only the pure result of chance; and one sees a thought emerge, always the same thought, from the abyss of facts and centuries."[12]

The importance to Staël of this theory of history is emphasized when, in her second preface to the book, she reiterates her claims, now citing a number of other writers who have professed the same theory in answer to her critics. It is a system, she says, that "promises to men on this earth some of the benefits of immortality, a limitless future, continuity without interruption!"[13] This passage specifies that the movement of history which Staël wishes to recount will be characterized not only by an upward linear progression but also by a particular articulation of events—they must be continuous, uninterrupted, their lines unbroken, smoothly linking from one to the next. But the passage also betrays the scarcely spoken skepticism Staël felt about her cherished theory. She says it "promises" various benefits.

In the Preliminary Discourse of her book (p. 208) Staël calls her theory a "une croyance philosophique" (a philosophical belief). At the same time she claims that it is not a "vain theory" but rather that it is based on the "observation of facts." She does not, however, state what those observations are, so that the word *belief* seems to fit well. What she says about this belief does not amount to a proof of its truth but rather to an appeal to its advantages. It serves to combat discouragement, the feeling that one's efforts are pointless. Thus Staël's attitude toward her theory of history is characterized both by an adamant insistence on the importance of its moral and emotional role and by an inherent implicit skepticism about its foundation in demonstrable fact. The story of perfectibility must be told and believed, but it is not necessarily a true story. Staël made a valiant effort to tell that story, but she does not manage to make it work smoothly and convincingly. The structure of the story being told works at cross purposes with that of the story Staël wanted to tell. Decadence taints perfectibility. Senselessness threatens sense. Circularity bends linearity.

Every story must have a beginning. Staël does not show as much interest in beginnings, though, as such eighteenth-century thinkers as Rousseau and Condillac, who discussed at length the origins of language, knowledge, and society. Rather she sets history in motion abruptly. Facts about our origins are missing; lacking anything upon which to base our ideas, we speculate in vain. Yet it is necessary to posit some sort of a beginning and some force that explains why there was a beginning at all. Staël brings in a quite general principle. She claims simply that "moral nature" acquires quickly what is needed. "For example, . . . language is the instrument that is necessary for the acquisition of all other developments; and, by a sort of miracle, this instrument exists."[14] The initial step of human kind is inexplicable; one can only appeal to some unknown force, a divine hand, a quasi-magic thrust into existence from nothingness. Once the elements of humanity and society are in motion, further developments come slowly, in steps, which lend themselves to study and to understanding. But the beginning leaps into being surprisingly, irrationally.

Staël's attitude toward the originators of Western civilization, for her, the Greeks, is decidedly ambivalent. This is a second factor that gets her story off to an uncertain start. She does not admire them as much as she does the Romans, saying that they, in disappearing from history, leave "few regrets" (part I, chapter 4). Yet emotions and thought, as well as the literature which expressed them, existed in a pristine state, uncomplicated by precedents, which can never be recaptured. Staël does show some nostalgia for this state. Regret for a lost past is not compatible with the theory of perfectibility that theoretically should involve looking ahead with anticipation and behind with the assurance that the past existed mainly to serve the present and the future. From the outset nostalgia coexists uneasily with perfectibility.

The main characters of the next episode are the Romans. If the theory of perfectibility is valid, then they must be both different from the Greeks (that is, the Romans must be superior to them), and different from modern France (that is, inferior to it). On the first point, Staël has little difficulty. Rome borrowed from Greece and integrated its borrowings into its own distinctive culture. On the second point, however, there are some obstacles. Modern France may be superior to ancient Rome, but not in all ways. Roman historical writing, for instance, is better than French. Or again, in many ways, France is neither better nor worse than Rome, but similar. To point out a few resemblances between ancient and modern times does not at first glance seem to threaten necessarily the theory of perfectibility. But if the examples of similarity become too numerous, then history will start seeming to repeat itself and thus be more like a circle than a straight line. That is why Staël, whenever she makes a comparison, is potentially endangering her entire hypothetical structure.

In fact, Staël does much more than point out resemblances. She sees a structural similarity between the history of the Romans and that of the French. Everyone knows and Staël repeats the story of the Romans, whose civilization flourished and then declined and fell.

One cannot talk about Rome without talking about decadence, that major enemy of perfectibility. Naturally, then, when Staël treats the fall of the Roman Empire she is working in an area mined with danger to her system. It presents a strong case for the countertheory to that of Staël: inevitable periodic decadence. "Some have claimed that the decadence of the arts and letters of empires must necessarily occur after a certain degree of splendor."[15] Staël combats this hypothesis by recourse to a distinction she was careful to make at the beginning of the account and which she reiterates throughout: that the arts are not indefinitely perfectible (the classical ideal of a "point of perfection"), whereas thought can progress indeterminably. This distinction can certainly guard perfectibility from the threat of decadence in the realm of the arts, but it provides no defense if decadence can be demonstrated in the realm of thought. Faced with this threat Staël makes a very dangerous move. "Moral nature tends to be perfected. Previous improvement is a cause for future improvement; this chain can be interrupted by accidental events that impede future progress but that are not the consequences of previous progress."[16] She introduces the element of chance, of accident, disconnecting the chain of events that, she had claimed, leads continually from one to the next. She has given up a great deal here, abandoned, in fact, the cornerstone of her entire claim, the uninterrupted continuity of progress. Yet she proceeds as if this capitulation had not taken place. She goes on to claim that whereas the Romans did indeed decline, decadence is not an inevitable thrust within history and that there is every reason to believe that it will not happen again. The argument is that decadence is not destined to occur; it comes as the result of certain causes, so that when the causes are eliminated or diminished the effect will cease or be attenuated. But the case is not very strongly argued. Reference is made to Montesquieu for factual proof of the thesis. Yet, as in her discussion of perfectibility, the appeal is not to demonstrable evidence but to emotional necessity; it would be too depressing to contemplate an inevitable succession of falls. Furthermore, in the case of at least one cause, that of the atrocities committed as the Roman Empire declined, it can only be demonstrated that that cause does not exist any more by eliminating the fact of the Terror. If one took this Terror into consideration, rather than refusing to consider it, as Staël suggests, one's conclusion would be quite different. The price of the proof is abstraction. And even so, Staël cannot bring herself to claim triumphantly that decadence no longer threatens, only that the threat has diminished in intensity.

Next, Staël has to deal with the "Dark Ages," with what appear to have been ten centuries of decadence, a period that would indeed seem to question the idea of perfectibility. But even in those times events were not left to chance development; a mysterious force was at work. The narrative language of the chapter on the Middle Ages (part I, chapter 8), depends on the functioning of some hidden but active intelligence. The force is strongly reminiscent of the one Staël used to set history in motion. The process of creation is described in terms similar to those used in the discussion of this process of re-creation after the neo-chaos which followed the fall of the Roman Empire. Staël must deny chance as an explanatory factor in the unfolding of history (and this in spite of her own occasional slips). But at the essential moments of articulation, as at the moment of creation, she cannot manage to assert and demonstrate a chain of cause and effect. She relies instead on a behind-the-scenes, mysterious power that energizes what might otherwise have remained in nothingness or reverted to it. Neither the thrust nor the processes of history seem to be marching along.

Halting and questionable as the progress has been up to this point, however, Staël moves on to the Renaissance. Here modern history begins. It is to be, she asserts, different from the past. Resolutely taking the side of the Moderns rather than the Ancients, Staël points to a new era that has already begun and which will now progress without further interruption. She calls upon the reader to look ahead. Looking back is associated with depression or discouragement, looking forward with renewed life, fecundity, hope, the excitement of voyage. Theoretically, whatever threats decadence may have posed before the Renaissance are now past, overcome. One may proceed into a continuously progressive future.

But that is not by any means how the story really goes on, for Staël soon arrives at the Revolution. "Thus time was marching toward the conquest of freedom . . . Ah! . . . Every time the course of ideas leads us to reflect upon the destiny of man, the revolution appears!"[17] The only answer to this despair is a renewed rhetorical exhortation: "Nevertheless, let us not succumb to this discouragement. Let us return to general observations."[18] Moreover, when Staël turns from the past to the future, in the second part of her work, projecting what further progress is foreshadowed in the events and developments of her own time, her projections do not seem to promise continuity and progress any more than her retrospections. It begins in this way: "I have followed the history of the human mind from Homer until 1789. In my national pride, I viewed the time of the French Revolution as a new era for the intellectual world."[19] The Renaissance was supposed to be a new era that was to proceed without interruption. But now there has been another interruption, the Revolution, and there is to be a second new era. Is history not repeating itself?

It certainly seems to be doing so. The similarities between the state of things at the fall of the Roman Empire and now, in the aftermath of the French Revolution, are overwhelming. The structure of the two situations is the same, and Staël brings it out very clearly herself. In the first case, the friendly force of history had to bring about a reconciliation between two opposing sides, the barbarian invaders from the north and the decadent invaded from the south. The linking factor was the Christian religion. In the second, contemporary, case, the opposing sides are the decadent aristocracy invaded by the lower classes. How, Staël asks, can they be reconciled? The problem is the same: opposing forces to be united. The very natures of the two sides in the two cases are parallel. And the solutions, Christianity in the first case and now, as Staël shows in the latter chapters of her book, enthusiasm, are strikingly similar.

As Staël says, in her projections of the future she has depended upon her observations about the past. Indeed, people say that one studies history in order to learn from it; no doubt that is in general a good thing to do. But within the system of Staël, when the past is so inescapably like the present, the backlash from learning the lessons of history is that history begins to look circular. There is a double bind here: one cannot profit from the contemplation of the past unless history does repeat itself; but in that event we must face the fact that past events may recur and with the same results as before, and recur again and again. That, for Staël, is a very depressing thought. "It is impossible to condemn thought to retrace its steps, without hope and with regret; the human mind, deprived of a future, would fall into the most miserable degradation. Let us then look for this future, in literary productions and in philosophical ideas."[20] Again, in the face of threatened decadence, the rhetorical exhortation. History does not have tense, not the past, nor the present, nor the future. It has only mode, and that mode is the imperative. It is the "let us affirm, let us look, let us not give up." In this book Staël wanted to make the past make sense by the power of the word, but she could not finally tell the story she wanted to tell. The chain of perfectibility is constantly buffetted by the fear of decadence. The projected future is a wish; the only hope for its realization is to write rhetorically in such a way that the reader will want to share the "philosophical belief."

Thus Staël's theory of history and her development of events and their causes are troubled, proceed by fits and starts, demonstrate the opposite of what she claims, and veer finally away from history into rhetoric. In her epistolary novel *Delphine*[21] projections just as optimistic meet with equally disappointing results. In the preface to her novel, Staël does not immediately announce a definite shape that it supposedly will have, but she does make her explanatory factor quite clear. Destiny is formed by morality. The moral life of the characters will determine the elaboration of their stories. "Fictions should explain to us, by our virtues and our feelings, the mysteries of our fate."[22] Whatever happens to us, mysterious as it may temporarily seem, is finally explainable, can ultimately be shown to spin out of what we are and do. In the novel, the reader can expect to find a linking of events which makes sense of their succession and direction. The implication is that if the characters are virtuous, their stories should be, like history, a continuous improvement. That, in any event, is the prediction the main character Delphine naïvely makes about herself as the novel opens. "I am entering the world with a good and true character, wit, youth and fortune; why would these gifts of Providence not make me happy?"[23]

But here is briefly what happens: When the hero, Léonce, and Delphine meet, the former is engaged to be married to a cousin of

Delphine, Mathilde de Vernon, who is also the daughter of the woman whom Delphine considers to be her closest friend, Sophie de Vernon. Since the announcement of the engagement has not yet been made nor all of the arrangements completed, Léonce would be able, at the beginning, to change his mind and marry Delphine instead of Mathilde. Certainly the two of them recognize very soon their irresistible attraction to each other. But a villain intervenes. Sophie de Vernon, it turns out, is a treacherous woman who has taken advantage of Delphine's friendship and generosity. Now she intends that her daughter will marry the wealthy and charming Léonce and uses Delphine's innocence, credulity, and spontaneity against her, once she has perceived that Léonce's preferences do not go toward her daughter. She tricks Léonce into believing that Delphine is involved with another man. Disappointed, Léonce quickly marries Mathilde (part I).

Delphine does not understand why Léonce has acted as he has, so that following the marriage there is a period of misunderstanding. At length, however, Léonce and Delphine both discover the truth about Madame de Vernon's perfidy, but too late: Léonce is already bound to Mathilde (part II). Delphine realizes that under the circumstances she should leave Paris, refuse to see Léonce, and thereby eliminate the risk of allowing their relationship to continue and deepen. But Léonce prevails upon her not to leave, and continually finding new excuses to blind herself to her duty, Delphine stays. The position of the would-be lovers becomes more and more untenable, so that finally Delphine manages to leave Paris without telling Léonce where she is going or indeed without even announcing her departure to him (parts III and IV).

Now, two more villains: one Monsieur de Valorbe, who wishes the reluctant Delphine to marry him, and Madame de Ternan, sister and eventually agent of Léonce's mother, whose aim it is to separate her son from the threat that Delphine presents to his marriage. Hounded by the first and perfidiously encouraged by the other, Delphine takes religious vows, (part V), ironically at the same time that Léonce is being freed from his marriage by the death of his wife. At this point it is Delphine who is bound and Léonce who is at liberty to marry. If only Delphine could be persuaded to abjure her vows . . . But she knows that Léonce would never be able to accept that solution: What would people say of his marrying a defrocked nun? The only real solution is the one that is worked out in each of two endings: the death of the lovers (part VI).

In *Delphine*, the claim is made that character leads to destiny. To some extent, that is true. To be sure, Delphine's character produces the spontaneous actions that turn out to be so compromising in the eyes of Léonce. This exchange of properties which results in chiasmus causes the lovers to be not so much star-crossed as character-crossed. The actions of the villains as well as those of characters who innocently, or at times with good intention but blunderingly, end by placing obstacles to the progress of the lovers are explainable and explained by the characters. But something else is at work in the formation of destiny that makes it depend not only on the tightly-conceived interaction of people but also, to an important degree, on chance and fate.

One can best see the design of *Delphine* by outlining the major actions of the plot.

a. Part I: Léonce marries Mathilde instead of Delpine.
b. Part II: Léonce and Delphine find out the truth about what has separated them.
c. Parts III and IV: Delphine leaves Paris.
d. Part V: Delphine takes religious vows, thus making marriage impossible.
e. Part VI: The lovers die.

The working out of these actions does not proceed always in the same way. In fact, there are two series of actions, viewed from this standpoint. Actions (a), (b), and (d) differ from actions (c) and (e). Novelistically, the first series is superior to the second. In the former case, Staël skillfully and gradually presents a number of characters whose complex interaction moves the story along. Essential here are the machinations of villains, Sophie de Vernon, first, and then Monsieur de Valorbe and Madame de Ternan. They take advantage of Delphine's well intentioned help for her friends, of her naïve trustfulness, and of her tendency to act spontaneously, without sufficiently foreseeing the repercussions for herself. In the case of the second series, however, there is little real story. At the beginning of part III and at the beginning of part VI, the climactic action is so predictable that the letters consist of a sequence of avoidance maneuvers that merely postpone the inevitable. The first series is more dynamic than the second.

The factors at work in the second series are malevolent chance and, on the part of the characters, an indecision that would put the most hardened procrastinator to shame. In part III, Delphine announces her departure three times, but in each case Léonce uses emotional blackmail, the threat that he will die if she leaves, and in each case she submits to his threats. In part IV, still knowing she should leave, she insists that her much-admired sister-in-law, Mademoiselle d'Albémar, decide for her. The latter, herself much influenced by Léonce's threats, decides that she should stay. But her staying becomes more and more problematic. Chance events make the situation as unendurable as possible, but still her decision is not forthcoming. Finally, Delphine reveals the truth about the feelings between herself and Léonce to Mathilde, whose ability not to see them make her a model wife for a faithless husband. But this action on Delphine's part is not an action at all. She describes her state of mind during the confession as irrational; she did not know what she was doing. Her "decision" was not based on a reasoning process but on an irresistible inner movement. Then in the aftermath of the encounter, Delphine depicts herself as a helpless victim, waiting for someone else, in this case, Mathilde, to make the final determination. Mathilde, not surprisingly, requires that she leave, but even now fifteen more letters intervene before the departure.

In these two parts (III and IV) the plot is not one of suspense, but of suspension. Whatever happens, happens despite the characters, not only the interventions of chance but even their own so-called actions. The inevitable outcome is postponed at greath length, so that the characters exist always in a state of waiting, of living-until, of uncertainty and loudly proclaimed helplessness, the victims not of themselves but of circumstance.

In fact, suspension is present also in the parts in which more really motivated action takes place. The moment of truth that concludes part II is postponed, for example, when by chance Delphine does not find the person to whom she needed to deliver an essential letter, and she trustingly, foolishly, gives it to Madame de Vernon to send. The latter takes advantage of the contretemps in order to keep the lovers separated and in darkness longer than would have otherwise been possible. In part V, Delphine takes the vows that will separate her from Léonce at the very time when he is becoming free; had she waited just a little while, the situation that seemed to be forcing her into that drastic solution could have been dispelled.

Not even the actions of villains have the expected force. Their actions represent negative and destructive forces, but they are at least dynamic, emanating from character, evil though it be. It is useful to compare Madame de Vernon to a character Staël probably had in mind when she created her, Pierre de Laclos' Marquise de Merteuil. The marquise, in working her evil designs on her innocent victims, intended and maintained her actions and her character to the very end. Madame de Vernon intended what she did, but she ends by repenting, explaining her motivations in such a way as to expiate her crimes, at least in the eyes of Delphine. The same is true of Monsieur de Valorbe. Even Madame de Ternan, who does not repent, gives a lengthy explanation of her actions, designed to attenuate the evil of her character. Staël, unlike Laclos, will not allow evil to persist in her book; she must purge it, explain it away, make it acceptable. But in this refusal of evil she is undercutting an essential active force, softening her plot, turning away from what she had used as a principle of story-advancing action.

Decision is postponed and finally thrust upon the characters; the plot depends on chance; the villains are defused. Where the characters and their actions should be present, if we are to believe that out of our essence spins our story, there are voids. The analysis of the plot gives negative view of human action that people are not involved in a series of events that either make sense or are related in a pattern of consequence.

The atmosphere of the novel confirms it. In fact, the book is a romance that bathes in the atmosphere of medieval chivalry. Conventional motifs from that system abound. On two major occasions, when she falls in love and when she travels into Switzerland upon leaving Paris, Delphine has the impression of a passage from the ordinary world into a new one, dangerous but perhaps promising transformation and salvation. In several scenes, she is depicted in a carriage, being led away from the old world by dizzyingly swift horses. There are what the characters take to be supernatural premonitions of the future: when Delphine has taken her vows, she accidentally breaks the portrait of Léonce, signaling, she believes, the coming of some ominous event. A wise older woman, latter-day crone, tries to help the heroine. A blind man represents a happiness into which the lovers are denied access and a warning of that denial. There are festivals, a masked ball, scenes in dark churches. The love of Léonce and Delphine is that of Tristan and Isolde, a love-passion which leads to death through a series of separations and reunions. Realistic scenes, that is, scenes in which the characters are shown in their social settings, do not lack. Yet actually society is not so much the background against which the story is played out as a stock character of medieval romance, the villain, "this modern fate,"[24] "an uncontrollable, irrational, destructive, counter-natural force."[25] Such conventional motifs set up certain expectations about destiny. A dark fate hangs over the characters, and it will not be carried out in linear, logical fashion. The arbitrary is in the service of the inevitable.

Are we, then, responsible for our actions? Apparently not, if the actions based on our characters are as fated as those visited upon us by others or by circumstance. But what does, finally, explain destiny? The book comments on the question but by no means addresses itself to it effectively. The plot explains nothing, gives no coherent vision of destiny, because the way events are articulated within it does not make sense of them. Naturally, the only appeal possible is to an obscure external force sometimes called chance and sometimes, fate. In *Delphine* the force is more openly acknowledged than in *On Literature*, where it is imbedded, implicit in the language but not overtly discussed. But it is, nonetheless, recognizable as the kind of agent *ex machina* that Staël brought in at crucial junctures of that story as well. Both books deal uneasily with consequence.

Whereas sequence of events caused Staël a great deal of difficulty in *On Literature*, the shape of destiny is clear in *Delphine*. That shape bears an interesting and revealing relationship to history as Staël tells it. The story in *Delphine* follows the archetypal pattern of Tristan and Isolde. The protagonists meet and fall in love despite the fact that one of them is already engaged to marry someone else. They share a moment of happiness and intimacy (in Staël the intimacy is spiritual only) but are separated by the marriage of one. However, they do come together later, (in the case of Delphine and Léonce, twice) but are again separated after each reunion. Their final encounter brings death. Thus the pattern is one of alternating presence and absence. In the description of the shared moments (six in all), several qualities are gradually developed and linked: bliss, timelessness,[26] music, and death.

The recurrence of the same motifs in each of the encounters creates a circularly shaped plot, consisting of a sequence of returns to and banishments from ideal moments. In shape, therefore, the story of Delphine strongly resembles the history of *On Literature*, not, to be sure, the latter's asserted movement of perfectibility, but its tendency to fall away from linear progression into a cycle of rise and fall.

Thus the story Staël wanted to tell—a story of temporal progress and comprehensible causality—becomes constantly distorted into another quite different one, characterized instead by circularity and senselessness. Despite the assertions she made about her conception of history on the one hand and the novel, as a genre, on the other, they both actually tell the same story. Some unwilled but inexorable pattern seems to impose itself, weakening the links of the desired narrations and molding them into a common shape. It is, then, in the very "weakness" of the plot that Staël expresses herself most strongly. Nancy K. Miller's work on novels by eighteenth-century women, often accused of implausibility and lack of verisimilitude, directs attention to this kind of strength: "The peculiar shape of a heroine's destiny in novels by women, the implausible twists of plot so common in these novels, is a form of insistence about the relationship of women to writing . . . The attack on female plots and plausibilities assumes that women writers cannot or will not obey the rules of fiction . . . but . . . the fictions of desire behind the desiderata of fiction are masculine and not universal constructs."[27] The case of Germaine de Staël illustrates and is illuminated by these perceptions.

The associations Staël spells out in her *Essay* are crucial: speculative philosophy, history, abstract, invented, and public are linked with the male; the opposites, imaginative fiction, concrete, imitative, private, are related to the female. In these two books she separates the two domains into two supposedly different works, thereby theoretically dividing herself into two people, the one functioning in man's terms with the mind of a man and the other in woman's terms with the sensitivity of a woman. Staël could not, of course, successfully execute such a polarized plan. One cannot function alternately in two preconceived modes. Rather, one functions always in the same mode, one's own, informed by the place in the world one occupies as male or female and by one's interpretation of that place. Thus, Staël could not finally set history aside as an idealized and abstract form that she could use to tell a story of progress and continuity. It is difficult to believe in a story one has not participated in and even more so to lend credence to a story that does not ring true when judged according to one's own experience.

It is to Staël's credit that she devoted considerable thought to the nature and relationship of the stories of man and of woman. In the *Passions* she states that love for woman is a story but for man it is an episode.[28] Man's story is public and recounted by history. In his story, woman, who belongs to private life, figures only incidentally, in those "vast empty spaces" that are not included in the narration of public events of the past. In man's story woman is present only in the absent parts— in other words, she figures not at all. If she tries to tell that story herself she will inevitably find herself not included in it. Can one tell a story from which one has been erased in advance? In *On Germany*, some ten years after the publication of the two books under consideration here, Staël put the matter somewhat differently: "Women try to arrange themselves like a novel; men, like a history"[29] This reflection implies that a woman will design her story along the lines of the private life she leads rather than in the manner of the story in which she has no part. This is in fact what Staël did in composing her two histories. She aspired to the telling of man's story in what she perceives as man's way, but she could not carry it off. She ends instead by telling twice the story whose structure she had personally experienced.

There is, however, one element in the book on history that

indicates that Staël was making an effort to go beyond the impasse she had reached in trying to tell two separate stories. This effort takes two forms in *On Literature*: the first is to find a place for women in male history; the second is to write a new story with parts for both men and women.

The search for a place within male history was most fundamentally for Staël a search for a place for herself, that is, a place for a special woman, different from others, more talented, more energetic, more ambitious, unwilling to be relegated to the domestic life that other women accept. At the beginning of her chapter on women, the reader may be led to expect a general treatment of the place of women in society and a call, like that of Mary Wollstonecraft, for improvement in the status of woman through education. But after this general introduction, Staël passes immediately to the subject of her real interest, revealed in the very title of the essay, "On Women Who Cultivate Letters" (part II, chapter 4). She particularly examines the place of woman writers in a monarchy and in a republic. As the essay draws to a close she depicts the vicissitudes of the female literary figure in a way all too obviously calculated to attract pity to herself. Politically, this chapter amounts simply to an appeal that some few, elite, superior women be allowed a role in man's history. The chapter does not foresee any impact on that history that would exceed its limits.

The second effort is more imaginative and may reach further. Staël promises in the introduction to show what impact the status ("mode d'existence") of women before and after the establishment of Christianity had on the development of literature. Such an initiative would potentially involve a new history that would integrate both man's story and woman's story into one story. Thus two inadequacies of history, as Staël saw it, would be overcome. No longer would there be vast empty spaces that remain when one tells public history only, thereby leaving out the private. No longer would woman's story be an often-omitted episode in a story in which she did not participate. Both man's and woman's story would thereby be completed, complemented, supplemented by each other.

That Staël even envisaged such a history is quite impressive. To this day it has not been written, although feminist historians are at work to increase the knowledge about women in the past to a point that would make it possible to attempt such an integration. That Staël did not succeed is not surprising. Even in her introduction one realizes that her insight has not gone far enough, for she writes of woman's influence in a list of many other factors that includes forms of government, religion, and climate that have had an impact on the history of literature. Obviously woman is not the focal point of her concern. Moreover, in this introduction, the influence of woman is subsumed under another apparently more influential category, the establishment of Christianity.

In the remainder of the book, Staël does not actually limit herself to woman's place before and after Christianity. Possibly she introduced her topic in such a timid and limited way in order to avoid criticism that she, as a woman, was giving inordinate attention to the place of women. Identifying herself with women, making common cause with "them," was not part of her approach. Her desire to write a book which would be admired by men and accepted as a piece of writing as fine as any man had done would have turned her away from any bolder move. Each mention of women in the work, in fact, has the same double movement which we are noting here: a claim rich in suggestions followed by an undercutting of those suggestions or of the claim. I will give a few examples of this phenomenon.

Staël states that in Homer there is little "true sensitivity." It seems, she says, that the ability to love has increased with other progress the human mind has made, especially in modern times when women are called upon to share man's destiny (part I, chapter 1, FD I, p. 212). The fact that the Greeks had only limited relationships with women, who were kept rigidly in certain roles, in turn limited the sensitivity and thereby the profundity of their works. Here she seems to be pointing toward a new society. A society that includes both men and women functions best. Any other society will be constrained and restricted, its works of art concomitantly vitiated. Yet only a few sentences later Staël specifies the role that she envisages for woman: she will be mentally equal, submissive because of love, "a companion who will be happy to dedicate her faculties, her time, her feelings, to complete another existence."[30] Here the particular kind of "sharing man's destiny" is specified. Woman is depicted in her traditional secondary and private role. Destiny still belongs to man, this second passage states clearly. Woman may share it but only by remaining in a derivative place.

Before Christianity, women were virtual slaves, Staël states. Christianity made them morally and spiritually equal (FD I, p. 239). This equality, limited as Staël indicates by her qualifiers, admitted women to the role they now have: they have not composed, she says, truly superior works but they have served the cause of literary progress because of what men have learned from them in their relationships. Or again, as Staël begins her discussion of contemporary literature, she stresses woman's influence. "All the feelings which they are permitted to have, the fear of death, regret for life, endless devotion, measureless indignation, enrich literature with new expressions."[31] The beginning of the chapter attaches great importance to women in the transformation of ancient into modern literature. Here again an attempt at integration of the private and the public is at least sketched. But the influence of women is limited (I, 151) to works of imagination and, within that category, to certain aspects—delicate sensibility, variety of situations, knowledge of the human heart. Furthermore, Staël's references to women are always in the third person, indicating a distancing and dissociation from the group to which she in fact belonged. In short, many times suggestions are made but their implications are immediately restricted to relatively small and delimited areas that are not outside the traditional realm of women.

Timid and consistently undercut claims bear witness to troubled and unresolved feelings, which are really at the heart of the narrative difficulties of *Delphine* and *On Literature*. In her chapter on women of letters Staël says "The existence of woman in society is still uncertain in many ways . . . Everything is arbitrary in their success as well as in their failures . . . In present society, they are, for the most part, neither in the order of nature nor in that of society."[32] Observing that her actions have unpredictable results, a woman may well find it difficult to believe in continuity and causality, to depict an order to which she does not belong, to speak with certainty from a position of uncertainty. Staël's desire to function within the world of men conflicted with society's dictates concerning woman's proper place. Her desire to believe that there was a forward-looking, progressive, continuous male story in which she might herself take some part, albeit indirect, conflicted with her observation of the story she seemed to be living out herself. In these two books she works in a troubled half-light with these conflicts. Her tremendous energy and ambition are still at work, but they become enmeshed in circularity and senselessness because she has found no resolution, no certain ground on which to stand and from which she can function. She refuses solidarity with other women, cannot find a satisfactory place for herself in man's world, and finds no way to reconcile the two.[33]

Staël was both bold and timid. Her audacity made her writing possible; her timidity undermined its effectiveness. The uncertain position of their author generates the peculiar status of these strong and yet insecure works. She had not enough courage to object to that status openly, not enough fear to accept it, and not enough blindness to ignore it. Here she has seen through to the true nature of woman's, of her own, story. She has told it once and again, always with the same structure, no matter what the difference in terms. Therein lies her deeply female vision and her implicit "j'accuse."

6. *A Topography of the Soul*

Crossings

"The genesis of *Corinne* comes about symbiotically with the genesis of *On Germany*," writes Simone Balayé in her edition of Staël's travel diaries.[1] The books are indeed a pair which contrast sharply with *Delphine* and *On Literature*. Madelyn Gutwirth calls *Delphine* the novel of the mothers and *Corinne*, that of the fathers.[2] Laurence Porter identifies the difference between the two expository works in this way: "The strongly assertive style of *De la littérature* reflects the belief that the truth, once stated, is obvious. The more tentative style of *De l'Allemagne* suggests that truth, so far as we can know it, is relative to subjective perceptions of the world."[3] It appears that the focus of Germaine de Staël's literary existence has changed.

Indeed, if *Delphine* and *On Literature* are books of time—of nostalgic looks backward toward a lost time, of attempts to tell how people and peoples move through time, of projections of a future time—*Corinne*[4] and *On Germany*[5] are books of space,[6] telling of countries: Germany, Italy, England, France. How Staël conceives of these countries is based on her observations, but beyond that, they are what she calls "regions of the soul" (II, 22. FD II, p. 117). The map of Europe becomes, during her exile from Paris, a topography of her inner world. Her books depict a movement that is not temporal but spatial, involving displacements between and among ways of being that these countries represent for her. Thus, both books tell not just what these places were like, but what they meant for her and what was the significance of moving from one to another. She gives exciting accounts of her spiritual journeys.

That these two books are characterized most strikingly by the "act of crossing over" brings immediately into focus their contrast with the "crossings" of *Delphine* and *On Literature*. There the crossings go against the wishes or the grain of parental figures. But these new crossings involve going somewhere else, looking for a new way of being, a new spiritual region. It is with these crossings that I wish to begin my discussion of the two books.

On Germany contains a powerful account of Staël's passage of the Rhine during her first—not entirely voluntary—trip to Germany, in 1803. Staël was exiled from Paris by Napoleon; her insatiable energies, denied their desired outlet in the political, social, and cultural activity of the capital, necessarily sought satisfaction elsewhere. Without exile, Staël would probably never have traveled extensively.[7] From childhood she had considered Paris to be the center of her existence, a place whose atmosphere was as necessary to her as the air she breathed. Her nomadic if comfortable life did not suit her, so that we are not surprised to find the tone of the passage somber. It is winter and one's first impression, she says, is sad. The moment of crossing the Rhine into Germany is described as a solemn one, its extraordinary quality emphasized by an imaginary voice that says simply but gravely: "You are out of France."[8] Simone Balayé has commented that "the passage of all borders impresses this traveler deeply."[9] Clearly this particular passage is no exception.

The leaving of one's native land ("le pays qui nous a vus naître"—"the country which witnessed our birth"), one's fatherland ("la patrie"), is a kind of death, a death to one's former self. Uprooted, one becomes someone else, a stranger to oneself. This is because, Staël goes on to indicate, one's existence, consisting of simple habits and intimate relationships, of serious engagements and frivolous pleasures, is disrupted. The fatherland provided the continuity among the elements of one's life and attested to its unbrokenness. In leaving it one undergoes a change, a renewal, yes, but a sad rebirth whose condition is death to the past, thereby, potentially, death to one's identity.

After this foreboding introduction, Staël recounts in specific personal detail her crossing of the Rhine, drawing closely on the account she wrote in her diary immediately after the event.[10] "Six years ago I was on the banks of the Rhine, waiting for the boat that was to take me to the other side; the weather was cold, the sky dark, and everything seemed to be a fatal omen . . . . There was on our ferry an old German woman, seated on a cart; she refused to get off of it even to cross the river. 'You are very calm,' I said to her. 'Yes,' she answered, 'Why make noise?' These simple words struck me; in fact, *why make noise*?[11] The elements of the archetypal hero's adventure are present here: the unusual and mysterious atmosphere, the departure from the familiar into the unknown, the presence of another being, here a wise old woman, who comments and indicates direction or gives advice. Although she does not initiate conversation, she irresistibly draws the attention of Staël, who cannot refrain from speaking to her. The remark evokes a reponse, which strikes Staël dumb: Why make noise? At first, she can only echo the words in her mind. Momentarily transfixed is this woman who had always made noise as a matter of course, as if it were the only natural thing to do. She had attracted attention, she had written and published, she had spoken up brilliantly in social situations—she had made a lot of noise. The silence of the old woman on the occasion of this solemn crossing seems to demand a justification. It requires that if after this death and rebirth she is to continue to speak in her new life she must explain why.

Whose voice is this? That of her mother who renounced making noise and of her father who strongly implied that she should do also? Or, coming from within herself, that of the mature writer who has earned her right to be so considered and who, standing as she is on the edifice of a career unfinished but already solidly in place, feels able to examine it critically? At this point in the text, in any event, Staël seems to reflect that her own making of noise had indeed caused her pain, as if it had attracted difficulties to her. She indulges in a moment of self-pity, not answering her own question, and then passes on. "But even if generations were to cross through life in silence, unhappiness and death would observe and attack them nonetheless.

Upon arriving on the opposite bank, I heard the horn of the postillons whose sharp, out of tune, sounds seem to announce a sad departure for a sad sojourn."[12]

Not a very promising new beginning, it seems. Yet if Staël turns a deaf ear to the old woman's question in this account, the strong and lucid visions of the book and of its companion piece *Corinne or on Italy* suggest that she was more able now to assert herself and to demand her own justification of herself despite parental voices. At the end of this chapter, which begins so unpropitiously, she indicates clearly what new approaches, new ideas, new forms the Germans have suggested to her. Her change in place has entailed a displacement of her interests and emphases. To die to one's former self is painful indeed, but to be reborn to a potentially new and different self is full of excitement and discovery. Staël's description of her passage of the Rhine strongly conveys both feelings.

But Staël depicts her crossing with a mixed affectivity that suggests that, not surprisingly, she has not entirely left the concerns of the past behind her. Unmistakably, parental voices are still resounding in her mind, from the other side of the rivers and oceans she has crossed. In *On Germany*, she writes chapters on three topics that she closely associated with her mother. Chapters 18 and 19 of the first part treat education, a topic which she had hesitated to discuss as early as her *Letters on Rousseau*. Staël is a parent now herself. Auguste was born in 1790, Albert in 1792, and Albertine in 1797, so that their education must have been on Staël's mind when she wrote *On Germany*. She seems freer now to examine the topic than earlier when, perhaps because of conflicts surrounding her own education, it had seemed to occupy dangerous territory. That motherhood itself was on her mind is strongly suggested by her treatment of that theme in three plays she wrote and presented in her home during this period.[13] Finally, she echoes her mother's book *Reflections on Divorce* (1793), which Suzanne Necker had written at least partly as a sermon to her wayward daughter during the unhappy first years of her marriage and at a time when the mother first learned of her daughter's relationships with other men. In chapter 19 of part 3, on "Love in Marriage," Staël expresses quite conservative ideas on female behavior: "People are right to exclude women from political affairs; nothing is more opposed to their natural vocation than anything that would put them in a position of rivalry with men, and success itself (la gloire) can be nothing more for a woman than a dazzling mourning for happiness."[14] She tells in the same chapter how painful a bad marriage is, how unjust the double standard for judgments of male and female conduct. But we recognize the shiftings of attitude that allow Staël to criticize parental attitudes while appearing to bow to them. She opposes the ease of divorce in Germany. "It is still better, in order to keep something on earth sacred, that there be in marriage one slave rather than two strong minds."[15]

Her father's presence is strongly felt here, too. She quotes a maxim of his, "In politics, it is necessary to have all the freedom which is compatible with order,"[16] and says "I would turn that maxim around."[17] She will "cross" the statement as she did her mother's in the epigraph to *Delphine*. "It is necessary to have all the taste which is compatible with genius." Here she seems to be demonstrating considerable mental freedom in the face of paternal dictums, changing his classical admonition into a romantic praise of genius.

But of course these are not the only signs of the presence of her father who was for her, in the words of Madelyn Gutwirth, "man writ large."[18] Staël introduces a lengthy section into part 2 of her book, chapters 12 "On Morality Founded on Individual Interest," and 13 "On Morality Founded on National Interest."[19] They are largely digressions from her main topic, Germany, and she uses them as a vehicle for criticism of revolutionary France and of the empire. Here she uses her father as an example of a man who, had he been heeded and followed, could have changed the course of events. She refers to several of his writings as well as to her own intimate knowledge of his character. Finally, in the next to the last paragraph of the book, when she is rising to a highly emotional climactic statement, she refers in reverent terms to her dead father, affirming his continuing presence in her life and her own intention to write the story of his life, a task she was not able to complete. In short, the peculiar and ambivalent presentations of father and mother continue in these books written from the other side of borders that separated her symbolically from them.

Corinne contains many crossings over and through water that figure new beginnings for the characters.[20] The most important of these signals the beginning of the artistic career of Corinne, celebrated Italian poet, improviser, dancer, actress. Corinne is the daughter of an English nobleman who, while traveling in Italy, fell in love with and married the Italian woman who became Corinne's mother. Lord Edgermond, the father, left Italy when his wife died, Corinne staying behind to be educated in the country of her mother. Upon her aunt's death, Corinne was taken to England to live with her father, his second wife, and their daughter, Lucile, Corinne's half sister. Immediately the dry, repressive, and repressed character of Lady Edgermond conflicts with that of the spontaneous, lively, and creative Corinne. Her father, whose return to England has brought out the English in him, is not able to protect Corinne from her stepmother's coldness and prejudice even during his lifetime; after his death she is faced with the choice of remaining in England, the land of the powerless father and the evil stepmother, or of returning to Italy, that of her real mother and her true self. Here it is the decision to make the trip, not the trip itself, which is highlighted. The crossing of the Rhine reveals the affectivity Staël associated with this stage of her life; Corinne's decisionmaking specifies the content of her thought.

If the right choice is not clear to Corinne, the terms of the decision are. To choose England is to consent to a purely domestic life spent in relative seclusion, in a small British town, married to the man her stepmother has chosen for her. It is to accept conformity to a rigid set of rules and conventions. It is to continue to identify herself as the daughter of an Englishman and to represent that family name. Such a life is repugnant to Corinne. She sees it as a living death, saying that a tombstone bearing her name could fulfill her role in such a society as well as she herself. Italy, the land of her true mother, offers a life in which she can pursue her work as an artist, a work enriched by the fact that she has two nationalities and the best of two quite different cultures. It promises freedom, independence, creativity, fame. What typifies England is the enclosed dark parlor and the tea service; Italy is epitomized by its beautiful language, the mother tongue of Corinne, and by the music the language fits so naturally. Italy is Corinne's home and away from it she feels like a branch with no roots.

It might seem that the right choice is quite obvious, but Corinne is strongly held by her desire to fulfill the expectations of her dead father and of her stepmother, unsympathetic and unprepossessing as she is. She feels ties also with her half sister Lucile, whom she loves and has tended for three years as a "second mother." Social respectability is not to be lightly renounced, the opinions of others not to be easily defied. Thus, though Corinne chooses Italy, she presents this decision not as totally voluntary but rather partly as the result of her stepmother's ill will, and partly as following the entreaties of her beloved servant Thérésine. The mood of her departure is not one of resolution but of reckless abandon. "I left in one of those moments when one gives oneself over to destiny."[20] She arrives quickly in Italy, barely mentioning the trip itself, leaving her name behind. She becomes as if dead in England and is reborn in Italy simply as Corinne, without a family name, without an identity of any kind, her past unknown. Under these conditions, she gradually becomes a great and celebrated artist.

The good mother dies when the child is only ten. We recall that the good relationship between Staël and Suzanne Necker lasted also only until Germaine was about ten years old. Just as the child must have felt that in entering adolescence she left the good mother behind and exchanged her for a bad one, so Corinne moves from mother to mother. The metaphor of a trip from Italy to England is making it possible for Staël to depict her relationship with her mother, a subject she never treats directly. There is a quite positive note here: the feeling on Corinne's part that if she can only get back somehow to the good mother her creativity will be released; in her "mother tongue," the language of her good mother, she will be able to speak. And in Italy she does speak.

The father plays a very different role in this spiritual journey from that generally attributed to the Necker of Staël's life. Here he is greatly admired but very much in the background, weak and unassertive. The more familiar Necker is present in the book not in Corinne's family drama but in that of Staël's other alter ego in the book, the Englishman who falls in love with Corinne, Oswald, Lord Nelvil. She is gradually telling all of her story here but dividing it between her two central characters. Oswald's passage of the English Channel on the way to Italy is a second important crossing in the book. "It is more difficult to leave one's fatherland when one must cross the ocean in order to go away from it; everything is solemn in a trip of which the Ocean marks the first stages: it seems that an abyss is opening up before you and that return could become forever impossible."[22] The description echoes the sad, solemn, and foreboding passage of the Rhine. The resemblance is not coincidental. When Staël wrote of the first trip into Germany she had to recall that it was then that her father died. Guilt over his dying during her absence was to haunt her for many years. Oswald suffers from guilt over his relationship with his father, who died while under the impression that his son had acted out of conformity with paternal wishes. If we had not noticed the similarity of Oswald's attitude toward her father and that of Staël herself, she brings it strikingly to our attention by quoting, as words written by Oswald's father, passages from Necker's *On the Importance of Religious Opinions*. Lest the shades of her father be offended by the role she attributes to paternal figures here, she incorporates him into her text, thus reaffirming her loyalty. Moreover, she can always argue with that shade that it is Oswald's father, not hers (that of the female figure Corinne) whose heavy presence causes her downfall.

In this way Staël was able to transfer her guilt over to the hero, thus apparently leaving her heroine the freedom to develop creativity fully, unfettered by such destructive feelings. Still, in the final analysis, the powerful father plays a negative role, in that Oswald's refusal to marry Corinne, a refusal that breaks her heart and puts an end to her creative power, is due to the stubborn obeisance he pays to his father's values and wishes even though they come to him, in fact, from beyond the grave.

In *Corinne* the passage into Italy, that is, into female creativity, is recounted in two moments, that of the heroine and that of the hero, as if its elements needed to be separated out rather than dealt with as a whole. The passages come to represent those psychological journeys one must take in order to leave early stages of dealing with one's family situation for more mature ones. By the time she wrote *Corinne* and *On Germany* both of Staël's parents were dead. Madelyn Gutwirth speaks of the "release" those deaths brought about for Staël in this way: "Freed from parental reproof and the fear of it, after twenty years of equivocation about her own nature, she here [i.e., in *Corinne*] dares to assert her own amazonian self."[23] Though the death of parents does not silence their voices within us, especially insofar as those voices echo society's expectations of us, it may provide space for movement. This seems to have been the case with Staël, for now she is moving more freely than she has done in the past into new or newly interpreted areas. In these books she deals more honestly and openly with her past than before and in so doing, she leaves it, crossing over from youth into maturity, removing inner obstacles to new places within the topography of her inner world.

Unity and Disunity

Thematically and structurally, there are strong continuities between Staël's earlier pair of works and this one, but an important shift in emphasis is taking place. Of Germans she says, "They made up for the interests which events supply by that of ideas."[24] In speaking of them she will partially abandon her interest in story and deal instead with ideas. The diachronic will be replaced in *On Germany* with the synchronic. This is not to say that Staël now repudiates the theory of perfectibility. She reiterates it, saying that those who deny it condemn man to the fate of Sisyphus, that fortunately one can perceive "a design, always the same, always followed, always progressive, in man's history."[25] But elsewhere she defines it less strongly than in *On Literature* saying that it means simply that human kind is "susceptible of education," and that one can show that "there are eras marked for progress of thought in the eternal road of time."[26] Moreover she quotes Goethe on perfectibility, who said that the human mind advances in a spiral (II, p. 202). The coexistence of her theory stated as strongly as she had stated it earlier with milder and transformed versions indicates that she does not attach the same importance to it now as she had earlier, that her thought has passed on, crossed over, to other concerns.

It is in *On Germany* that the statement we have already examined regarding story and history in women and men is found, but to quote it in its entirety is to illustrate the shift in emphasis that is occurring here. "Women seek to arrange themselves like a novel, and men like a history; but the human heart is still quite far from having its most intimate relations penetrated. Someday perhaps someone will tell sincerely everything he has felt, and people will be astonished to learn that most maxims and observations are erroneous, and that there is an unknown soul beneath the one we are recounting."[27] History and story are both arrangements, organized presentations of the self that, the passage implies, obscure it. The "most intimate relations" (in its dual meaning of "relationships" and "narrations") have not been revealed by those accounts. If the human heart were understood, the inapplicability of maxims would be exposed and something as yet mysterious ("une âme inconnue"—"an unknown soul") might be uncovered. The story is not the form in which that revelation will be made.

Because of her crossings, Staël begins to drop her interest in history and story and to turn her attention to the personality of people or of peoples, and indeed of herself. This is, to be sure, not a new interest. In *On Literature* Staël constantly characterized the peoples who played parts in her story of literature. But now these characterizations become the major focus of interest; story is no longer the fundamental structure, not even in the novel *Corinne*, which of course has a story line. In describing her crossings Staël stressed that leaving reminders of the past behind disintegrates the identity, makes one feel that one is leaving one's past on the other side of the waters. Such an act has its positive side: the past can become encrusted on the self in such a way as to block or immobilize it. When the past falls away, one emerges apprehensive, fearful, and vulnerable but open, flexible, ready for change, or at the very least, ready to get acquainted with oneself anew.

Precisely because Staël is no longer surrounded by reminders of the past, she is asking herself what she is like, what is this "unknown soul" beneath the soul whose story one tells. Her parents are dead; she is in exile. That she feels deeply threatened is reflected in the recurrence of the theme of madness in these two books. In *Corinne* Oswald performs several acts of derring-do on his way to Rome, one of which is to save inmates of a madhouse from fire. Staël describes the faces of madmen with a feeling for telling detail that is seldom present in her writing. Observation of madness riveted her attention. Corinne herself feels threatened by madness. In Naples, after she knows that Oswald has read the story of her life and while she awaits word from him regarding whether anything in that story will prevent their union, she wanders under the mercilessly hot sun. The heat and her emotional state create vertigo in her, and she is close to madness. Later, when she knows Oswald will not choose her over fidelity to his family, she writes to an Italian friend, "I would pass for mad if I did not have the sad gift of observing my madness."[28] In *On Germany* as well as in *Corinne*, Staël links madness with sorrow. She thinks of the Rousseau of the *Rêveries d'un promeneur solitaire*, "this eloquent depiction of a being who is a prey to an imagination stronger than he."[29] She recalls that he felt he was hated and persecuted, the object of everyone's envy and the victim of a conspiracy that extended from the lower classes to kings, that all his friends had betrayed him, that even their favors were in fact traps laid to catch him. Then she imagines what consolations a highly socialized person on the one hand and a religious person on the other would have to offer to such a man. The Staël of 1788 had identified herself with Rousseau and his work. The feelings she attributes to him here were also feelings she herself might well have had during her estrangement from Napoleonic France and at the time when she was deeply disturbed at having been abandoned by Benjamin Constant. She is depicting her own life and its effect on her mental and emotional health, and imaginatively seeking different types of comfort. She speaks also of the effects of suffering as entailing the feeling that nature itself has been overturned. "Everything . . . seems an over turning of nature, and no one has suffered without believing that great disorder exists in the universe."[30] To believe so is to be threatened with madness.

Early on in her career Staël had shown interest in madness. Her "Madwoman of Sénart"[31] depicted a crazed woman rushing madly from stranger to stranger asking what about her made her so unlovable. It seems natural that in this period of instability in her life this interest would become acute and internalized. Because of the threat of disintegration, of personal disorder, with which this period of displacement confronted her, Staël came to feel that what is really interesting is the structure and not the story of the soul. Therefore, a major concern of these two books is not the telling of a story but the examination of unity and order, locked in struggle with disunity and disorder. In this struggle unity is sometimes valorized as the provider of sanity and strength. But at other times Staël sees in disunity a potentiality for liberation, a way out of the confinement into which rigidly established categories may bind a person or a nation. This structure—unity engaged with disunity—underlies the development of a variety of themes in these books, and its elements are combined and assessed in a number of different ways.

In *On Germany* Staël imagines a new story entirely, one that does not develop according to the linear principle of perfectibility, the basis of *On Literature*, but rather on a succession of "enthusiasms." The concept plays an important part in both of the crossing books in that it is a source of unity. Etymologically it means, as Staël says, "god in us." For Staël it connotes some great idea in which the people of a time believe totally—emotionally, intellectually, spiritually. Because all participate in the same belief, it unites each with all and thus provides stable meaning as well as a link of the one with the many. Enthusiasm fills one with exalted feelings and puts one at peace with oneself and the world. This is an active peace in that it launches the individual and the group toward great accomplishments.[32] Enthusiasm is, then, a fundamentally unifying factor. Tracing the history of the world, Staël sees four different eras: "heroic times, which founded civilization; patriotism, which made the glory of antiquity; chivalry, which was the warlike religion of Europe; and the love of freedom, whose story began toward the time of the reformation."[33] The problem in France since the early seventeenth century, she says, is the lack of a common enthusiasm. One is needed now; it seems that the appropriate enthusiasm is that for freedom, but it is not widely enough shared to fulfill its function at this time.

Both of her books reach toward and end with fervent bursts of religion and enthusiasm. The motivation she claims she had in writing *On Germany* in particular was to express and inspire enthusiasm in her readers. Speaking of writers for whom writing is simply a mechanical sort of occupation, she asks, "Do they know with what hope one is filled, when one believes that one is demonstrating, by the gift of eloquence, a profound truth, a truth that forms a generous link between us and all souls in sympathy with ours?"[34] She wants to feel and to be able to express the impact of enthusiasm, which is to bring about a oneness within the self and with others. "As soon as man is divided within himself, he feels life only as an ill; and if, of all feelings, enthusiasm makes us happiest, it is because it unites more than any other all the strength of the soul into the same center."[35]

There is indeed, then, as Simone Balayé says, in both the poetics and the esthetics of Staël the idea of unity.[36] These books valorize and seek unity on both the personal and the collective levels as a refuge from the threat of madness and as the basis for a new political world. But just as the desired pattern of perfectiblity was undermined by discontinuity and decadence in *Delphine* and *On Literature*, disunity puts unity into question. To examine how and why this happens, it is necessary to consider Staël's dual meditations on unity, that of the inner oneness of the individual or of the nation and that of the relationship between and among individuals and nations.

Staël views individuals and nations as similarly structured. (This is why one can read her books about people or about peoples comparatively.) She states in *On Germany*, "Difference in language, natural boundaries, memories of the same history, everything contributes to create among men those great individuals we call nations; certain proportions are necessary for their existence, certain qualities distinguish them."[37] Both individuals and nations are wholes made up of parts that work together to form an essence. In order to describe either type of entity, therefore, one looks for the particular properties and shows how they add up to the total essence. Their languages, their sizes, their histories make them different, but their basic structures are the same.

Staël had been working according to such a model at least since *On Literature*. There, she described each nation that played a part in her story by enumerating the qualities which emanated from the circumstances of its statehood and by characterizing its fundamental way of being. She proceeds in a similar way with Germany and Italy, but now the descriptions are more complex. Character seemed relatively simple to define to the Staël of the turn of the century. In *On Literature*, she said "One need seek out in a people, as in a man, only his characteristic trait; all the others are the effect of a thousand different strokes of chance: that one alone constitutes its being."[38] Certainly such a situation makes definitions and descriptions easy to make, but the Staël of *On Germany* has ceased to believe that things are quite that simple. "Each character is a new world for those who are able to observe with subtlety, and I do not know, in the science of the human heart, any general idea which applies completely to particular examples."[39]

This new skepticism of generalities was inspired in Staël partly no doubt by observing the "unknown soul" of the self she was discovering in her travels. Moreover, close observation of, for example, the Germans, made it impossible for her to attribute to them one characterizing trait as she had in *On Literature*. That trait was melancholy. Instead, she sees that up close their complexity rather than their simplicity strikes one. Their character is impossible to seize under one general rubric. In Germany one sees a strange assembling of characteristics rather than one unified character. "The mind of the Germans and their character appear to have no communication with each other: the one suffers no limits, the other submits to all yokes; the one is very enterprising, the other very timid."[40] Similarly, the Italians are adept and powerful in the exercise of the arts but lack strength of character as far as nation and society are concerned. The reason for these apparent contradictions is the inability on the part of both peoples to influence political events, since both belong to weakened and fragmented countries. Circumstance, then, can cause discord in the very essence of a person or of a people by generating contradictory properties. To find the one defining trait would be in such cases quite impossible. Character does not always lend itself to a simple essence/property, whole/part model, Staël seems to have discovered.

The coexistence of divergent traits in the character of a person or of a people is to some degree positive and enabling, but it has its dangers even in the best of cases. Corinne's home, Oswald thinks when he first sees it, unites the best of three countries: France, England, and Italy. Corinne herself has two nationalities. (In passing, let us note that the issue of nationality was very alive for Staël personally. She was of Swiss parentage, but French by birth, experience, and inclination. Efforts to establish French nationality occupied her acutely at certain moments of her life, especially because of the instability of the government.) Part of her artistic strength and personal charm depends on this admixture. Yet finally it will be her undoing. In *On Germany* Staël speaks several times of the debilitating effects of trying to unite incompatible traits. For example, Frederick II of Prussia tried to unite German and French traits and in so doing undercut both.[41]

Totalizing, or the bringing together of properties into a single essence, is as problematic on the national level as on the level of personal characteristics, as one sees in comparing the political organization of France to that of Germany or Italy. Both of the latter countries are fragmented into loosely associated groups, whereas France is strongly centralized in one place, Paris, and by one man, Napoleon. Each arrangement has its positive and negative features. Strength is found in unity; what is divided, as the proverb claims, does not conquer. However, Germans and Italians, because they lack a strong center of political power, develop inner qualities to a greater degree. Continual action, in which the French may engage, makes thought superficial, though it strengthens character. The act of centralizing, like that of totalizing, has its importance, but it involves dangers.

The case of Frederick of Prussia, half French and half German, bespeaks not only the negative effects of such unhappy combinations on a person but also the potential harm the merging of countries and of people can bring about. Staël is considering the interactions among the traits of a single entity and the interrelationships of entities among themselves. In *On Germany* she expressed two ideas which were to some extent at odds with each other. One was that the French have much to learn from the Germans, that the converse is also true, and that, therefore, a totalizing, a bringing together, an integration of the qualities would be desirable. The other was politically motivated. During this time Napoleon the conqueror was pursuing his dream of a new French hegemony over Europe. Staël wanted to oppose the realization of that ambition. Therefore, she takes great care when she depicts the interaction she desires between the two countries. She envisions not an empire but an association in Europe, in which each country would keep its independence. To unite countries under the same rule would be to bring about a loss of the identity of each. "If Germany were united with France, it would follow also that France would be united to Germany, and that the

French of Hamburg, like the French of Rome, would alter by degrees the character of the compatriots of Henry IV: the conquered would gradually modify the conquerors, and all would finally lose in the process."[42] She presents the matter in such a way as to appeal to the French sense of identity, though naturally, as she also says, all identities would be in danger.

In like manner it is harmful and inappropriate to "transport" the qualities and works of German literature directly into France. What succeeds on the stage of one country would most frequently fail in another. The novels of one country, which depict, of course, its mores, would not be effective if copied by another. One studies foreign literature for general, not specific, inspiration. "The big advantage that one can find in studying German literature is the movement of emulation it gives; one must look there for the strength to compose oneself, rather than for ready-made works one can transport elsewhere."[43] In short, political or literary totalization is totalitarian, and Staël opposes both, defining very precisely the desired impact of her own attempts to transport knowledge of Germany into France.

Totalizing in the personal realm, at its most intimate, is love. One transports one's feelings to another person and hopes to bring that person's feelings over to one's self in return. The dream of lovers is a merging of what were two separate souls into one. It is not surprising that the structures of unity and disunity are fundamental in *Corinne* as well as in *On Germany*. The novel is at once a story of lovers and a guide to Italy—its monuments, its character, its literature, its artistic achievements. Staël takes care to unite these two parts of her book into a whole by having the events of her story happen in places that reflect or symbolize the particular nature of the event. The attempt is made to "unite history and poetry with landscape," to use a phrase attributed to Corinne as she describes her favorite kind of painting.[44]

When Corinne and Oswald first meet and recognize their attraction to each other, Corinne begins to introduce him, and the reader, to Rome. She begins by showing buildings and ruins, which must be appreciated from the outside. Gradually she moves to the inside of the museums and churches, thus suggesting the increasing intimacy of the relationship that is developing between the guide and her beloved tourist. She speaks of the marks history has left on Rome; at this early stage of their relationship their own histories have not yet emerged to trouble it so that the past seems pleasurable to contemplate. Yet all throughout the section on Rome there are references to "la cattiva aria," the noxious air coming into Rome from the outlying marshes that is believed to encroach more and more upon the city as the summer advances. This "bad air" represents the dangers inherent in the relationship of the lovers.

Two crucial scenes immediately precede the moment when the lovers exchange information about their pasts, information that will ultimately separate them and destroy their hopes for a future together. One is a masked ball, representing the covering of a reality less cheerful than the costumes of the revelers suggest. This carnival of mardi gras gives way then to Corinne's celebration of holy week, prefiguring death. Thereafter, Corinne and Oswald go to Naples where the actual revelation is to take place. Naples is described as a savage city inhabited notably by people who know nothing, not even their own names, who are uncivilized and represent, therefore, passion out of control. Oswald and Corinne go up a mountain and peer into the volcano inside.

After the revelations but before the rupture between them, Oswald and Corinne go to Venice, the archetypal city of illusion. After her return from England where she has witnessed Oswald's betrothal to another woman, approved of by his father, Corinne sojourns alone in Florence, situated in the center of a country whose past has long since been destroyed. So also has Corinne's brilliant past as an artist been obliterated by her unfortunate love. Beatrice Le Gall, who has studied Staël's descriptions of the landscapes in *Corinne*, maintains "the description constitutes infinitely more than a framework for the novel and never constitutes a diversion. It is an itinerary of symbolic significance."[45] Maria Lehtonen, in her study of Staël's imagery, in like manner emphasizes the *correspondances* between nature and man and between soul and body, citing Staël's own formulation, that the world is the work of a "pensée unique," a "single thought."[46] This statement is true, but the integrations of plot and scene are carried out in quite a mechanical way, as even this brief account of some of them may suggest. There is indeed an attempt to make "the microcosm reflect the macrocosm," as Le Gall puts it.[47] However, all too easily does the weather change from sunny to stormy when the lovers begin to quarrel. The effort at making of these two elements a harmonious whole is clear, but the harmonies achieved have a contrived and artificial ring. This is a first sign that totalization will give Staël as much trouble in this book as in *On Germany*.

The interpersonal relationships end in failed attempts at harmony. Because Corinne is England and Italy united, Oswald feels at first that she will provide a continuity missing in his life, that is, that she will enable him to unite his British self, his submission to duty, his strict standards of conduct, with an Italian self he feels coming out in him especially when he goes to Italy, a passionate, romantic self. Corinne, in fact, is presented as a conveyer of continuity. She is the link among her friends, as one of them comments.[48] It seems that her own integration of disparate elements makes it possible for her to bring about harmonies in those about her. But this is not what happens. Corinne cannot give her lover what she unconsciously provides for her friends. The nature of love makes the dream of lovers impossible. "There must be harmony in feeling and opposition in character so that love may be born both of sympathy and of diversity."[49] The characters of Oswald and Corinne are indeed opposed, as were those of Delphine and Léonce. He cannot give up social respectibility. She cannot love in a restricted domestic setting. They fatally love each other, but they cannot come together in any smooth and continuous way. Love seems to promise totalization more than anything else, but it is quite unlikely to bring it about.

In *Corinne* love not only does not win out; it also destroys Corinne. At the beginning of thebook, Corinne is honored on the Capitoline hill. She receives a Petrarchan crown and then improvises before an adoring crowd. Her talents, combined with her exposure to two quite different cultures, have given her special powers of creativity. The novel, however, is a künstlerroman in reverse. Corinne's crown falls when she sees Oswald for the first time. Later in the novel she crowns him for a heroic act he has performed. Still later, in a moment of intense suffering over their lost love, she falls down, hitting and cutting her head. She bitterly points out that a crown once adorned this now bleeding head.

Her dual nationality has been somehow to blame. That the affair with Oswald could so completely disintegrate her personality must be because her duality made her especially vulnerable, all the more so with a man to whom one of the components of her personality corresponded. The novel calls upon us to feel pity for Corinne and to view Oswald as something of a charming and sensitive cad. But it does not entirely suggest that the love of Oswald and Corinne would have been a good thing for them if it had worked out. "Talent requires an inner independence true love does not permit," reflects Corinne.[50] Madelyn Gutwirth has beautifully developed this theme. In her "Du silence de Corinne et de sa parole,"[51] she shows how the conditions that made Corinne's speaking possible are destroyed by England and by love. In another study, Gutwirth states that as early as her work on the passions she "subliminally perceived that the fictional dominance of love . . . was an instrument for maintaining women in a state of subservience and in that permanent latency which had baffled her own development."[52]

Love, it seems, is structured like totalitarian governments. Just as the creativity of the Germans and the Italians, as well as that of Corinne, is related to the fragmented and diffuse organization of their governments and of their characters, so also the artist must not participate in a strongly centralized, integrated oneness with another. Germans, Italians, and artists, all owe their creativity to their political powerlessness and to their foregoing of a character centered both within itself and with another person. Staël was fundamentally suspicious of unity or oneness both politically and personally.

What, then, is suspect about unity, especially in books that in many ways value it so highly? The answer lies in Staël's conflicting feelings about where her loyalties were properly to be placed. Freedom, the enthusiasm she suggests as that of the present and the future, has existed only in political organizations that were unamenable to effective roles for women. "When there are, as in England, great interests to discuss, societies of men are always animated by a noble common interest; but in countries where there is no representative government, the presence of women is necessary in order to maintain all feelings of delicacy and purity, without which the love of the beautiful may be lost. The influence of women is more salutary to warriors than to citizens; the reign of the law does without them better than that of honor."[53] That is, when there is a strong government in which citizens take part, men involve themselves in it and have less need of women. Their "love for the beautiful," the fine, the worthwhile, is energized by participation in events. The "reign of law," a political situation characterized by well-developed and sharply defined institutions, excludes women. The "reign of honor," the feudal period, in which political arrangements were less centralized, included women because it needed their influence. The reign of law involves a rigid separation between the private, or domestic, and the public spheres. Corinne could not live in England, the country mentioned in the passage just quoted, where this division of labor between men, who act in the public realm, and women, who must remain in the private, was rigidly enforced. In Germany, Staël indicates, feudal or chivalric social arrangements opened a more important place for action by women.

This insight, for which Staël found her original inspiration in Montesquieu,[54] is quite perspicacious. Modern historians of women, beginning in the 1940s with Mary Beard and continuing to the present in England with Joan Kelly and in France with Régine Pernoud, have studied the Middle Ages in an attempt to find out whether women had more opportunity for participation, more room for action, than during and after the Renaissance and, if so, what structures made that possible.[55] Such researchers look for the answer to such questions in social structures rather than in the kind of indirect and inspirational influence toward which Staël instinctively turned. But the fact that her thought on history and woman's place in it led her to the Middle Ages indicates that at this point in her career she was able to handle the question not only more skillfully and suggestively than in *On Literature* but in a way that has its intrinsic value, whose implications have not been adequately explored to this day.

Staël was a man's woman who wanted to participate in his world in any way she could. Less openly, though, she was a woman who understood that to praise the "enthusiasm of freedom" was to undermine her own position still further, to work toward a world in which she would have even less place than in the present one. Again, as in *Delphine* and in *On Literature*, we find her professing what she cannot believe and believing what she does not want, perhaps does not dare, to profess.

Overtly, in her actions and on the surface of her writing, she seems to take the position that the interests of the world of men should be furthered by all. True action takes place there; one cannot be said to be active except insofar as one takes part in it. Thus if freedom, unity, totalization, or centered strength is what is best for *mankind*, then the pursuit of those things should engage the best efforts of man and woman. Staël mustered her loftiest flights of eloquence as well as every type of activity in which she could conceivably become involved toward the aim of participating in man's world.

But those efforts encountered inner resistance. She could not support such aims wholeheartedly, as much as she may have wanted to do so. That inner resistance asserted itself constantly, making her question concepts in which she claimed belief. A persistent lucidity within her whispered that there was another side to those issues, that she was not acting in her own interests as a woman. From that lucidity comes a continual crosscurrent in her writing that makes it question the validity of the idealized concepts it claims to support. Out of the conflicts generated in this way come flashes of brilliant and fundamental insights. The first crosscurrents in Staël's writing were those that opposed themselves to her strong impulse to write. The sense that the same image applies to her writing at this point in her career suggests that the instinct to write in a woman's way, in woman's interest, is now asserting itself against those earlier forces, although incompletely and rather timidly still.

Staël understood that this new story, based not on temporal continuities but on a succession of enthusiasms, does not fit woman any better than that of perfectibility. She knows that the structure of unity is to be desired but that those unified entites the world has known have tended to close ranks against women. For woman's energies to be able to flow, there must be spaces, which only disunity, discontinuity, can leave open. Without being conscious of doing so, Staël is nonetheless undoing what she perceives as male values—

progressive continuity in time, political and personal unity. The fluctuations of position regarding these issues are attributable to Staël's indecision about which side she should take, indeed, about which side is truly hers.

Finally still another insight is at work here, shaking the affirmations of unity and order. As those concepts are undermined, what begins to emerge in their place is a valorization of multiplicity wherein not only oneness but also duality is shattered into manyness. While Staël is still writing her books in pairs, and will continue to do so, the rigid male/female dichotomy which she had tried to establish earlier no longer seems to be a preoccupation. *Corinne* and *On Germany* resemble each other in their surface qualities more than do *Delphine* and *On Literature* in that both are presentations of countries and cultures. Here it is not that one member of the pair questions the assertion of the other and brings its inconsistencies to light. Rather, the books echo each other's questions. This complementarity suggests that the male/female dualism is loosening its grip. She seems less concerned, then, with establishing a definable, stereotypical sexual writing identity. Her writing is none the less feminine in that her concerns are still generated from her womanhood, which continues to energize her creativity and to prod her to look for the openings through which her own voice can be heard. Paradoxically, she may indeed even be freer to conduct those explorations now that her differentiations can be more supple than before. Dualism is another model that comes into question once unity is no longer the accepted structure, the uncertainties here also generative of both intuition and apprehension.

New Regions, New Identities, New Voices

The aim of asserting unity was no more successful than claims for continuity, with, in both cases, resultant anxieties and insights. Similarly, on the other side of the boundaries that separated Staël from her past, thus provoking such anxiety about personal integrity, she discovered that she could imagine and live temporarily within other, hypothetical identities in which her voice could speak in new ways. In order to come to an understanding of those new identities, one must examine closely the characteristics of the countries that inspired them. It is striking that while traveling in Italy and Germany, which she had depicted as very different in her celebrated distinction in *On Literature* between the literature of the north and that of the south, she now finds them very much alike in basic ways. Their similarities have been implicit in much of what has been said here, but I would like to recapitulate them briefly.

Both Italy and Germany lack political unity. Neither has a strong central government that unites different parts into one nation. In Italy, there are various states that differ greatly from each other in character and customs.[56] Germany is an aristocratic federation with no common center. The fragmentation that results from decenteredness has both advantages and disadvantages. Negatively, the countries and their citizens find their power to act undermined. Germans lack energy and character, which must be grounded in devotion to the country. To be sure, they have many fine qualities, "but their gracious and obliging eagerness to serve power pains one who loves them and who thinks that they are the most enlightened speculative defenders of human dignity."[57] Rome, with a similar political situation and a history of many defeats, provides an ideal setting for "those who no longer have the ambition, nor the possibility of playing a role in the world."[58]

The past of the two countries is more illustrious than the present. Corinne reminds Oswald, who has attacked the current debility of Italians, that once, under the Romans, the country was "the most military of all, the most jealous of freedom among the medieval republics, and, in the sixteenth century, the most illustrious in letters, sciences, and the arts."[59] In her travel journal, Staël quotes Alfieri's assessment of the nature of Italians after the French conquest, "We are slaves, but slaves still trembling with rage."[60] The monuments of Germany recall centuries of chivalry. "The whole country resembles the home of a great people which have long since departed."[61] The link between Germany and an even more distant past is introduced in Staël's first chapter, which Laurence Porter eloquently calls "an impressionistic landscape."[62] "The multitude of forests indicates a civilization which is still new . . . . Germany offers still some traces of an uninhabited nature . . . . It seems that time moves there more slowly than elsewhere."[63] To visit either country is to move among traces of the past, to return to lost times, even to enter a land where time itself does not move according to the temporal laws of modern countries.

Finally, both countries excel in liberal arts, that is, in those endeavors involving imagination and fantasy rather than attention to practical detail and applicability of ideas. The art of improvisation, whether in music, in words, or both is highly developed in each. This art requires freedom, spontaneity, and ease of thought. Shorn of political power, the inhabitants of both countries have creative powers, all the more unfettered for being removed from places of power in the "real" world. Because they cannot act in the political arena, they displace their energies onto that of the arts and of philosophy.

The reason why Staël saw such striking resemblances between countries that, theoretically, should be quite different lies in the fact that she found in her travels what every traveler ultimately finds: herself. Madelyn Gutwirth, Marie-Claire Vallois, and Simone Balayé have all spoken of the correspondance between woman and Italy.[64] The characteristics Germany and Italy have in common, they also share with woman as Staël viewed her, that is, with herself. The discoveries her passages make possible are self-discoveries.

The third chapter of *On Germany* is entitled "Women." The positioning of this chapter in the book seems significant in that the treatment of women is placed very near the beginning rather than near the end, as in *On Literature*. This placement suggests that the topic was coming toward the forefront of her interests, able to do so because the metaphorical topic of the book itself is women. The chapter begins with general comments on women, before moving to the more specific subject, German women, which is of course more closely related to the literal theme of the book, Germany. Her characterization of women contains exactly the same four elements as those of Germany and of Italy. "They hold onto life only by links of the heart, and when they wander it is still by a feeling they are carried away. Their personality is double."[65] This is to say that women are fragmented; their being is not unified, not complete within itself; rather it is split, divided, fragmented. Moreover, women are decentered, because their hold on life takes place through links they establish with something outside themselves. They have no center, or if they do, it does not function as a center. "The destiny of women remains always the same, their soul alone makes it. Political circumstances do not influence it at all."[66] Like Italians and Germans, women are removed from the political arena. Men of countries that exercise political power are called upon to exercise their own power and become the stronger, the more energetic, for it. But women in all countries are the same, since they do not in any event exercise any direct power. In that way women can be appropriately figured by the Italians and the Germans.[67]

Further, women are more associated with the past than with the present. While men are engaged in activities, "women cultivate their minds, and feeling and revery preserve in their soul the image of all that is noble and fine."[68] The idea of "preserving" indicates the keeping of what is lost when one moves ahead to other activities. Women, like Germans, live in a time lost for men; they are the conservators of what would otherwise be forgotten. Finally, like Italians and Germans, women excel in the liberal arts. The chapter on women ends with a brief discussion of conversation, no doubt the liberal art in which Staël herself most excelled. Conversation, as Madelyn Gutwirth points out and as Carol Peterson has recently developed most beautifully,[69] is, like the improvisation in which the Germans and the Italians are so skilled, an art associated with women. A strong reason for the excellence of all three groups in this free and spontaneous form of selfexpression is their very powerlessness to act.

Staël has said in *On Germany* that her new interest, replacing the attempt to tell a story, is the search for the "unknown soul," and that this search will be carried out in the form of confession. Confession was not a mode she favored, as her journal and her *Letters on Rousseau* make clear. But in these two books, because of the resemblance with the situation of woman she sees in them, one can find out a great deal about her that she did not reveal in any other place or in any overt way. Her approach is indirect, oblique, metaphorical. She identifies herself with the peoples whom she is to discuss and tells of herself through them.

In *Corinne*, writers, like all Italians, are in the position of women, unable to affect their society and their government.[70] Her criticism of their style, attributed to the Englishman Oswald, is quite severe. Their language, he contends, is not conducive to effective prose style.[71] "Most of your prose writers today have a language so declamatory, so diffuse, so abundant in superlatives, that one would say that they all write on command, with received phrases, and for conventional nature; they do not seem to suspect that to write is to express one's character and one's thought."[72] Italian prose has the very qualities one finds in Staël's own prose: rhetorical flourish, hyperbole, banality, inauthentic self-expression. That Oswald's statement is to be read as self-criticism by Staël becomes evident when, in Corinne's answer to him, she explains why Italian writers write as they do in terms unmistakably parallel to her description of the plight of woman.

> Unfortunate circumstances having deprived Italy of its independence, people there have lost all interest in the truth, and even, often, in the possibility of saying it. The result has been to delight in words, without daring to approach ideas. As one was certain not to be able to obtain by one's writings any influence on things, one wrote only in order to show off one's wit, which is the surest way to end up by not having even wit; for it is in directing one's efforts toward a nobly useful objective that one finds the most ideas. When prose writers cannot influence in any way the happiness of their nation, when one writes only to distinguish oneself, when, finally, it is the means which are the end, one winds oneself around in a thousand ways, but one does not go forward.[73]

The history of Italy, like that of woman, is marked by a fall: it was independent, but now it is dependent; once Italian writers had influence, but they lost it. And that fall, that loss, has an inevitable effect on language: wit is undercut, direction twisted, words emptied of meaning because they are devoid of potentiality for action.

The association Italy/woman means that if we listen carefully, we will hear Staël's voice as she speaks of Italian writers: she will really be speaking of herself, covertly, but with more lucid perception and less gesturing than elsewhere. In *Corinne*, she is enabled to move into her most extraordinary self-criticism and self-expression. In order to hear them, one must be attentive to shifts in level of reference. In the passage just quoted, for example, one recognizes the voice as that of the witty Frenchwoman ("Showing off wit . . . is the surest means of not even having wit"); or that of the high-minded idealist and moralist ("by directing one's effort toward a nobly useful objective"); or that of the cultural critic analyzing Italian civilization. These discourses shift from one into the other from sentence to sentence, phrase to phrase. Insistently surfacing, though, there is the obliquely self-expressive voice of Staël: once she shows how her situation is parallel to that of the Italians, whenever she speaks of them she speaks of herself, as if the closeness of the identification is such that while sometimes she remembers to keep her distance and to talk about Italians, at others she merges with them and speaks confessionally.

The passage on Italian comedy is superb from this point of view. The subject of the passage is why the Italians did not excell in that genre. As it begins, words like *poetry, joy, and inoffensive gaiety* are associated with Italian literature. Such qualities do not make comedy, where the jokes (*plaisanterie*) are "based on something sad." Staël refuses this kind of comedy. From the beginning of the passage she is on the side of the Italians. She gradually identifies with them even more intimately, to the point of moving into indirect confession.

> It is not that the Italians fail to study the men with whom they deal, nor do they fail to discover, more subtly than anyone, most secret thoughts; but it is in the spirit of conduct that they have this talent, and they do not as a rule make a literary use of it. Perhaps they would not like to generalize their discoveries, to publish their perceptions. In their character they have something prudent and dissembling which perhaps advises them not show, by their comedies, what they use to guide themselves in specific relationships, not to reveal, by witty fictions, what can perhaps be useful in circumstances of real life.[74]

In *On the Character of M. Necker and on His Private Life*,[75] Staël tells us that her father had composed many comedies in his youth but did not publish them precisely because he decided to participate in public affairs. In a sense, she saw him as refusing to reveal what he knew about human foibles. We know that she associated herself closely with him, so that when we read of the Italians we know we are reading about Staël and also about her father. She suggests that the comedy the Italians would have written (that Staël would have written, if she had written comedy) would be poetic, joyous, inoffensive. They have not written comedy but not because of lack of perspicacity and penetration. The reason given for this bizarre inaction—not doing something one would be quite capable of doing—has little to do with Italians; it is a projected reason of Staël herself. She says that they/she use(s) the kind of knowledge comic writers put in comedies for the actual conduct of their lives. The more speculative she becomes, the more she voices herself. The key words *prudent . . . dissembling . . . not showing . . . not revealing*, are interspersed with three *perhaps*. The words sketch a manner of behaving appropriate to the condition after the fall into a world where action is not direct but tortuous. Immediately following this passage is a reference to Machiavelli, the very archetype of the advice to act in a manner that, through its very prudence and dissimulation, would bring a power the actor could not attain otherwise.

In the passage on Italian tragedy, to choose another example, one sees the same shift from general comment on the mythical Italians to personal statement, the surfacing, in other words, of the voice. "Our poets refine and exaggerate feeling, whereas the true character of the nature of Italians is a rapid and profound impression that would be expressed better by silent and passionate actions than by an ingenious language. In general, our literature expresses our character and our mores little. We are a nation much too modest, I would almost say too humble, to dare to have our own tragedies, composed with our own history, or at least characterized from our own feelings."[76] Here the apparent contradiction between what the Italians are really like and how their words turn out—the opposition in short between language and realization—leads to a quite surprising generalization to explain why someone might not write a given type of work: it has to do with self-depreciation, the sense of one's own lack of worth and intrinsic interest, more feelings related to a fall. Here again, Staël can quietly and obliquely, perhaps even unwittingly, speak without posing and with astonishing lucidity about what she has not accomplished in writing, about powers and perceptions she thought she had and yet could not use, about a voice which never fully spoke.

A voice, in order to speak, must have access to a language. As early as the *Story of Pauline* Staël had suggested that her native tongue was compromised as a vehicle of self-expression because when speaking it she activated the voices of parental figures whose fundamental message was that she should remain silent. Staël's travels brought with them a renewed and more immediate need for and interest in modern languages, especially English, German, and Italian. She was an enthusiastic student who believed deeply in the value of acquiring some measure of competence in foreign languages. "When I began to study German, it seemed to me that I was entering a new sphere."[77] Such was the impact of the study of German on her, as she says in *On Germany*. In *Corinne* one of her characters counters the Frenchman the Count d'Erfeuil, to whom Staël attributes a closed mind on the beneficial effects that the study and assimilation of foreign literatures can have. She has one of her Italian characters say, "The literature of each country reveals . . . a new sphere of ideas. It is Charles V himself who said 'A man who knows four languages is worth four men.'"[78] "New spheres" or "new regions of the soul" were precisely what Staël was discovering in her travels. It is language that opens them. In new spheres, one feels that one is a new person. She says, "It is amusing to pronounce foreign words: one listens as if it were another person speaking."[79] If in living in a new region and speaking, hearing spoken a new tongue, one feels like a new person, perhaps one can find some means of escape from the constraints of the mother tongue. Staël could express, even confess, herself while imagining herself to be German or Italian. In like manner, she explored the expressive possibilities of languages other than her own. Germans and Italians are hypothetical selves for her. In her two books she often evaluates various modes of communication with respect to their power to make self-expression possible, examining the advantages and disadvantages of several means of expression by trying them out.

One of the well-known facts about Staël is that she grew up in her mother's salon, where exciting conversation helped to develop her mind and personality and attached her permanently to the intellectual and personal pleasures of social life. She excelled and reveled in conversation, experiencing her exile from the Parisian world where this art was most fully exercised as a kind of amputation of a needed part of her life. The inhibitions and interdictions associated with the written word, the exercise of which is a male prerogative, did not plague the use of the spoken word. Her affection for the Prince de Ligne, a portion of whose works she published along with a preface she wrote herself,[80] may be due in some measure to her capacity to distinguish qualities in him she sensed also in herself, for she had this revealing remark to make about him: "But those who are not under the charm of his presence analyze as an author a person whom it was necessary to listen to while reading because the very faults of his style are graces in conversation. What is not always grammatically clear becomes so by its appropriateness to the conversation, the sensitivity of the look, the inflection of the voice, everything, in short, that gives to the art of speaking a thousand times more resources and charms than to the art of writing."[81] This comment suggests that there was a Staël whom, of course, we will never know, one who dealt freely with words while working within a language she perceived as her own. Oddly, one does not even catch a glimpse of this artist in her fictional works, where she was apparently not able to write conversation effectively. Dialogue in *Delphine* and *Corinne* is stilted, resembling exchanged monologue rather than animated give-and-take. It is rather in her expository works that one sees the conversing Staël at work. A critic with an enumerative and mathematical bent could easily make a list of many phrases such as "but someone may object" or "you will say to me" or "frequently one says," phrases which indicate that, as she composed, she was conversing with an imaginary interlocutor, and that this fantasied conversation energized the onward movement of her writing.

Lucia Omacini, who has studied Benjamin Constant's notations on Staël's manuscript of *On Current Circumstances* . . . , tells us that he consistently suggested the omission of such comments,[82] finding, presumably, that they were inappropriate to the rhetoric expository writing requires. In an account that may or may not be apochryphal, Charles-Julien Lioult de Chenedollé, at one time a frequent visitor at Coppet, claims that when Staël was writing *On Literature* she would introduce the topic of a chapter one evening as a dinner conversation, treat the subject herself improvisationally, and incite guests to do the same. The next day she would write the chapter, but, Chenedollé claims, her improvisations were always more brilliant that what she wrote.[83] Conversation, the skilled use of the spoken word, is perhaps more closely associated with women than with men. It is regrettable that Staël did not explore more extensively the integration of her spoken style into her written style. This innovative approach might well have enriched her writing and made it more distinctive, more closely expressive of the specificity of her own female personality.

Yet in "On the Spirit of Conversation" (*On Germany*, part I, chapter II), her attitude is decidedly ambivalent. On the one hand, she speaks of conversation in very positive terms.

> In all classes, in France, people feel the need to chat: the word, there, is not only, as elsewhere, a means of communicating one's ideas, feelings, and activities, but it is an instrument one loves to play and which animates the spirits, like music in case of some peoples, and strong drink in that of others.
>
> The kind of well-being an animated conversation makes one feel does not exactly lie in subject of this conversation; neither the ideas nor the knowledge one may be developing in it is the source of interest. It is a certain way of acting upon each other, of pleasing each other mutually and quickly, of speaking as soon as one thinks, of enjoying oneself immediately, of being praised without having had to work for it, of showing one's mind in all nuances by the accent, the gesture, the look, finally of producing at will a sort of electricity which makes sparks fly, relieves some persons of the excess of their vivacity, and awakens others from a painful apathy.[84]

What is remarkable here is the extraordinary release of energy and totality of self-expression that the spoken word makes possible. Its effect is explicitly compared to that of music, alcohol, and electricity, while the implicit relationship with sexuality is evident. Unlike the written expression of those without political power, conversation is action, "une manière d'agir." Rather than the disheartening feeling that one's words do not count, the speaker feels pleasure with the interlocutor and within herself, effectiveness and rewarding reinforcement. Within conversation, while using the spoken word, one finds at least temporary relief from those very emotional states that were troublesome for Staël in the previous passages, from an "excess of vivacity," which we may associate with the frustration which comes from insufficient and inefficacious self-expression and from the "painful apathy" known as depression, constantly threatening and undercutting. In this quasi-theatrical setting, a joyous energy and power are unleashed and realized in a satisfying form of action.

Yet, as the description and analysis of conversation continue, its darker side appears.

> They [i.e., Germans] do not hear a word without drawing a conclusion, and do not conceive that one can treat the word as a liberal art, which has no aim nor result but the pleasure one finds in it. The spirit of conversation sometimes has the disadvantage of altering sincerity of character; it is not a premeditated but an improvised trick, if one can express oneself this way. The French have put in this genre a gaiety which makes them likeable; but it is nonetheless certain that the most sacred things in the world have been shaken by grace, at least by the kind of grace that turns everything to ridicule.[85]

Serious objections are made here to conversation as a satisfactory means of communication. It undermines sincerity rather than makes it possible. It is good that it is a liberal art, free from the necessity of leading to direct consequence. Yet, as such, it turns toward the realm of game, in which one plays with words, ideas, and positions without demanding at all times that these be expressions one is willing to follow up with action, or thoughts one truly wishes to see realized. Thus, the conversed word becomes removed from one's character, one's essential self, one's recurring principles. The very presence of the interlocutor requires a continual adjustment or adaptation of the self to the other and a wearing away of one's own individuality. It is good also that the spirit of conversation is gay and full of grace. But gaiety and grace are associated with lack of basic values and even with mockery, which is really an attitude of at least indifference and even hostility to principles and people. Just beneath the exhilaration one actually experiences in the act of conversation is the haunting thought of the insincerity and anger with which it is tinged. The voice that is making itself heard through conversation is not finally a true, strong, personal one. Staël comments, "In a country where chatting has so much influence, the noise of words often covers the voice of conscience."[86] Thus, Staël's mother tongue, the spoken word, in which a woman functions—theoretically—beyond the confines of male prerogative, is a compromised language. Perhaps because it does allow for some expression of hostility, it obscures the traces of that threatening feeling with insincerity.

Throughout the chapter on conversation, this peculiarly French phenomenon is constantly contrasted with German self-expression. The comparison continues in chapter 12, entitled "On the German Language in its Relationship with the Spirit of Conversation."[87] Staël states, "The Germans find a kind of charlatanism in the brilliant expression, and choose rather the abstract expression, because it is more scrupulous and more nearly approaches the very essence of truth . . . .

Its tiresome construction, its numerous consonants, its scholarly grammar, permit it no grace in suppleness; and one would say that it stiffens itself against the intention of the one is who is speaking it as soon as one wishes to make it serve to betray truth."[88] Two sets of contrasts are being made. The first is the dichotomy brilliant/abstract. "Brilliant" in Staël's vocabulary means vivid, concrete, depictive of external, visible reality. She valorizes abstraction, claiming that general terms, by eliminating the particular, capture and communicate a truth beyond specific reality. Certainly Staël admired German and indeed all the languages of the north, for which it serves as archetype. Her own style resembles her description of German in those countless passages where she employs a language of conceptual generality. At the same time, her second dichotomy, supple/stiff, puts the total adequacy of such expressions into question. Its very rigidity seems to exclude a desirable flexibility. The use of German is not a liberal art, like that of French conversation. One would encounter in speaking German the same sort of difficulty Pauline experienced in dealing with a meaningful language that involves reflexivity: the impossibility of saying one's own more complex truth completely. The speaker who weighs the advantages and disadvantages of German and French conversation reaches an impasse where it seems unsatisfactory, finally, to liberate one's language from meaning and just as undesirable to function within meaning.

Each of these languages, then, is defective, lacking, deficient. The total personality cannot be expressed through them. If a language could be devised that would combine the positive characteristics of each, then their insufficiencies would be repaired and a single satisfying entity created. Music is such a language, able to combine the positive characteristics of the other two.[89] It causes a feeling of gaiety, like conversation, but a gaiety that no longer has its sharp, threatening edge because it is integrated with a more thoughtful melancholy. At the same time, the melancholy does not turn to depression. "Music is such an ephemeral pleasure, one so much feels it escaping as one feels it, that a melancholy impression is combined with the gaiety that it causes; but also, when it expresses sorrow, it still inspires a sweet feeling . . . . It has the fortunate powerlessness to express any base feeling, any artifice, any lie . . . . Even misfortune, in the language of music, is without bitterness, without distress, without irritation."[90] Music manages to bring about an integration of qualities that seemed incompatible in the discussion of German and French conversation. Its language provides the model for effective self-expression, a model which depends on the combining of apparently self-exclusive elements. In it one may experience gaiety without hostility, melancholy without depression, action without insincerity, truth without regidity.

Therefore, music inspires a feeling of competence and potentiality for action, whereas in speaking German and French one is always limited or constrained. "There is no longer any emptiness, no longer any silence around you, life is full, the blood runs rapidly, you feel in yourself the movement which an active life gives, and you need not at all fear, outside of you, the obstacles which it [an active life] dreads."[91] This wordless language involves a totality of expression which words can never attain. Staël's cousin, who wrote a brief biography of her, said that she was very sensitive to sound and quotes her as having exclaimed on one occasion: "That's poetry! What I like about it is that there is not one idea."[92] Music inspires at least the illusion of activity. "No word can express this impression; for words drag after primitive impressions, as prose translators after the steps of the poets."[93] A sensual, again sexual, excitement is aroused when one listens to music. One is in immediate contact with fundamental experience. Suddenly one is no longer haunted by the threat of inactivity, impotence, ineffectiveness, stasis. Nothing separates impression from expression. One feels fearless, active, fulfilled, empowered.

Yet because it is wordless, in a sense music is not a language at all. Unlike the languages that Staël characterizes as deficient, music has a fullness to overflowing that does not need the intermediacy of words. The moment there are words, there are obstacles between the speaker and herself, between the speaker and the listener. That is why Pauline chose a wordless world. Only music is totally what French conversation could only partially be: a liberal art. Language inevitably becomes concerned with truth-value, whereupon, because one has tried to link language with truth, rigidity sets in, or alternatively, a carelessness for truth that arouses vulnerability, hostility, and guilt. It is condemned to remain in a state between an insouciant freedom from meaning and subservience to it. In the intermediate domain which it occupies, self-expression cannot take place. Staël is deeply skeptical about the medium of language which, in fact, does not satisfactorily mediate. Beginning by perceiving the inadequacy of language for woman, Staël ends by radically questioning the nature of language itself.

Thus, no written language will ever make possible the excitement of speech exercised in the presence of an interlocutor, nor can words ever attain the immediate effect of the wordless language of music. But in her vision of Italian poetry, Staël comes close to imagining a mode of expression that captures those most fervently desired qualities, and it is here that her search for a language is most nearly realized. In book VII of *Corinne*, "Italian Literature," the heroine describes Italian poetry by contrasting it with English, in a version of Staël's distinction between the literatures of the north and those of the south.

Doubtless there is not in our poets this profound melancholy, this knowledge of the human heart which characterizes yours; but this kind of superiority belongs rather, does it not, to philosophical writers than to poets? The brilliant melody of Italian is more suitable to lustre of exterior objects than to meditation. Our language would be more appropriate for depicting furor than sadness, because reflected feelings require more metaphysical expressions, while the desire for vengeance animates the imagination and turns sorrow outward. Cesarotti has made the best and the most elegant translation of Ossian which exists; but it seems, in reading it, that the words themselves have a festive air which contrasts with the somber ideas which they recall.[94]

Staël's description of English reminds one, as did her description of German, of her own written language. Its object of interest is the inner world; the affectivity associated with it is that of depression; the way of thinking is meditation and reflection, that is, turning toward the inside and holding up a mirror to the emotional life; and all of this brings along an abstract manner of speaking. This cluster of characteristics is, in fact, identical with the one which, in her own language, undercuts effectiveness, an affectivity marked by the threat of depression and a style of abstract generality. The traits of Italian, in every way different from those of English, stand as an ideal lacking those compromising elements. The Italian poet is interested in the outside world; the way of thinking involves turning away from the self; within the gamut of its affectivity openly expressed rage and lightness and joy do not exclude one another; and his style is animated and imaginative, particular rather than general.

Staël associates Italian with music: "One lets oneself be charmed by our sweet words . . . as by the murmur of waters and the variety of colors."[95] She indicates its potentiality for imitative harmony: "The measure of the lines, the harmonious rhymes, these rapid endings, . . . imitate sometimes the light steps of dance; sometimes more serious tones recall the noise of the storm or clatter of weapons."[96] And she concludes that Italian is pure pleasure. "Finally our poetry is a marvel of the imagination, one need look there only for pleasures."[97] Like conversation, it is a liberal art; but unlike it, gaiety and rage are compatible within it. Indeed, it most closely resembles music, the model for effective language, in its ability to integrate opposing forces creatively. It is well-known that Staël admired the north and felt kinship with it. Yet as she describes Italian here, the attitude and tone convey a feeling of liberation and of joyous discovery. Free from an excessive turning in upon itself, free from distorting anger into what Madelyn Gutwirth has called "wrathful sorrow,"[98] Italian turns to the outside and depicts what is there openly, limpidly, unreflexively, directly, specifically. For a woman to be able to express herself, this is the language she would need, a language in which she could name her own world and speak of her rage.

An analysis of what is wrong does not automatically bring a cure. Staël does not manage to speak Italian in *Corinne*. Anger is indeed distorted into depression here. Corinne claims that she does not want vengeance upon Oswald. She takes the suffering upon herself, slowly dying of a broken heart. The narrator ends her story by asking, rhetorically, whether Oswald regretted what he had done, whether, in England, he ever thought of Italy and his Italian love. Like Corinne, Staël refuses overt condemnation, saying only that she does not know what his subsequent feelings were, and "I do not want, in this respect, to blame or to absolve him."[99] That she blames him, in fact, is quite clear. Yet neither she nor her heroine is openly angry, so that the affectivity that dominates the last parts of the book is depression. Staël is still not dealing well with anger, though her description of her imagined Italian language suggests that she at least suspected that unexpressed rage has a debilitating effect.

Nor does she manage to speak Italian in those parts of the book that most demanded poetry. She may well have been intimidated by the kind of scorn that Gilbert and Gubar show the "woman poet" attracted in the nineteenth century.[100] Corinne's improvisations (book II, chapter 3, FD I, pp. 665–668 and book XX, chapter 5, FD I, pp. 861–862) do not actually exhibit the qualities Staël wished the reader to associate with Italian poetry. The reader is told not to expect to feel the full impact of Corinne's talent, for the narrator has been obliged to render into French prose the beautiful verses of Corinne, so that one can only imagine their effect in the original. In like manner, Staël herself was able to give only translations of herself in this book because of the indirect way of voicing herself that she consistently preferred to the direct. Her reader can only guess at those patterns of thought that her language obscures as much as it reveals.

Nonetheless, in *Corinne* and in *On Germany* Staël has crossed over, with dread and excitement, into new lands. There she has met up with the self she had always known but also with new selves, new languages, new voices. Using the countries and people she found as metaphors, she succeeded in expressing herself more fully and more interestingly than ever before. She has avoided the threat of madness, the disintegration of the personality, which her exile and the end of her youth seemed to hold, by meditations on the nature and desirability of integration itself. Most importantly, she has found effective, if oblique, ways of discovering and voicing the unknown soul.

7 *The Right to Sincerity*

In 1810 Germaine de Staël was forty-four years old. She had been in exile since 1802, so that the preceding decade had not been an easy one for her. However, it had been a period of considerable creativity and success in her literary career. She had published three major works. *Corinne* in particular was immensely well-received and made its author even more celebrated throughout Europe than she had been before. It was on this occasion that Staël took the unprecedented step the significance of which Madelyn Gutwirth has spoken: she bought a big writing desk, the first one she had ever owned.[1] Before this time, she had always written at a portable desk she could take with her from room to room. It enabled her to carry on household tasks while continuing to write, as well as to obscure the amount of time she was devoting to this activity, in deference to her father's wishes. Her cousin, Albertine de Necker de Saussure recounts that on this occasion Staël told her, "I really want a big table, it seems to me that I have the right to one now."[2]

That she viewed the acquisition of a writing desk as a right is quite interesting. The French and American revolutions had sparked intense discussion of political rights in the Western world, and of course this was a matter much on Staël's mind. Now she was thinking of her own rights as a writer. What had earned the right to a desk was the success of previous work, Staël says, thus indicating that she felt that as long as she was an unproven writer, one who had not been rewarded by great acclaim, she would not be justified in declaring herself to be one at all. It is useful, no doubt, to recall that Jacques Necker, who had made mock of her early ambitions and withheld support for her career, had died in 1804. His death, while deeply mourned by the adoring daughter, seems to have provided more freedom of action than she had previously felt she had. In any case, the student of Staël cannot but wonder, contemplating this momentous purchase, how many male writers await public approval and the death of a parent before feeling that they have the right to use a desk.

That the continuation of her career was very much on her mind during this period is evident even in the plays she wrote with no intention of publication, purely for the entertainment of her household and guests.[3] Three of these pieces are comedies, in which she depicts the power of theater, playfully reflecting on the art. In *Captain Kernadec, or Seven Years in One Day*, written and presented in 1810, a comedy-within-the-comedy is used to trick the obstreperous Captain, who was standing in the way of his daughter's marriage. Signora Fantastici, in the 1811 play that bears her name, recruits players for her informal troop by giving them the parts they have always wanted to play in life. Finally, a young woman arranges to have a puppet stand in for her, thus proving finally to her father that her suitor, who prefers what he takes to be a quiet and obedient woman to his fiancée, is not the right man for her (*The Mannequin*, 1811).[4] In each case, women use theatrical artifices as means to their ends. Their self-reflective nature gives witness to an introspective artist, looking in upon herself as she creates. The fourth play of this period, also written in 1811, is a short tragedy based on the legendary life of Sappho, the poet personifying the archetypal woman writer. This play deals with sources of poetic inspiration and their interrelationship with Sappho's life. Even in her leisure, literary creativity occupies Staël's mind in these seven last years of her life, 1810 through 1817.

In the work Staël produced for publication in these years, she was to some extent laying claim to still more rights, beyond the quite practical one of buying a desk, by writing books about topics that had seemed to be outside of the realm of women. Most notably, she tackled two subjects she had been wary about: politics and confession. At the same time, she was reviewing work already done and working within patterns already established in her previous writing.

I am particularly interested in examining to what extent she was able to seize firmly, to hold, and to realize the rights she was beginning to suspect were hers.

The year 1810 seemed to promise still another success to go along with that of *Corinne*, since *On Germany* was now ready to appear. But Staël met with unexpected obstacles. Though initially it had seemed that the book would be published without difficulty, quite suddenly it became apparent that Napoleon would not allow it at all, and that, further, he had decided to exile its author more severely than ever. She was either to travel to America or to return to Coppet, her Swiss home, and not to leave it by more than two leagues.

Staël was dismayed. She had been working on this book for six years, felt joy on completing it, and had plans to send it to people all over Europe. "I attached great value to this book, which I thought would make new ideas known in France."[5] In saying "I had flattered myself that my book would have an honorable success,"[6] she was no doubt making an understatement of her hopes for it. When it became clear that the book was not to be published, Staël felt robbed, stripped of her "literary existence."[7] Needless to say, her ordinary existence was also to undergo a profound change. She at first planned to spend the time of this latest exile in England, but Napoleon, who feared, not without reason, that that country would provide her with an effective base of operation for writing against him, took precautions to close it to her. Staël decided to return to Coppet, where after a long period of hesitation she finally made plans to go to England anyway, but through Germany, Russia, and Sweden. On May 23, 1812, Staël left Coppet for her unwanted and perilous trip.

She carried with her a new manuscript, the personal account of her exile. Upon her arrival in Stockholm, in September of 1812, she took out her manuscript and started working on it again. At the same time, she began work on two other books. She wrote *Reflections on Suicide*[8] and published it in Stockholm. The dramatic rupture in her hopes and plans she had undergone since 1810 seems to have reminded Staël of her experiences of the 1790s. That, too, had been a time of cruel political events and of the impossibility of publishing certain works. Perhaps this is why the *Reflections* remind one so strongly of her major work of that earlier period, *On the Influence of the Passions.*[9] Indeed, although the immediate inspiration for the work came from the celebrated suicide of the German poet Kleist, Staël seems to be thinking back. "I praised the act of suicide in my work on the *Influence of the Passions* and I have always repented since then for my thoughtless word."[10] She might have added that *Delphine*, too, had been criticized for its apparent permissiveness regarding suicide. Clearly this work retracts what she had said before and makes a strong contrary statement. Furthermore the work ends in a dramatic scene that features Jane Gray, heroine of Staël's play of 1787, published in 1790. Here again she is reaching into past work and past thought for her inspiration. Certainly one reaction to displacement is to look backward, to rethink old questions, and to review the answers one gave to them before.

But Staël is not, by this time, a person who spends an excessive amount of time looking back. The account she gives in her continuation of the autobiographical manuscript she had brought with her, and which was to become *Ten Years of Exile*,[11] suggests that during her travels she was planning a third pair of works which would take up questions treated in her previous two pairs and find new approaches to them. For some time, she had been doing research for a new writing project quite different from any writing she had done before. She mentions this project in *Ten Years of Exile*. At one point in her trip, it seemed not advisable for her to pursue her plan to reach England by the north and that she would be obliged, instead, to choose a route through Constantinople. This would have been a trip of forbidding dimensions to be sure, but Staël says: "I consoled myself for this big trip by thinking about a poem about Richard the Lion-Hearted which I propose to write, if my life and health are adequate to the task."[12] This would be an epic in prose and would depict "the mores and the nature of the Orient."[13] It would be dedicated to "a great era of English history, when the enthusiasm of the Crusades was replaced by the enthusiasm for freedom."[14] Staël believed that one could not write of places one had not seen, so that when friends convinced her not to choose this route, she postponed and eventually abandoned her plans.[15] But she makes it clear that she had in mind to write a third great fictional piece. Its expository companion, as Simone Balayé says, would no doubt have been called *On Russia*,[16] for though her stay there was brief, she quickly became fascinated with the Russians and saw in them, as in the historical period of Richard the Lion-Hearted, answers to some questions that were uppermost in her thoughts.

With intense and increasing alarm, Staël had watched Napoleon's conquests, first of France and then of other European countries. The promise of freedom the Revolution had made at great cost seemed entirely revoked, never to be realized. In the Russians Staël saw hope for stopping Napoleon's advances and a possible return to the principles in which she believed, that is, establishment of an English-style constitutional monarchy in France, and the end of Napoleon's hold on Europe. This is what she says of them: "There is in this way of being some relationship with savages; but it seems to me that now European nations have vigor only when they are either what is called barbarian, that is, not enlightened, or free. But these nations which have learned from civilization only indifference for this or that yoke, as long as their fireplace is not troubled by it; these nations which have learned from civilization only the art of explaining away power and rationalizing slavery, are made to be conquered."[17] Her concern here is the search for a place, or perhaps more accurately for a state of being, that would lend itself not to the acceptance of despotism but to the insistence on liberty. Her thought becomes grounded, as it had been at the turn of the century, in a diachronic mode, now coexisting with the synchronic. She envisages a spectrum beginning with the savage or uncivilized and stretching by degrees to the civilized. Along this continuum, she wonders, where is the human being in a state most resistant to tyranny, most demanding of freedom? The Russians are situated along this gamut in a position nearer to the savage. They will, therefore, prove more vigorous in their resistance. The Europeans are close enough neither to the strength of the wild nor to that of the truly civilized. Thus, they have fallen into a slavery they can justify with the clever words civilization teaches one to use. The Russians represent a state less developed than that of the Europeans, which may in this case be more conducive to actions of courage.

This is the same line of thought to be developed in her epic poem.

There Staël is also looking at history for an answer to current problems. She intends to depict a certain moment, when what she calls the "enthusiasm for freedom" first appeared in England. Perhaps this moment holds an answer to the question she is asking. If one can define that state of history in which the taste for freedom appears, perhaps by working toward a recreation of those circumstances, one can make it live again. This attempt seems to have formed the basic motivation for both of these new works.

The two geographic and political regions to be treated in the books differed in Staël's view in such a way as to provide her the chance to develop further the issue of women's status. She writes, "The Russians did not take part in the time of chivalry; they had nothing to do with the crusades . . . . The Russians, in societal relations, so new for them, do not distinguish themselves by the spirit of chivalry, as the peoples of the West conceive it; but they have always proved to be terrible against their enemies."[18] We recall that Staël had suggested earlier that the European Middle Ages provided a greater arena for female participation than the modern era. That she now selects this very time as the subject of her study indicates, perhaps, that she intended to pursue that perception, contrasting with the age of chivalry a country that, while bearing some similarity to it, lacked the element of chivalry itself. This would have provided an excellent focus for further meditation on woman and action. Of course we will never know what if any development Staël would have given to this theme. Neither of the works under consideration here was written. But to state their presence, if only in the form of seeds, is to witness the consistency and creativity of Staël's literary imagination. She repeats patterns of the past, as she has done before, but with variations that allow expression of new concerns and insights.

If Staël did not complete these projects, she did write another pair of closely related works: this *Ten Years of Exile* and her *Considerations on the Principal Events of the French Revolution*,[19] the third work begun in Stockholm in 1812. It is in *Considerations* that Staël makes her final attempt to do political writing, whereas in *Ten Years of Exile* she tries her hand at autobiography. Together, then, they are the place where Staël will or will not exercise the rights of a mature, established writer to venture into whatever subject matter she chooses, even if those subjects have appeared to be forbidden lands in the past. The relationship between these two books is not the same as that between the two pairs already written and the projected third pair. We are not dealing here with one fictional and one discursive piece whose themes and structures echo and question each other. But these two works were written at the same time and there is a dynamic relationship between them.

Staël describes the genesis and the development of her *Considerations* in these terms: "I had first begun this work with the intention of limiting it to the examination of the political acts and writings of my father. But, as I advanced in my work, I was led by the subject itself to trace, on the one hand, the principal events of the French Revolution, and to present, on the other, the tableau of England, as a justification of the opinion of M. Necker, concerning the political institutions of this country. Since my plan had grown, it seemed to me that I should change its title, though I had not changed my objective."[20] Staël thus links the *Considerations* project to her intentions, particularly conceived after her father's death in 1804, to write the story of his life. But almost immediately, it seems, the project became associated with two related subjects. In this way, the original "Political Life of Jacques Necker" becomes three works in one: the story of Necker's life, the "principal events" of the Revolution, and the English political system. She chooses a title under which all three of the subjects can be subsumed and writes a different book from the one she originally had in mind.

Once she reconceived the book about her father in the way described, it began to take on a very close relationship to her *Ten Years of Exile*, the memoirs on which she had been working even before her trip. She found that she was recounting the same events in both books, since she, like her father, had lived through the Revolution and the Napoleonic years. In fact, as the two books stand today, many of the same events are recounted in each. But she decided to remove certain narratives from her own memoirs and insert them into the book that was originally her father's life story. In a sense, this seems to be an act of filial piety and self-sacrifice, that is, to subtract from one's own "life" in order to enhance one's father's. *Ten Years of*

Exile was never finished, partly because she gave it up to pay primary attention to the *Considerations*. In her memoirs only two periods of what were to be, in fact, twelve years of exile are recounted, 1800–1804 and 1810–1812. Part of her work was removed, other parts were never written. Thus her own memoirs lie dismembered, in disconnected pieces that were not to find their unity. In another way, however, her "sacrifice" turns out to be tinged with a certain aggressiveness. The more of her own memories she puts into her "father's story" the more that story becomes, really, her own. In *Considerations*, to be sure, Necker is given a major role in all events in which he took any part at all. His figure looms very large; his actions and ideas are exalted; he is depicted as the savior and then as the potential savior of France. But we are told just as much about Staël's own role as about her father's. The book of the father has to some extent become the book of the daughter.

This partial take-over of the father's book suggests that Staël had, at this point, a freer attitude toward the societal restrictions on women's writing than before. Middle-aged now, a celebrated author, Staël seems to feel she has earned the right to tell her own story, as she does in both of these books. In addition she has assumed the privilege, heretofore reserved for men, of writing a political work. The woman who, in the 1790s, could not see her way clear to writing about politics, now does so.

She places her political statement in a historical context. Like many people, Staël became increasingly interested in history as she grew older, and her interest became more focused. When she was a young woman, the historical facts she had at her disposal tended toward the general. Her theory of history was schematic and even naïve. But by the time of *Considerations*, she seems to have studied history in more detail and asked of it specific questions. If one compares the historical reflections of *On Literature* with those of *Considerations*, one sees that in the former work she was intent upon making the history of literature fit into a preconceived scheme of things, perfectibility, whereas her approach in the latter is quite different. Here she poses as her principle of proceeding that freedom is not a new idea, but rather a quite old one that was lost over a long period of French history, particularly during the apogee of the

French monarchy in the seventeenth century. She claims that before that time kings had been sensitive to the cause of freedom. Thus she is looking back in time, asking what periods were most propitious for freedom.

In these later works or sketches of works, she does not discuss the status of women explicitly, but the subject seems to be involved, at least implicitly. In *On Literature* it was in the past that she saw greater spheres of action for women, specifically in the chivalric Middle Ages. One can imagine a synthesis of these two lines of thought, in which she would have linked her more general search for the conditions of freedom with the quest for conditions conducive to female participation.

She apparently did not agree with those of her feminist contemporaries who had tried to get their movement started during the Revolution, and who believed it a good time for the achieving women's demands. We know, certainly, that she did not join them.[21] John Cleary has studied Mary Wollstonecraft's active disapproval of certain stances Staël took.[22] If one wishes to attribute her nonparticipation to factors other than masculinism or cowardice, one could argue that her analysis of history caused her to conclude that current initiatives for freedom and woman's struggle for rights were not of a piece. Or, less generously, one could maintain that she always saw the status of women as a by-product of or as dependent on other social or political phenomena that were of primary importance to her. Thus, she would not be disposed to ask for women's rights themselves but rather to look for conditions under which they might develop. Although she does not pursue that line of thought, the rudiments of it are at least suggested here. But in the final analysis she has not written into her political work a statement on the political status of members of her own sex.

In fact, while one senses a certain loosening of the grip of convention on Staël here, it would not be true to claim that she ventures forth into forbidden literary lands, unfettered by the chains of the past. She does not exercise her newly found right to political writing freely. *Considerations* does not really declare itself as the "great political work" that in some ways it is. It is certainly more than memoirs, even of Necker or of Staël. It contains historical information, designed to put the events of the present into perspective, analyses of contemporary events, and a lengthy discussion of British history and government. But its anecdotal nature does not allow the text to remain long on a theoretical level. It is an uneven work, not in its quality but in its focusing on subject matter, or on some unified level of subject matter. The interest and liveliness of the work lie precisely in this unevenness, but that is also what keeps it from being a political work in the traditional sense.

Looked at from the standpoint of memoirs, neither of the works is entirely satisfactory because, to put it baldly, Staël does not tell the truth. A comparison between what she has to say about her role in the French revolutionary period and the role which historians can prove she actually played reveals a vast discrepancy between her claim and reality.[23] Briefly, Staël was politically quite active, for example, in trying to divert the Napoleonic thrust for power and to replace Napoleon with some more acceptable figure, notably Bernadotte. Once disillusioned with Napoleon (and she tends to push back in time the moment when that disillusionment first occurred) she used every means at her and her friends' disposal to undermine him, and yet when she finds herself pursued and persecuted by him, she prefers to present herself as an innocent victim. It does seem odd that she would have felt that this passive image was a more attractive one than that of the actively participating political figure, although the ridicule that Henri Guillemin heaps upon her for it seems entirely exaggerated.[24] As Barbara Watson points out, "The most essential form of accommodation for the weak is to conceal what power they do have."[25]

Staël not only misrepresents her political activity, she also omits events of a personal nature. For example, she attributes to procrastination and indecision her delay in leaving Coppet to escape from Napoleon's harrassment. While it is understandable that she put off the difficult resolution to begin a grueling and dangerous trip, surely the fact that she gave birth to a child on April 7, 1812, makes the May 23 date of her departure seem less than leisurely. To be sure, the child in question was illegitimate, so that she had reasons for remaining silent about its birth, but this incident illustrates that we are dealing with very selectively recounted events.

No doubt all authors of memoirs choose to relate certain events and to omit others as well as to impose their own interpretations, the ones they wish to leave to posterity, upon what happened to them and what they did. In Staël's case the pattern of interpretation and omission indicates continuing discomfort with confessional forms, even at a time of her life when authors commonly think of writing in that form. Certain roles and activities were for Staël subjects that women do not discuss about themselves. Instead, one hides rather than reveals them, as she said in criticism of Rousseau. Staël has changed less than it might appear from the embarrassed young girl who tore up excessively revealing pages of her journal. She has earned the right to a new desk but not entirely to these new subjects.

Thus, political science and confession are genres that Staël could not write effectively, even when she did find the freedom to work within them. In these two books her most powerful writing is not in those forms but rather in the metaphorical mode she had been gradually working out since the work on the passions and which she used to great effect in *Corinne* and *On Germany*. I have been claiming that *Considerations* and *Ten Years of Exile* are a dynamically related pair, and so they are. But they are by no means equal in metaphorical power for a reason that has to do with the question under discussion: the right to self-expression. *Considerations* is an interesting book for the modern reader in that it makes the French Revolution come alive through its vivid eyewitness accounts and its judgments that bear the marks of the headiness and uncertainties of immediately experienced events. Staël was quite right, and signaled the real strength of her work, when she said in her introduction, "Perhaps specific circumstances are more helpful in making known the spirit and the character of the time one wishes to describe."[26] But throughout the book, and especially in the last of its six parts, Staël's discussion of England, the texture is singularly flat, lacking in the resonances that make so many Staëlian texts exciting. Her narrative seems one-dimensional, without echoes of other matters palpably present and yet unstated. This lack of resonance is by no means true of *Ten Years of Exile*. Here the descriptions are endlessly suggestive, leaving the reader the impression that what has been said is symbolic of feelings left unsaid, perhaps not even fully thought out by the writer herself. Evidently, what Staël saw in Russia had the same profound impact on her thinking that her contact with Germany and Italy had had, unleashing parallels with her own emotions that allowed her to express them through the metaphor of the country, the language, and the people in a way she never felt appropriate in direct language. This fact may seem odd.[27] After all, England, the country under discussion in *Considerations*, was no doubt the one she admired most, with the exception of France itself. Russia was politically important to her in its potential for stopping Napoleon, but she hardly knew the country and, in many ways, she did not admire it.

However, it was Russia and not England that allowed her to express her continuing concerns. The once and still admired Germans had proved to be a disappointment to her. Staël is still preoccupied, as she has every reason to be in 1812, with the threat to the integrity of European nations posed by Napoleonic totalitarianism. The structures that formed her thought as she wrote her earlier works, the relationship of the part to the whole and of properties to essence, are at work here. In every country she visits, she is worried by any evidence she sees of inappropriate alliances that may undermine the internal unity of its people. She sees such an undermining in the case of the Tyrolians, who by their history and customs, she says, should be a part of Switzerland and yet are now attached instead to Austria. They have a "need to be a nation" (p. 145), still unsatisfied. Even in the Russians she perceives a similar problem. Speaking of Peter I's Europeanization of his country, Staël asks, "Was he right to erase, as much as he could, Oriental mores from his country? Should he have placed its capital in the north and at the extremity of his empire?"[28] The character of a people is distorted when it is not respected and built upon rather than thwarted. Staël still believes, as she did in *On Germany* and *Corinne*, that strength comes from the uniting of characteristics, but she still also fears inappropriate and destructive unity or totalization on the personal and the national levels.

Unusual as the comparison may seem, the connection in Staël's mind between the Italians and the Russians is made so frequently that it cannot be missed. At times the resemblance is implicit only. "There is patience and activity in this nation, gaiety and melancholy.

One sees united in them the most striking contrasts, and that is what causes one to predict great things of them."[29] It is only by reflecting that these were the very qualities associated with the Italians that one makes the connection. Or again: "Nature, all around Petersbourg, is like an enemy who seizes his rights again as soon as man ceases for a moment to fight against him."[30] One must remember here that it was in exactly such terms that Rome, surrounded by "bad air," was described. But often, the association is made explicitly.

> The Russians who live in Petersbourg are like a people of the South condemned to live in the North . . .[31] People of the lower classes . . . transport the mores of the "lazzaroni" of Naples to the sixtieth degree of latitude.[32]
>
> One recalled Rome in seeing Moscow, not of course that the monuments are of the same style, but because the mixture of the solitary countryside and magnificent palaces, the grandeur of the city and the infinite number of temples, give to the Asian Rome some relationship with the European Rome.[33]

This comparison signals Staël's ability to identify with the Russians in the same way as she did with the Italians, perhaps not because of any intrinsic similarity between them, but more nearly because of the similar circumstances in which she found herself in visiting the two countries, creating a need to project herself on her surroundings in her exile and to express herself through them.

In Staël's mind, Italians and Russians seem related to the Orient. "Russians have, I believe, much more in common with the peoples of the South or rather of the Orient, than with those of the North. What is European about them has to do with court manner, the same in all countries; but their nature is Oriental. One feels, in Russia, at the door of another land, near this Orient from which so many religious beliefs come and which still holds in its breast incredible treasures of perseverance and reflection."[34] This new element is extremely important. The Russians are more than a repetition of the Italians; they seem in some way new for her. Their very language transports one into a new world.

> All these names of foreign countries, of nations that are almost no longer European, awaken the imagination in an unusual way.[35]

> The Slavic language is unusually resonant. I would almost say that it has something metallic about it; you think you are hearing brass struck when the Russians pronounce certain letters of their language, completely different from those of which Western dialects are composed.[36]

Because of this difference Staël thought, not wrongly as it turned out, that in them she had found the force of resistance she was searching for during her trip. They became the national counterpart to the resistance she felt she had in her own personality. Furthermore, they became also the third nation through which Staël could express herself, metaphorically, in a strong way.

Through them, she tells us that she is a person of singular strength shot through with unexpected weakness. Let us begin with strength.

> Their nature has not been changed by the rapid civilization which Peter I has given them; it has up to now formed only their manners; fortunately for them, they are still what we call barbaric, that is to say, led by an often generous, always spontaneous, instinct, which admits reflection only in the choice of means, and not in the examination of the end: I say "fortunately for them" not because I wish to praise barbarianism; but I designate by this name a certain primitive energy, which alone can replace in nations concentrated strength of freedom.[37]

This quite civilized person, who did not feel that as a woman she enjoyed freedom of action, sees in the Russians, and perhaps hopes she can find in herself, a substitute for it: "primitive energy." Only sheer strength can provide the generating force for people or peoples who, for whatever reason, live under despotism.

The Russians have this strength, but they also have other less admirable characteristics, also corresponding to Staël's self-perception. They are, in the first place, superstitious. "They are more capable of superstition than of emotion: superstition is related to this life, and religion to the other; superstition is linked with fatalism, religion with virtue; it is by the liveliness of earthly desires that one becomes superstitious, it is on the contrary by the sacrifice of these same desires that one is religious."[38] Staël depicts herself as well as the Russians in this statement.[39] Even if the reader did not recall how many events in Staël's fiction and nonfiction as well seem to her to be fatal premonitions or favorable signs, in this very book she speaks of her own superstition: "One experiences a kind of superstitious fright that leads one to consider all honest people as victims."[40] But Staël sees here a quality in the Russians she has even more deeply in common with them than primitive energy and superstition. Like them, she is given to dissimulation. Once again, the Italians come to mind; they, too, were presented as dissimulating their true thoughts and for similar reasons as the Russians, that is, political weakness. Echoing her discussion of Italian, she says of the Russian language: "The sweetness and brilliance of the sounds of their language are remarkable even to those who do not understand it; it must be very appropriate for music and poetry . . . . Their works, up to now, are composed half-heartedly, and never can such a vehement nation be moved by such shrill harmonies."[41] People characterized by energy and strength can feel violent emotion and so it is with the Russians. But their literary production is superficial, imitative. This astonishing contrast has to do with the discrepancy between the felt and the expressed. Their literature is not adequate to express them. But the problem of dissimulation does not end there. Staël perceives herself capable not only as dissimulating to others but even to herself. She tells us that she was so taken by the beautiful things she was seeing in Russia that "I forgot the war upon which the fate of Europe depended."[42] The Russians seemed to behave in a similar way: "One finally learns the truth but the habit of remaining silent is such among Russian courtiers that they dissimulate the night before that which is to be known the next day."[43] The habit of dissimulation does not stop at the level of a game played with others. One ends by playing it with oneself as well. Such a dangerous habit is neither consciously nor arbitrarily acquired. It comes from being in a position of powerlessness. "The refinements of civilization alter in all countries sincerity of character; but when the sovereign has the unlimited power to exile, to emprison, to send one to Siberia, etc. etc. his power is too great for human nature. One can meet men proud enough to disdain favor, but one must have real heroism in order to brave persecution, and heroism cannot be a universal quality."[44]

The Russians are not always heroic; Staël knew that she was not always heroic either. In *Ten Years of Exile* she says of herself, "I could not dissimulate to myself that I was not a courageous person; I have boldness of imagination but timidity of character."[45] A timid person like the woman Staël, who must play out her life against a great power, in this case derogatory attitudes toward women writers, frequently finds herself in the position of lying. It is this mixture of "primitive energy," strong, even superstitious imagination, and dissimulation that make the Russians such an inspiring subject for Staël. Once again she can express herself in the way she does best, covertly, metaphorically, dissimulating her own feelings, those feelings one would rather conceal than reveal, under the cover of national characteristics. This is why her depiction of the Russians is so very strong, so alive and resonant with significance for her and for the reader.

In this same book we learn why writing about the English is not nearly so exciting to her, nor what she has to say about them so exciting to us. Especially in the last fifty pages of *Ten Years of Exile*, Staël frequently refers to the British in such a way as to make them appear as a counterpoint to the Russians.

> The English, with this admirable uprightness distinguishing all their actions, render as exact an account of their reversals as of their successes, and enthusiasm is sustained in them by truth, whatever it may be. The Russians cannot yet attain this moral perfection, the result of a free constitution.[46]

> The English give in their newspapers the most exact accounting, man by man, of the wounded, of the prisoners, and of those killed in each encounter: noble candor of a government which is as sincere toward the nation as toward its monarch . . . .[47]

The English stand in sharp contrast to the Russians. The perfect sincerity of the former puts in stark relief the misrepresentations of the latter. But the contrast is not attributed to some innate moral superiority on the one hand or degradation on the other. The cause lies rather in political organization. Under a free government, sincerity is possible; under despotism, dissimulation is necessary, even becomes a habit of the soul.

Thus, it is possible to admire sincerity in a general way but to acknowledge that not everyone is in a position to be sincere. In fact, sincerity is not particularly admirable in a person who has power. Staël remarks that a man once said to her, concerning Napoleon's agent, the prefect of Geneva, "Don't you find that the prefect declares his opinions with great frankness?" "Yes," she reports having answered him, "he says with sincerity that he is devoted to the powerful man; he says with courage that he is on the strongest side. I do not feel the merit of such a confession."[48] A truly courageous statement would be one sincerely made by a person without power. Ironically, sincerity is possible only in those for whom it is impossible. The sincerity of a strong person does not count; it is too easy to be sincere from a position of strength. But only the most extraordinary of persons in a position of weakness can be sincere, and then not in any consistent way. Staël admires the British for their rectitude, but she cannot identify with them because she, under the power of Napoleon, under the power of society over women, does not find herself in the position of freedom. Therefore their example does not apply to her, admire it as she may. This is why when she speaks of them in *Considerations* her prose does not have the energy and excitement of that identification with the subject which makes it alive with meaning for the writer.

A passage in the *Considerations* that, unlike many others, does have this kind of vivacity bears directly on the question of the right to sincerity. She describes in this way the situation of Louis XVI in the period between his removal from Versailles to Paris and his death, that is, between 1789 and 1793:

> The king was conducted to Paris in order to adopt at City Hall the revolution which had just taken place against his power. His religious calm kept in him as always his personal dignity, in this circumstance as in everything that happened later, but his authority existed no longer. . . . The apparent hommage rendered then to the dethroned sovereign is revolting to generous people, and never can freedom be established by the false situation of the monarch or the people: One must be within one's rights in order to be within one's sincerity.[49]

If people are not in a rightful position with respect to one another, sincerity is impossible on everyone's part. Staël is identifying herself here with the dethroned king; his fall resounds with the fall she felt she endured upon "entering into the world" and discovering that she, like the king, had lived in an artificial world whose falseness she discovered painfully. She felt that she did not have the right to sincerity, because she was not within her rights as a citizen and as a woman. It was not possible for her, therefore, to choose freely the subjects she wished to treat or to say openly about herself whatever she wanted. Instead, she had to write with caution, as one sees her doing in even these last of her works. This mixture of strength and weakness is documented by reference to the syntax of Staël by Lucia Omacini. Her increased use of the mode "pouvoir" (to be able) conveys a sense of strength, but decreased occurrence of "vouloir" (to want) suggests discouragement.[50] She weaves into and out of political science, the subject which she greatly wanted to treat, hiding the traces of her own thought behind personal anecdotes and beneath the shadow of her father. Her apparently autobiographical works are neither less nor more confessional than any of her other pieces. In all of them her truth is expressed indirectly, its traces almost lost among apparently unrelated subjects.

In 1814 Staël finally returned to Paris. She continued working on *Considerations*, bringing their narration through the restoration of the monarchy 1815, after Napoleon's second fall. She traveled once more to Coppet and to Italy, where in addition to *Considerations* she pursued her project on Richard the Lion Hearted. In an Italian journal she published *On the Spirit of Translations*.[51] Here she exhorts the Italians once more to look for their destiny in the arts, since they cannot find their "active principle of interest" in the world of politics. Simone Balayé points out Staël's disappointment with Italy during this last visit. "The debris is absorbing the ruins," she observed. And further, "The habit of remaining silent or of speaking only on command has made a kind of progress which leaves the commander little left to desire."[52] She was never able to make her last projected journeys, to Sicily, Greece, and Palestine.[53] *Considerations* and *Ten Years of Exile* were unfinished on July 14, 1817, when Germaine de Staël died.

8 *Conclusion*

The story of the literary existence of Germaine de Staël is perhaps not as flamboyant as the one her biographers tell, but it is thought-provoking for those who wish to understand and to give meaning to the phrase "woman writer." Her work has a remarkable coherence that substantiates the shape she determined in her *Letters on Rousseau*. She continued to run up against the obstacles and to pass through the openings she perceived then. The persistent urge to write she felt so profoundly throughout her life constantly brought her into a confrontation with a cluster of warnings and interdictions about the writing woman. This confrontation molded her work into a configuration quite distinct from that of her models and her contemporaries. She had to work out for herself a different rhetoric than theirs and to function experimentally, feeling her way along, within genres. As a result she continued the breakdown of traditional generic boundaries that had already begun in the eighteenth century, but she did so more radically than her male contemporaries.

A woman writer is forced, in spite of herself, to take experimental approaches because she is an outsider to the largely male domain in which she is trying to participate. It is not surprising, then, to find a woman writer who uses forms or genres from what, from the standpoint of man's literature, would be called the past or the future. Only when a large number of women writers are studied in detail will critics and historians of literature be able to write the history of woman's literature, whose past, present, and future will not necessarily follow that established by men. At that point, we may finally come to appreciate and valorize the qualities of a literature forged by a person whose society opposes her creation of it.

The career of Germaine de Staël is an important piece of evidence in that enterprise, for she was not satisfied to remain within the generic and topical boundaries usually reserved for women, and she was not willing, as her female contemporaries were, to accept those boundaries. She wanted to present herself validly as a serious writer rather than as a frivolous "lady novelist."

There is some evidence that at least some women writers today feel as menaced by being in that category as did Germaine de Staël more than a century and a half ago. In two of Margaret Atwood's works, for example, *Lady Oracle* (1976) and *Bodily Harm* (1982), the main character is by profession a writer, a novelist in the former book, a journalist in the latter, whose subject matter is limited to what are ordinarily considered female-associated topics. It is as if in creating characters who are what she does not want to be Atwood is exorcising the figure of the lady-writer, which, apparently, poses a threat to her identity as a writer. Germaine de Staël was engaged in a similar activity when she created her pairs of male and female books. Thus, both past and contemporary woman writers find it difficult to overcome the time-honored association of serious writing with maleness.

On this point, however, the example of Germaine de Staël turns out to be instructive. In Staël's efforts to move beyond the traditional realm of the woman writer through her works in male/female pairs, she proved, finally, only one thing: a writer, man or woman, writes only out of a single writing identity. In each of Staël's pairs she did not create separate male/female visions of human life, but only one vision from her own vantage point as a woman. If she intended to show that man's history develops in in linear progression and a woman's is characterized by discontinuity, she did not demonstrate that at all. Rather she showed that, for her, history has only one shape, the shape of a woman's life story as she perceived it. If she intended to praise centralization, a unifying enthusiasm, a oneness within the self and with others, she finally and simply could not do so. Instead, despite her intentions, she questioned such concepts as exclusive of or harmful to women, glimpsing at the same time the liberation from dualism that multiplicity might bring.

Her example suggests that at least as long as there is a female place in society there will be a female writing identity and that women writers will write out of it, no matter what our intentions may be. It suggests further that insofar as women writers write as women the writing will be strong. That Staël partially did so and partially did not is what gives her writing its particular quality. The reader struggles along, the feminist reader despairingly so, through pages of the style that Paul de Man so accurately said was characterized by "banality, dissimulation, and self-serving sentimentality."[1] One tires so easily of generalized and idealized statements whose connections with anything recognizably real seem never to have been established or to have been severed. What is the subject here, one wonders. Where is the author? But then, suddenly, something can happen in the text, something that is so exciting that all the hours one has restlessly or hopelessly spent are rewarded. Quite suddenly the text ceases to be a thin crust covering a vast emptiness. Layers of reality and sense accrue to its surface of the text, undergirding it with substrata through which the substance of meaning ripples and resounds. The reader is then aware of hearing the voice of Germaine de Staël, which even the considerable noise of her words cannot drown or crowd out.

What makes the sounding of this voice possible is Staël's discovery of a personal rhetoric that allows her to speak of herself through apparently unrelated and impersonal topics. Not all topics, of course, energized her writing in this way. But as she grew into her maturity as a writer, roughly speaking in the first decade of the nineteenth century, she became more and more adept at finding those that did. Perhaps she had become more sure of exactly what she wanted to say about herself. Or perhaps time and practice had enabled her to work out a mature style. The decisive fact is that Staël proved herself as a writer, yes, as a woman writer, in the strong and positive meaning of that term, by evolving such a style and by speaking through it.

In that woman's voice, she was able to comment on a number of topics in an astonishingly perceptive way. Chief among them are history, unity, and language. Her meditations on the first of these subjects occupied her thought from the early nineteenth century, with *On Literature*, until her untimely death cut off her pursuit of the suggestive line of thought in which she was then engaged. Even as she wrote of man's history, she allowed herself, however intermittently, to try to imagine woman's history. Her thought ranged from timid suggestions regarding how women fit into man's history to a search for a time when women and men might participate in the making of history together. If it must be said that Germaine de Staël did not develop the implications of her own thought, at least one can add that historians today still have not exhausted its implications. With respect to the second, unity, this writer who so vociferously professed belief in a world integrated into oneness because it is the product of a single idea constantly and increasingly undermined that belief. It is as if she needed to loosen the tight unity that excludes woman in order to open cracks through which we might slip and which we might eventually widen into places of significance for ourselves.

But it is in the area of language that Germaine de Staël carried out her most urgent research. The execution of her other aims depended, after all, on access to a language that would be conducive to thought and expression. It was precisely the threat of not being able to find an adequate way of speaking from a woman's vantage point that haunted Staël throughout her career.

Germaine de Staël is, in fact, among the foremothers of contemporary feminist writers, many of whom are deeply interested in the relationship between woman and the written or spoken word. The concern is that the very language women speak has been elaborated in a patriarchal world, so that from our mouths come words which are not entirely ours, which have been deeply marked with the imprint of structures within which our existence is peripheral. Two examples of contemporary women engaged in the struggle called for by that interpretation are Monique Wittig, in France, and, in America, Mary Daly.[2] Both have gone so far as to imagine and to compose parts of a woman's dictionary that contains newly coined or newly defined words. Germaine de Staël would have found such initiatives odd and radical, although her own writing was done in something of the same spirit.

Certainly there is no evidence that she experienced as a personal failure her feeling that she was unable adequately to express herself.

As we have seen, she linked it rather to woman's status and story, and searched for an effective and fulfilling language. She depicted woman as being condemned to speak meaninglessly, in the words or with the ideas of others, or, alternatively, to speak meaningful truth but in so doing to risk censure. She painfully acknowledged that man is the linguistic as well as the political legislator. He assigns meanings and values. The dictionary, to put the matter in contemporary terms, is of his authorship. The language in which Staël finally found that she could speak was an oblique and indirect one indeed. The texts written in it are dispersed, nearly hidden, among others that do not carry her voice, in which she speaks someone else's language. In the language of someone else one can make noise, but one cannot truly speak.

Germaine de Staël did more than find a covert way of speaking, a kind of do-it-yourself rhetoric with which she could, in a rough and ready way, express herself. She analyzed the nature of the problem and examined what kind of language would be an enabling one for woman. She understood that in order to forge a woman's language she would have to engage in the most fundamental linguistic activity, that of nomination. She would have to make her own meanings, to call the world by her own names. Moreover, she would have to find some way to express her fury. Only when the paradoxically destructive/constructive power of rage is unleashed can one speak truthfully. To transmute rage into depression or self-pity is to direct one's anger inwardly, toward oneself, not outwardly, toward what provoked it. Only by confronting anger may one escape from the internal conflict between meaninglessness and meaningfulness. Thus, the founding of meaning and the expression of fury make each other possible and open the way to effective language.

Staël herself could only imagine such a language and point toward it. The effect of her own texts is vitiated by a debilitating obliqueness, though it is the discovery of that obliqueness that makes it possible for her to speak authentically at all. Once one learns to translate her indirect language, one begins to hear a genuine and penetrating voice that bespeaks a personal vision of what woman's language must become. The woman must dare to name her own world and to speak out her rage.

The strongest evidence for the existence of woman's literature and the highest praise I can offer to the memory of Germaine de Staël is that she wrote like a woman, even though she did not set out to do so. I have tried to show in this book how she did, after all, reject a male writing identity, not because she did not want to assume one but rather for the most basic of reasons, that she could not write out of an identity that was not hers. She did not write man's history because try as she might she did not believe in it. She did not work within man's rhetoric because it was not consonant with her own voice. Not daring to express herself in her inherited language, she looked for other languages, other identities, through which she might truly speak. That is why beneath the noise of borrowed words, imitated forms, and bogus sexual identity, one can hear the timid but strong voice of Germaine de Staël.

Notes
Bibliography
Index

Notes

Foreword

1. Maréchal, Sylvain, *Project for a Law Prohibiting Women from Learning to Read* (Paris: Chez Massé, 1801). My translation.

2. See Evelyn Sullerot, *Histoire de la presse féminine en France, des origines à 1848* (Paris: A. Colin, 1966), 110.

3. Virginia Woolf, *A Room of One's Own* (London: Hogarth Press, 1929), 157.

Preface

1. *Oeuvres Complètes de Madame la Baronne de Staël, publiées par son fils* (Paris: Firmin Didot, 1861 [hereafter cited as FD]) vol. II, 368; *Dix Années d'Exil*, part II, chapter 2.

2. Sandra M. Gilbert and Susan Gubar, *The Madwoman in the Attic: The Woman Writer and the Nineteenth Century Literary Imagination* (New Haven and London: Yale University Press, 1979), 362.

3. Madelyn Gutwirth, *Madame de Staël, Novelist: The Emergence of the Artist as Woman* (Urbana: University of Illinois Press, 1978), 200.

1. Introduction

1. Collections of articles reflecting these various approaches and containing bibliographies are as follows: Elizabeth Abel, ed., *Writing and Sexual Difference*, (Chicago: University of Chicago Press, 1982); Elaine Showalter, ed., *The New Feminist Criticism: Essays on Woman, Literature and Theory*, (New York: Pantheon Books, 1985); Gayle Greene and Coppelia Kahn, eds., *Making a Difference: Feminist Literary Criticism*, (London: Methuen, 1985); and Elaine Marks and Isabelle de Courtivron, eds., *New French Feminisms*, (Amherst: University of Massachusetts Press, 1980).

2. It is not, however, the nationality but rather the theoretical proclivity of the critic that determines the tradition to which she belongs. For example, the volume edited by Hester Eisenstein and Alice Jardine, *The Future of Difference: The Scholar and the Feminist* (Boston: G. K. Hall, 1980) illustrates the commitment of a number of American critics to French theory.

3. Two outstanding examples of criticism of this type are Elaine Showalter, *A Literature of Their Own: British Women Novelists from Bronte to Lessing* (Princeton: Princeton University Press, 1977); and Helen Moglen, *Charlotte Bronte: The Self Conceived* (New York: W. W. Norton: 1976).

4. Toril Moi, *Sexual/Textual Politics: Feminist Literary Theory* (New York: Methuen, 1985), 50–88.

5. This duality of heritage and influence is reflected in the title of the book of Simone Balayé, *Madame de Staël: Lumières et Liberté* (Paris: Klincksieck, 1979). Roland Mortier has studied her heritage in his "Madame de Staël et l'héritage des Lumières," *Clartés et ombres du siècle de Lumières* (Geneva: Droz, 1969), 125–33, for example. Outstanding among articles studying her nascent romanticism are Laurence M. Porter, "The Emergence of a Romantic Style: From *De la littérature* to *De l'Allemagne*," *Authors and Their Centuries*, ed. Philip Crant, French Literature Series no. 1 (Columbia: University of South Carolina Press, 1974), 129–42; and Madelyn Gutwirth, "Corinne et l'esthétique du camée," *Le Prèromantisme: Hypothèque ou Hypothèse*, ed. Paul Viallaneix (Paris: Klinksieck, 1979), 153–68.

6. Susan Sniader Lanser and Evelyn Torton Beck make the latter point in their "[Why] Are There No Great Women Critics And What Difference Does It Make," *The Prism of Sex: Essays in the Sociology of Knowledge*, edited by Julia A. Sherman and Evelyn Torton Beck (Madison: University of Wisconsin Press, 1979), 79–91.

7. A recent biography in French is by Ghislain de Diesbach, *Madame de Staël* (Paris: Librairie Académique Perrin, 1983). A useful overview for English-speaking readers is Renée Winegarten, *Madame de Staël* (London: Berg Publishers, 1985).

8. Ellen Moers, *Literary Women* (New York: Anchor Books, 1977).

9. Hélène Borowitz, "The Unconfessed Précieuse: Madame de Staël's Debt to Mademoiselle de Scudéry," *Nineteenth Century French Studies*, nos. 1–2, (Fall/Winter 1982), 32–59.

10. Gutwirth, *Staël, Novelist*, 165–66.

11. Joanna Kitchen, "La littérature et les femmes selon Madame de Staël," in *Benjamin Constant, Madame de Staël, et le Groupe de Coppet*, edited by Etienne Hofman (Oxford: The Voltaire Foundation and Lausanne: Institut Benjamin Constant, 1980), 401–25.

12. For Staël's influence on Edgeworth, see Marilyn Butler and Christina Colvin, "Maria Edgeworth et *Delphine*," *Cahiers Staëliens*, nos. 26–27 (1979): 77–91.

13. Rebecca West, review of *Madame de Staël: Mistress to an Age*, by Christopher Herold *Encounter*, 18 no. 1 (July 1959); 67.

14. Noreen J. Swallow, "The Weapon of Personality: A Review of Sexist Criticism of Madame de Stael," *Atlantis* 8 no. 1 (Fall 1982): 79.

15. Gutwirth, *Staël, Novelist*, 286.

16. Simone Balayé, "A propos du Préromantisme: Continuité ou Rupture chez Madame de Staël," in *Le Préromantisme: Hypothèque ou Hypothèse*, edited by Paul Viallaneix, 154. (Paris: Klincksieck, 1975). (On a trop souvent refusé de la traiter comme un écrivain à part entière.)

17. de Diesbach, p. 43.

18. Georges Poulet, "La pensée critique de Madame de Staël," *Preuves*, no. 190, (December 1966): 27–35. (J'admire donc je suis, c'est à dire je me découvre dans le sentiment d'admiration que j'éprouve.)

19. Georges Poulet, "*Corinne* et *Adolphe*: Deux romans conjuguées," *Revue d'Histoire Littéraire*, no. 4 (July–August, 1978):596.

20. Jean Starobinski, "Suicide et mélancolie chez Madame de Staël," in *Madame de Staël et l'Europe*, 242–52 (Paris: Klincksieck, 1970) pp. 242–52. This article appears also in *Preuves*, no. 190 (December 1966):41–48.

21. Jean-Albert Bédé, "Madame de Staël et les mots," *Madame de Stael et l'Europe*, 317 (Paris: Klincksieck, 1970). (A coup sûr on aurait assez vite épuisé le nomenclature de ses procédés: ceux-ci ne se distinguent ni par la nouveauté, ni par la variété.)

22. Paul de Man, "Madame de Staël et Rousseau," *Preuves*, no. 190 (December 1966): p. 36. (Le langage analytique de Mme de Staël est capable des pires aberrations: banalité, dissimulation, sensiblerie intéressée, rien n'y manque.)

23. Virginia Woolf, *A Room of One's Own*, 1929. Reprint (New York: Harcourt, Brace, World, 1963), 59.

24. The major works of these two critics are cited above. Further references to them are to these books, unless otherwise stated.

25. Madelyn Gutwirth, "Madame de Staël, Rousseau, and the Woman Question, *Publications of the Modern Language Association*, no. 86, (1971):109.

26. For a fuller account of the childhood of Germaine de Staël, see Béatrix d'Andlau, *La Jeunesse de Madame de Staël, de 1766 à 1786, avec des documents inédits* (Geneva: Droz, 1970).

27. Madelyn Gutwirth traces the origins of this conflict and sketches its consequences, pp. 39–41.

28. Sandra M. Gilbert and Susan Gubar, *The Madwoman in the Attic: The Woman Writer and the Nineteenth Century Literary Imagination*, 45–92 (New Haven and London: Yale University Press, 1979).

29. Gutwirth, p. 39.

30. Judith Kegan Gardiner, "On Female Identity and Writing by Women," in *Writing and Sexual Difference*, edited by Elizabeth Abel, 177–91 (Chicago: University of Chicago Press, 1982).

31. Nancy Chodorow, *The Reproduction of Mothering: Psychoanalysis and the Sociology of Gender* (Berkeley: University of California Press, 1967); Carol Gilligan, *In a Different Voice: Psychological Theory and Women's Development* (Cambridge, MA: Harvard University Press, 1982).

32. Quoted in Toril Moi, *Sexual/Textual Politics: Feminist Literary Theory*, (New York: Methuen, 1985), 173. First published in "Choreographies: An Interview with Christie V. McDonald," *Diacritics* 12, no. 2 (Summer, 1982): 76.

33. See the discussion of Julia Kristeva in Toril Moi, 150–73.

34. Mary Jacobus, "The Question of Language: Men of Maxims and *The Mill on the Floss*," in *Writing and Sexual Difference*, edited by Elizabeth Abel, 37–52 (Chicago: University of Chicago Press, 1982).

35. Nancy K. Miller, "The Text's Heroine: A Feminist Critic and her Fictions," *Diacritics* 12, no. 2, (Summer, 1982):53.

36. Simone Balayé, "Absence, Exil, Voyage," *Madame de Staël et l'Europe* (Paris: Klincksieck, 1970), 236. (Il y a une contradiction entre ce qu'est Mme de Staël, la façon dont elle se voit, s'analyse, et l'apparence, le spectacle qu'elle offre involontairement et à la postérité.)

37. Barbara Watson, "On Power and the Literary Text," *Signs: A Journal of Woman in Culture and Society* 1 (Autumn 1975): 113.

38. Gilbert and Gubar, p. 169.

39. Le bruit des paroles couvre souvent la voix de la conscience. *Corinne*, part I, chapter 11; FD II, p. 25.

40. Marie-Claire Vallois, "Les Voi(es) de la Sibylle: Aphasie et discours féminin chez Madame de Staël," *Stanford French Review* 6 no. 1 (Spring 1982):48.

41. Gutwirth, p. 196.

42. Gilbert and Gubar, p. 155.

43. Vallois, p. 37. ([Son écriture romanesque] se double de la parole autobiographique qu'elle camoufle aussitôt.)

44. Un livre est toujours fait d'après tel ou tel système, qui place l'auteur à quelque distance du lecteur. On peut bien deviner le caractère de l'écrivain, mais son talent même doit mettre un genre de fiction entre lui et nous. (FD II, p. 260).

45. On the influence of Voltaire, see James F. Hamilton, "Madame de Staël, Partisan of Rousseau or Voltaire," *Studies on Voltaire and the Eighteenth Century*, no. 106 (1973):253–65.

2. *The Threat of Silence*

1. Notes sur l'enfance de Mme de Staël," *Occident et Cahiers Staeliëns* 2, no. 1 (June 30, 1933):42. Nous ne jouâmes point comme des enfants; elle me demanda tout de suite quelles étaient mes leçons, si je savais quelque langue? je lui dis que oui. Si j'allais souvent au spectacle? Je lui dis que j'y étais allée trois fois dans ma vie; elle se récria, me promit que nous irions souvent; mais qu'au retour il faudrait écrire le sujet des pièces que nous aurions vues; et ce qui nous aurait frappées, que sa mère l'exigeait. J'y consentis volontiers et lui

répondis; "Ce sera comme quand je reviens du sermon" elle me dit "c'est singulier, quelle ressemblance! et moi aussi je fais l'extrait des sermons que j'entends; oh, comme nous nous amuserons! comme nous serons heureuses! il faudra nous écrire tous les matins."

2. d'Andlau, pp. 103–10.

3. "Mon Journal," *Occident et Cahier Staeliëns*, 1, no. 3/4, (October 15, 1932):236; and as reedited by Simone Balayé in *Cahiers Staeliëns*, no. 28 (1980): 69–70. In this issue there is also an article about the journal by Jean Starobinski, pp. 25–32. Si maman avait écrit je suis persuadée qu'elle aurait acquis une très grande réputation d'esprit; mais mon père ne peut pas souffrir une femme auteur et, depuis quatre jours seulement qu'il me voit écrire son portrait, l'inquiétude lui prend déjà et m'appellerait (sic) dans ses plaisanteries "Monsieur de Saint-Ecritoire." Il veut me mettre en garde contre cette faiblesse d'amour-propre. Maman avait fort le goût de composer, elle le lui a sacrifié. 'Représente-toi, me dit-il souvent, quelle était mon inquiétude; je n'osais entrer chez elle de peur de l'arracher à une occupation qui lui était plus agréable que ma présence. Je la voyais dans mes bras poursuivre encore une idée.' Ah! qu'il a raison! que les femmes sont peu faites pour courir la même carrière que les hommes, lutter contre eux, exciter en eux une jalousie si différente que [sic] celle que l'amour leur inspire. Une femme ne doit avoir rien à elle et trouver toutes ses jouissances dans ce qu'elle aime! . . . Malheur à nous quand nous renversons l'ordre de la nature!

4. The discussion of Madelyn Gutwirth, pp. 39–41, is relevant in this connection.

5. This passage and those to follow are from the previously cited "Mon Journal," p. 76 (1932) and pp. 57–58 (1980). Le coeur de l'homme est un tableau qu'il faut voir à la distance où le sage ordonnateur de la nature l'a placé. (*De l'Administration des Finances*, vol, II). Tourne le feuillet, papa, si tu l'oses, après avoir lu cet épigraphe; ah! je t'ai placé si près de mon coeur que tu ne dois pas n'envier ce petit degré d'intimité de plus, que je conserve avec moi-même.

6. Je voulais faire entièrement le journal de mon coeur, j'en ai dechiré quelques feuillets.

7. Il est des mouvements qui perdent de leur naturel dès qu'on s'en souvient, dès qu'on songe qu'on s'en souviendra; il semble que l'on serait comme les rois, ils vivent pour l'histoire, et l'on sentirait pour l'histoire.

8. Malheur à celui qui peut tout exprimer, malheur à celui qui peut supporter la lecture de ses sentiments affaiblis.

9. Pour lui viendra plus grand malheur encore, [qù]à celui qui, ayant assez d'eloquence pour enflammer son papier du même feu qui dévorait son coeur, déchirerait encore ses feuillets et détournait ses yeux de son image.

10. Pour moi cependant je ne rougis pas de mon coeur, et seule dans le silence des passions, je le sens sous ma main battre encore pour l'honneur et la vertu.

11. For discussions of the other short stories written around this time, see Madelyn Gutwirth, pp. 52–75. Simone Balayé discusses the story "Mirza," pp. 25–27.

12. We should note in passing the very strong similarity of this story to Choderlos de Laclos' *Les Liaisons Dangereuses.* Staël was sixteen years old in 1782, when Laclos' book appeared. There exists no record in her correspondence or in her journal that she read the novel. She mentions it only once, much later, in *De l'Allemagne*, in most unflattering terms (part 1, chapter 4). Madelyn Gutwirth points out the debt of "Pauline" to the novelistic work of Samuel Richardson and Jean-Jacques Rousseau, pp. 54–58.

13. Ces climats brulants où les hommes, uniquement occupés d'un commerce et d'un gain barbares, semblent, pour la plupart, avoir perdu les idées et les sentiments qui pourraient leur en inspirer l'horreur. (FD I, p. 88)

14. Il avait lu quelques romans; il lui parle leur langage. (P. 88)

15. Cette enfant était devenue une amante passionnée; son jeune langage était celui de la plus noble éloquence. Peut-être pouvait-on s'apercevoir qu'elle s'exaltait elle-même sur son sentiment pour qu'il diminuât sa faute à ses propres yeux; mais tout ce que l'amour peut imaginer de plus élevé, de plus romanesque, elle le développa à Théodore. (P. 89)

16. Aucun sentiment factice n'était entré dans son âme, aucun de ces mouvements qu'on excite en soi pour pouvoir se permettre en conscience de les montrer aux autres. (P. 90)

17. Un état de trouble et de désespoir, dont la violence surpassait et les forces et les réflexions de son âge. (P. 88)

18. Cette vertu que je connais mal mais dont le nom m'était cher. (P. 90)

19. Madame de Verseuil parla longtemps à Pauline: elle éprouvait, en l'écoutant, une impression impossible à rendre; son âme se développait, des sentiments jusqu'alors incertains, confus, s'eclaircissaient et se fixaient; elle entendait le langage qu'elle avait désiré sans le connaître; elle voyait ouverte devant elle la route qu'elle avait cherchée; elle retrouvait dans madame de Verseuil le caractère qu'elle s'était représenté comme une chimère, dont elle avait conçu l'idée sans en avoir rencontré l'exemple. (P. 91)

20. Viens, suis-moi dans une autre contrée; mets l'immensité des mers, mets une éducation vertueuse entre ton enfance et ta jeunesse. (P. 91)

21. Les erreurs de ma jeunesse, le tort plus grand encore d'avoir pu te les cacher, ont flétri pour jamais cette félicité qui, par sa perfection même, ne pouvait souffrir d'altération. En mourant, je me crois digne de toi; l'excès de ma passion t'est prouvé; . . . Vois, Edouard, si je ne suis pas heureuse d'anéantir ainsi toutes les barrières qui séparaient ton âme de la mienne.

Nous nous réunirons dans le ciel, et jusqu'à ce moment mon image restera dans ton coeur, comme elle y fut jadis. (P. 100)

22. Le coeur d'une femme n'est dans toute sa perfection que quand il s'ignore lui-même; et les impressions qu'elle reconnaît, les émotions qu'elle se retrace n'ont jamais la même energie. (P. 95)

23. Paul Hoffman, in his *La Femme dans la Pensée des Lumières* (Paris, 1977), pp. 559–60, makes a similar point regarding Rousseau's attitude toward women, "guilty as soon as they showed themselves."

24. In "Corinne et l'esthétique du camée," p. 245.

25. Gutwirth, p. 99.

3. *The Pedestal and the Statue*

1. Harold Bloom's *Anxiety of Influence* was limited to patriarchal literary lineage. Gilbert and Gubar discuss the adaptability of his suggestions to inquiries concerning the female literary tradition, pp. 46–53; their entire book illustrates the use to which they put those suggestions. Mine is a similar undertaking, on a more limited scale.

2. *Correspondance Littéraire*, April 1786, p. 472. Quelques conversations sur la manière de faire des synonymes, auxquels le livre de l'abbé Roubaud avait donné lieu, ont fait naître à madame l'ambassadrice de Suède l'idée de s'essayer dans ce genre d'écrire. Cet essai a paru un modèle.

3. Suzanne Curchod Necker, *Mélanges extraits des manuscrits de Madame Necker* (Paris, Pougens, 1798), vol. I, pp. 220–21. La noblesse de caractère est une qualité différente de la générosité: on peut être noble sans être généreux ou généreux sans être noble; on peut aussi réunir ces deux mérites à la fois.

4. *Correspondance Littéraire*, April 1786, p. 472–73. On est franc par caractère, on est vrai par principes: on est franc malgré soi, on est vrai parce qu'on le veut. La franchise interrogée souvent ne peut pas garder un secret: mais la vérité étant une vertu, cède toujours le pas à une vertu d'un ordre supérieur alors qu'elle le rencontre.

5. *Correspondance Littéraire*, June 1786, p. 519. "La peinture d'un sentiment exalté jusqu'à la folie."

6. Their very title, *The Madwoman in the Attic*, underscores the theme.

7. In "Mon Journal," August 11, 1785, p. 237 (1932) and p. 71 (1980). Tenez, Monsieur, je vais vous montrer comme on danse avec une demoiselle dont on est amoureux.

8. André Corbaz, *Madame Necker: Humble Vaudoise et Grande Dame* (Paris: Payot, 1945).

9. Vallois, pp. 37 and 39–43.

10. Les mouvements de ses yeux . . . exprimèrent . . . le retour de ses idées, mais les mots lui manquaient. Elle remuaient les lèvres; une puissance

surnaturelle semblait lier sa langue; elle faisait des efforts inutiles, et tous ses traits peignaient l'impatience et la douleur. (P. 521)

11. Vous voyez . . . je pense, je pleure, mais je ne peux plus parler. (P. 521)

12. Gutwirth, "Madame de Staël, Rousseau, and the Woman Question," p. 100.

13. Suzanne Curchod Necker, vol. I, p. 147. Tant qu'*Héloïse*, *Emile*, toutes ces divines et essentielles portions de Rousseau, seront entre mes mains, je ne puis regarder la vie de leur auteur que comme un faible accessoire et il semble qu'on doit jeter un voile sur les défauts de ce père de la vertu.

14. James F. Hamilton, "Madame de Staël, Partisan of Rousseau or Voltaire," *Studies on Voltaire and the Eighteenth Century* 106 (1973):263.

15. Jean Starobinski points out the affiliation of the work to the genre of the "éloge" in his "Critique et principe d'autorité (Madame de Staël et Rousseau)," in *Le Préromantisme: Hypothèque ou Hypothèse?*, p. 331.

16. For a discussion of Necker's "Eloge," see Henri Grange, *Les Ideés de Necker* (Paris: Klincksieck, 1974), 21–25.

17. Gilbert and Gubar, pp. 148–52.

18. "Mon Journal," pp. 235–36 (1932) and pp. 68–69 (1980).

19. Ces lettres sur les écrits et le caractère de J. J. Rousseau ont été composées dans la première année de mon entrée dans le monde; elles furent publiées sans mon aveu, et ce hasard m'entraîna dans la carrière littéraire. Je ne dirai point que j'y ai du regret, car la culture des lettres m'a valu plus de jouissances que de chagrins . . . (Seconde Préface, F.D. I, p. 1)

20. Madelyn Gutwirth points out the Necker/Rousseau association, to be developed in some detail here, as well as the ambivalence of Stael's attitude toward Rousseau as a commentator on women's abilities and prospects, in "Madame de Staël, Rousseau, and the Woman Question."

21. Quel est le grand homme qui pourrait dédaigner d'assurer la gloire d'un grand homme? Qu'il serait beau de voir dans tous les siècles cette ligue du génie contre l'envie! que les hommes supérieurs qui prendraient la défense des hommes supérieurs qui les auraient précédés, donneraient un sublime exemple à leurs successeurs! Le monument qu'ils auraient élevé servirait un jour de piedestal à leur statute. (Letter 6, p. 24)

22. Lucia Omacini, "Pour une typologie du discours staeliën: les procédés de la persuasion," in *Benjamin Constant, Madame de Staël, et le Groupe de Coppet*, edited by Etienne Hofman (Oxford: The Voltaire Foundation; Lausanne: Institut Benjamin Constant, 1982), 378.

23. Balayé, p. 28. Cette étude sur Rousseau, la plus remarquable sans doute à cette époque, est bien une manière de réfléchir sur elle-même en allant à la rencontre de l'écrivain qui la touche de plus près.

24. Il n'existe pas encore d'éloge de Rousseau; j'ai senti le besoin de voir mon admiration exprimée. (FD I, p. 1)

25. J'aurais souhaité sans doute qu'un autre eût peint ce que j'eprouve. (P. 1)

26. Mais j'ai goûté quelque plaisir en me retraçant a moi-même le souvenir de l'impression de mon enthousiasme. (P. 1)

27. Peut-être ceux dont l'indulgence daignera présager quelque talent en moi me reprocheront-ils de m'être hatée de traiter un sujet au-dessus même des forces que je pouvais espérer un jour. (P. 1)

28. Comment consentir a s'attendre? (P. 1)

29. Il est remarquable qu'un des hommes les plus sensibles et distingués par ses connaissances et son génie ait voulu réduire l'esprit et le coeur humain à un état presque semblable à l'abrutissement; mais c'est qu'il avait senti plus qu'un autre toutes les peines que ces avantages, portés à l'excès, peuvent faire éprouver. C'est peut-être aux dépens du bonheur qu'on obtient ces succès extraordinaires, dûs à des talents sublimes. La nature, épuisée par ces superbes dons, refuse souvent aux grands hommes les qualités qui peuvent rendre heureux. Qu'il est cruel de leur accorder avec tant de peine, de leur envier avec tant de fureur cette gloire, seule jouissance qu'il soit peut-être en leur pouvoir de goûter! (Letter 1, p. 3)

30. Enfin, il croit à l'amour, sa grâce est obtenue. (P. 4)

31. Ces vains talents littéraires qui, loin de les faire aimer des hommes, les mettent en lutte avec eux . . . cette puissante force de tête, cette profonde faculté d'attention dont les grands génies sont doués. (P. 5)

32. Cet abandon sublime, cette mélancolique douleur, ces sentiments tout puissants, qui les font vivre et mourir, porteraient peut-être plus avant l'émotion dans le coeur des lecteurs, que tous les transports nés de l'imagination exaltée des poètes. (P. 5)

33. She returns to the subject in *De l'Allemagne*, (On Germany), part I, chapters 18 and 19, as part of her presentation of German culture. Her continuing interest in the topic is illustrated in the review she wrote of a work on education by Maria Edgeworth, published by Simone Balayé in the *Cahiers Staëliëns*, n.s. no. 7, May, 1968. See also E. Causse, *Madame de Staël et l'Education* (Paris, 1930).

34. Balayé, p. 30. Mais aussi son propre père pareillement rebelle aux tentatives en ce genre de sa femme et de sa fille, et toute une société qui accorde à regret que les femmes puissent écrire des romans et des vers.

35. Compare for example this statement from *De la Littérature*, (On Literature), part I, chapter 1: L'origine des sociétés, la formation des langues, ces premiers pas de l'esprit humain, nous sont entièrement inconnus, et rien n'est plus fatigant, en général, que cette métaphysique qui suppose des faits à l'appui de ses systèmes, et ne peut jamais avoir pour base aucune observation positive. (The origin of societies, the formation of languages, these first steps of the human mind, are entirely unknown to us, and nothing

is more tiring, in general, than this metaphysics which supposes facts to support systems, and can never have as a foundation any concrete observation.) (FD I, p. 210)

36. L'enfant dont l'esprit n'est pas au niveau de sa mémoire retiendra ce qu'il n'entend pas, et cette habitude dispose à l'erreur. (Letter 3, p. 11)

37. Que j'aime cette éducation sans ruse et sans despotisme, qui traite l'enfant comme un homme faible et non comme un être dépendant! (P. 11)

38. Avec quel soin n'interdit-il ces motifs d'émulation et de rivalité qui préparent d'avance les passions de la jeunesse! (P. 12)

39. C'est l'éloquence de Rousseau qui ranima le sentiment maternel dans une certaine classe de la société . . . . Le bonheur de l'enfant dépend de sa mère: hélas! Un jour peut-être elle le pressera vainement contre son sein; ses carresses ne feront plus renaître le calme dans son âme. (P. 12)

40. In the last lines of the passage quoted, Staël is obviously thinking of herself as a mother. Her first child, Gustavine, was born on July 22, 1787, during the time when Staël was writing the letters on Rousseau. She was a weak child who was to die on April 7, 1789.

41. For discussions of Staël's childhood and education, see Catherine Huber's "Notes sur l'enfance de Madame de Staël;" Albertine de Necker de Saussure's "Notice sur le caractère et les écrits de Madame de Staël," in *Oeuvres Posthumes*, FD II, pp. 4–8. See also Beatrice d'Andlau, *La Jeunesse de Madame De Staël*; and Madelyn Gutwirth, pp. 24–45.

42. Un plan sans défaut à l'imagination, p. 16.

43. Celui qui nous a fait connaître tout ce qu'on peut obtenir par la méditation. (P. 16)

44. Qu'on place au-dessus de l'ouvrage de Rousseau celui de l'homme d'état dont les observations auraient précédé les théories, qui serait arrivé aux idées générales par la connaissance des faits particuliers, et qui se livreraient moins en artiste à tracer le plan d'un édifice régulier, qu'en homme habile a réparer celui qu'il trouverait construit. (Letter 4, p. 16)

45. Balayé, p. 32. Rousseau et son père, l'écrivain et l'homme d'Etat, ces deux faces du génie, resteront deux pôles de sa pensée de femme subtilement torturée par le désir de concourir au bonheur de l'humanité et cantonée dans le rôle d'écrivain.

46. Ah! Rousseau, quel bonheur pour toi, si ton éloquence se faisait entendre dans cette auguste assemblée! Quelle inspiration pour le talent, que l'espoir d'être utile! Quelle émotion différente, quand la pensée, cessant de tomber sur elle-même, peut voir au-devant d'elle un but qu'elle peut atteindre, une action qu'elle peut produire! Les peines du coeur seraient suspendues dans de si grandes circonstances. (P. 17)

47. Cet ouvrage n'a pas sans doute ce caractère d'élévation qu'on souhaiterait à l'homme qui parle de lui-même. . . ; mais il semble qu'il est

difficile de douter de sa sincérité; on cache plutôt qu'on n'invente les aveux que les *Confessions* contiennent. (Letter 6, p. 18)

48. "Mon Journal," p. 80 (1932) and p. 63 (1980). L'élévation de l'âme est de toutes les qualités, la plus rare; mon père est presque le seul homme qui la possède dans toute son étendue. (P. 80)

49. Ah! maintenant un inutile attendrissement se mêle à l'enthousiasme qu'il inspire. (Letter 6, p. 24)

50. Si la calomnie osait aussi les attaquer, ils auraient d'avance mis en défiance contre elle, émoussé ses traits odieux. (P. 24)

4. *The Moralist and the Legislator*

1. Simone Balayé discusses these works and their political context, pp. 63–73.

2. Madelyn Gutwirth in "Forging a Vocation: Germaine de Staël on Fiction, Power, and Passion," in the *Bulletin of Research in the Humanities* 86, no. 3 (1983–1985): 242–54, discusses both the *Passions* and the *Essay*.

3. On pensera peut-être qu'il y a de l'empressement d'auteur à faire paraître la première partie d'un livre quand la seconde n'est pas encore faite. (FD I, p. 107)

4. Gilbert and Gubar, p. 316.

5. For a straightforward account of the place of this piece in late eighteenth-century discussions of the poetics of the novel, see Arnaldo Pizzorusso, "Madame de Staël et *L'Essai sur les fictions*," in *Madame de Staël et l'Europe*, (Paris: Klincksieck, 1971), 273–85.

6. Suzanne Curchod Necker, *Réflexions sur le divorce*, (Lausanne, 1815), with *Rapport sur l'état de France fait au roi* of Chateaubriand, originally published in 1794.

7. Gilbert and Gubar, p. 134.

8. Ibid., p. 145.

9. Deux ouvrages doivent se trouver dans un seul: l'un étudie l'homme dans ses rapports avec lui-même; l'autre, dans les relations sociales de tous les individus entre eux. (P. 108)

10. Ce qui est grand se retrouve dans ce qui est petit, avec la même exactitude de proportions: l'univers tout entier se peint dans chacune de ses parties, et plus il paraît l'oeuvre d'une seule idée, plus il inspire de l'admiration. (FD I, p. 109)

11. *De l'Influence des Passions*, FD I, p. 109.

12. In the article cited above, Madelyn Gutwirth connects the *Passions* with the moralist tradition which includes La Bruyère, p. 244.

13. Espérer qu'à travers tant de livres sur la morale, celui-ci peut encore être utile. (P. 172)

14. L'espoir sans la crainte, l'activité sans l'inquiétude, la gloire sans la calomnie, l'amour sans l'inconstance. (P. 110)

15. Autant le moraliste doit rejeter cet espoir, autant le législateur doit tâcher de s'en rapprocher. (P. 110)

16. Gutwirth, p. 97.

17. Mais si les accidents de la vie ou les peines du coeur bornaient le cours de ma destinée, je voudrais qu'un autre accomplit le plan que je me suis proposé. (P. 109)

18. Cet ouvrage, que je ferai, ou que je voudrais qu'on fît (P. 110)

19. See the brilliant critical edition of this work and its excellent introduction by Lucia Omacini.

20. La nature et la société ont déshérité la moitié de l'espèce humaine; force, courage, génie, indépendance, tout appartient aux hommes; et s'ils environnent d'hommages les années de notre jeunesse, c'est pour se donner l'amusement de renverser un trône; c'est comme on permet aux enfants de commander, certains qu'ils ne peuvent forcer d'obéir. (Section I, chapter 4, p. 137)

21. So stated, for example, the sarcastic critic David Glass Larg, *Madame de Staël: La Vie dans l'Oeuvre (1766–1800)* (Paris: Champion, 1924), 40.

22. Starobinski, "Suicide et mélancolie chez Madame de Staël," p. 255.

23. Simone Balayé, "Fonction romanesque de la musique et des sons dans *Corinne*" *Romantisme* 3 (1972):23–24.

24. Martine de Rougement, "L'activité théâtrale dans le Groupe de Coppet: la dramaturgie et le jeu," in *Le Groupe de Coppet* edited by Simone Balayé and Jean-Daniel Candaux, (Paris: Champion, Geneva: Slatkine, 1977), 275.

25. Simone Balayé, "Fonction romanesque de la musique et des sons dans *Corinne*," p. 24.

26. Les idées générales cesseraient d'avoir une application universelle, si l'on y mêlait l'impression détaillée des situations particulières. Pour remonter à la source des affections de l'homme, il faut agrandir ses réflexions en les séparant de ses circonstances personnelles: elles ont fait naître la pensée, mais la pensée est plus forte qu'elles; et le vrai moraliste est celui qui, ne parlant ni par invention, ni par réminiscence, peint toujours l'homme et jamais lui. (Section 2, chapter 2, p. 152)

27. J'ai rêvé plutôt qu'observé: que ceux qui se ressemblent se comprennent. (Section 1, note preceding chapter 4, p. 133)

28. Mais à vingt-cinq ans, à cette époque précise où la vie cesse de croître, il se fait un cruel changement dans votre existence: on commence à juger votre situation, tout n'est plus avenir dans votre destinée; et les hommes réfléchissent alors s'il leur convient d'y lier le leur. (Introduction, p. 114)

29. Qui, cependant, se trouvent souvent réunis aux qualités les plus éminentes. (P. 119)

30. Semblable au vent brulant d'Afrique, sèche dans la fleur, abat dans la force, courbe enfin vers la terre la tige qui devait croitre et dominer. (Section 1, chapter 4, p. 138)

31. Les individus de la même classe que soi, qui se sont résignés à n'en pas sortir, attribuant bien plutöt cette résolution à leur sagesse qu'à leur médiocrité, appellent folie une conduite différente. (Section 1, chapter 1, p. 117)

5. *History and Story*

1. Balayé, p. 248.

2. The critical edition of this work is Madame de Staël, *De la littérature considérée dans ses rapports avec les institutions sociales*, edited by Paul van Tieghem (Geneva: Droz, 1959).

3. Des femmes has recently published an "édition féministe" of *Delphine*, edited by Claudine Herrmann (Paris: Des femmes, 1981).

4. "A propos du 'préromantisme': continuité ou rupture chez Madame de Staël," p. 168. (L'Oeuvre critique et politique de Madame de Staël propose, construit, réconforte, pendant que l'oeuvre romanesque détruit en exprimant l'angoisse de l'écrivain.)

5. Gutwirth, pp. 77–80 and 157.

6. Un homme doit savoir braver l'opinion, une femme s'y soumettre. (FD I, p. 334)

7. Gutwirth, pp. 108–10 and 113–21.

8. Balayé, pp. 136, and 243. (Il y a pour ses romans des fins tragiques, pour ses oeuvres philosophiques et politiques des fins qui ne sont jamais des fermetures. . . . une différence fondamentale d'orientation entre ces deux manières d'exprimer son propre génie.)

9. James Hamilton, "Structural Polarity in Madame de Staël's *De la litterature*, *French Review* 50, no. 5 (April 1977):706–12.

10. En parcourant les révolutions du monde et la succession des siècles, il est une idée première dont je ne détourne jamais mon attention: c'est la perfectibilité de *l'espèce humaine*. Je ne pense pas que ce grand oeuvre de la nature morale ait jamais été abandonné; dans les périodes lumineuses, comme dans les siècles de ténébres, *la marche graduelle de l'esprit humain* n'a point été interrompue. (Discours Préliminaire, FD I, p. 207)

11. Lucia Omacini, "Pour une typologie du discours staëlien," p. 379.

12. Le temps nous découvre un dessein dans la suite des événements qui semblaient n'être que le pur effet du hasard; et l'on voit surgir une pensée, toujours la même, de l'abîme des faits et des siècles. (Part I, chapter 8; F.D I, p. 236)

13. Promet aux hommes sur cette terre quelques-uns des bienfaits d'une vie immortelle, un avenir sans bornes, une continuité sans interruption! (P. 198)

14. Par exemple, . . . le langage est l'instrument nécessaire pour acquérir

tous les autres développements; et, par une sorte de prodige, cet instrument existe. (Part I, chapter 1. FD I, p. 210)

15. On a prétendu que la décadence des arts, des lettres et des empires, devait arriver nécessairement après un certain degré de splendeur. (Part I, chapter 7. FD I, p. 234)

16. La nature morale tend à se perfectionner. L'amélioration précédente est une cause de l'amélioration future; cette chaîne peut être interrompue par des événements accidentels qui contrarient les progrès à venir, mais qui ne sont point la conséquence des progres antérieurs. (Part I, chapter 7. FD I, p. 234)

17. Ainsi marchait le siècle vers la conquête de la liberté . . . Ah! . . . Toutes les fois que le cours des idées ramène à réfléchir sur la destinée de l'homme, la révolution nous apparaît. (Part I, chapter 9. FD I, p. 245)

18. Ne succombons pas néanmoins à cet abattement. Revenons aux observations générales.

19. J'ai suivi l'histoire de l'esprit humain depuis Homère jusqu'en 1789. Dans mon orgueil national je regardais l'époque de la révolution de France comme une ère nouvelle pour le monde intellectuel. (Part I, chapter 1. FD I, p. 288)

20. Il est impossible de condamner la pensée à revenir sur ses pas, avec l'espérance de moins et les regrets de plus; l'esprit humain, privé d'avenir, tomberait dans la dégradation la plus misérable. Cherchons-le donc cet avenir dans les productions littéraires et les idées philosophiques. (Part II, chapter 1. FD I, p. 289)

21. For a discussion of the novel's epistolarity as well as of its revelation of Staël's depiction of the Revolution, see Madelyn Gutwirth, "La *Delphine* de Madame de Staël: Femme, Révolution, et Mode Epistolaire," in *Cahiers Staëliens*, nos. 26–27 (1979):151–65.

22. Les fictions doivent nous expliquer, par nos vertus et nos sentiments, les mystères de notre sort. (FD I, p. 335)

23. J'entre dans le monde avec un caractère bon et vrai, de l'esprit, de la jeunesse et de la fortune; pourquoi ces dons de la Providence ne me rendraient-ils pas heureuse? (Part I, letter 3. FD I, p. 341)

24. Balayé, p. 136.

25. Gutwirth, p. 106.

26. I take the desire to stop time altogether to be a more fundamental mode of temporal sensibility than the "hâte de vivre," the desire to make time move more quickly, isolated and analyzed by Georges Poulet, *Etudes sur le temps humain*, 1946. Reprint (Paris: Plon, 1956), 194.

27. Nancy K. Miller, "Emphasis Added: Plots and Plausibilities in Women's Fiction," *Publications of the Modern Language Association*, 96 no. 1 (January 1981):44, 46. This article has been reprinted in *Feminist Criticism:*

Essays on Women, Literature, and Theory, 339–60 edited by Elaine Showalter, (New York: Pantheon, 1985), 339–60.

28. Section I, chapter 4. F.D. I, p. 137.

29. Les femmes cherchent à s'arranger comme un roman, et les hommes comme une histoire. (Part III, chapter 18. FD II, p. 217.)

30. Une compagne de la vie, heureuse de consacrer ses facultés, ses jours, ses sentiments, à compléter une autre existence. (Part I, chapter 8. FD I, p. 212)

31. Tous les sentiments auxquels il leur est permis de se livrer, la crainte de la mort, le regret de la vie, le dévouement sans bornes, l'indignation sans mesure, enrichissent la littérature d'expressions nouvelles. (Part I, chapter 9. FD I, p. 243)

32. L'existence des femmes en société est encore incertaine sous beaucoup de rapports . . . . Tout est arbitraire dans leurs succès comme dans leurs revers . . . . Dan l'état actual, elles ne sont pour la plupart ni dans l'ordre de la nature, ni dans l'ordre de la société. (Part II, chapter 4. FD I, p. 301)

33. Two articles which treat Staël's attitude toward women in society are Madelyn Gutwirth, "Madame de Staël, Rousseau, and the Woman Question," and Joanne Kitchen, "La littérature et les femmes selon Madame de Staël." The latter, in the main, juxtaposes passages in which Staël treated the subject, whereas the former is marked by reflection and analysis.

6. *A Topography of the Soul*

1. Simone Balayé, *Les Carnets de Voyage de Mme de Staël, contribution à la genèse de ses oeuvres* (Geneva: Droz, 1971), 98. In this indispensable volume, Balayé follows the genesis of the works under discussion here, publishing the notes made chiefly by Staël herself during the trips and indicating how the books were generated by the travel experiences. (La genèse de *Corinne* se fait en symbiose avec la genèse de *De l'Allemagne*.)

2. Gutwirth, p. 157.

3. Porter, p. 133.

4. Claudine Herrmann has edited *Corinne* (Paris: des femmes, 1979) as well as *Delphine*. Of great value is Avriel Goldberger's translation of *Corinne* (New Brunswick, NJ: Rutgers University Press, 1987).

5. A good and easily available edition of *De l'Allemagne* is the edition by Simone Balayé, 2 vols. (Paris: Garnier, 1968).

6. Madelyn Gutwirth discusses time and space as modes in *Delphine* and *Corinne*, pp. 189–90. Simone Balayé studies spaces and places in *Corinne* in "Corinne et la ville italienne, ou l'espace extérieur et l'impasse intérieur," *Mélanges à la mémoire de Franco Simone* III (1984), pp. 33–50.

7. Balayé, pp. 97–110.

8. Vous êtes hors de France. (Part I, chapter 13. FD II, p. 28)

9. Balayé, "Absence, exil, voyages," pp. 233. (Le passage de toute frontière impressionne profondément la voyageuse.)

10. *Carnets de Voyage,* pp. 28–30.

11. J'étais, il y a six ans, sur les bords du Rhin, attendant la barque qui devait me conduire à l'autre rive; le temps était froid, le ciel obscur, et tout me semblait un présage funeste. Il y avait dans notre bac une vieille femme allemande, assise sur une charrette; elle ne voulait pas en descendre même pour traverser le fleuve. "Vour êtes bien tranquille!" lui dis-je. "Oui," me répondit-elle, "pourquoi faire du bruit?" Ces simples mots me frappèrent; en effet *pourquoi faire du bruit?* (Part I, chapter 13. FD II, p. 28)

12. Mais quand des générations entières traverseraient la vie en silence, le malheur et la mort ne les observeraient pas moins et sauraient de même les atteindre.

En arrivant sur le rivage opposé, j'entendis le cor des postillons, dont les sons aigus et faux semblaient annoncer un triste départ vers un triste séjour. (Part I, chapter 13. FD II, p. 28)

13. *Agar dans le désert*, 1806; *Geneviève de Brabant*, 1808; and *la Sunamite*, 1808.

14. On a raison d'exclure les femmes des affaires politiques et civiles; rien n'est plus opposé à leur vocation naturelle que tout ce qui leur donnerait des rapports de rivalité avec les hommes, et la gloire elle-même ne saurait être pour une femme qu'un deuil éclatant du bonheur. (Part III, chapter 19. FD II, p. 218)

15. Il vaut encore mieux, pour maintenir quelque chose de sacré sur la terre, qu'il y ait dans le mariage une esclave que deux esprits forts. (Part III, chapter 19. FD II, p. 219)

16. En politique, il faut toute la liberté qui est conciliable avec l'ordre. (Part II, chapter 14. FD II, 78)

17. Je retournerais la maxime.

18. Gutwirth, p. 44.

19. "De la morale fondée sur l'intérêt personnel" and "De la morale fondée sur l'intérêt national."

20. Compare Simone Balayé, p. 147.

21. Je partis dans un de ces moments où l'on se livre à la destinée. (Part XIV, chapter 3. FD I, p. 788)

22. Il en coûte davantage pour quitter sa patrie quand il faut traverser la mer pour s'en éloigner; tout est solennel dans un voyage dont l'Océan marque les premiers pas: il semble qu'un abîme s'entr'ouvre derrière vous, et que le retour pourrait devenir à jamais impossible. (Part I, chapter 1. FD I, p. 654)

23. Gutwirth, p. 161.

24. Ils ont suppléé à l'intérêt des événements par l'intérêt des idées. (Part I, chapter 13. FD II, p. 29)

25. Un dessein toujours le même, toujours suivi, toujours progressif, dans l'histoire de l'homme. (Part III, Chapter 21. FD II, 222)

26. Susceptible d'éducation. Il y a des époques marquées pour les progrès de la pensée dans la route éternelle du temps. (Part IV, chapter 2. FD II, p. 227)

27. Les femmes cherchent à S'arranger comme un roman, et les hommes comme une histoire, mais le coeur humain est encore bien loin d'être pénétré dans ses relations les plus intimes. Une fois peut-être quelqu'un dira sincèrement tout ce qu'il a senti, et l'on sera tout étonné d'apprendre que la plupart des maximes et des observations sont erronées, et qu'il y a une âme inconnue dans le fond de celle qu'on raconte. (Part III, chapter 18. FD II, p. 217)

28. Je passerais pour insensée, si je n'avais pas le triste don d'observer moi-même ma folie. (Part XVII, chapter 2. FD I, p. 822)

29. Cet éloquent tableau d'un être en proie à une imagination plus forte que lui. (Part IV, chapter 6. FD II, p. 241)

30. Tout . . . semble un renversement de la nature, et nul n'a souffert sans croire qu'un grand désordre existait dans l'univers. (Part IV, chapter 6. FD II, 221)

31. "La Folle de Sénart" was discussed in chapter 1, above, and is found in the *Correspondance Littéraire* of June 1786.

32. Frank Paul Bowman, in *Le Christ romantique* (Geneva: Droz, 1973) discusses the concept of enthusiasm in Staël, especially in his chapter 7, p. 222.

33. Les temps héroiques, qui fondèrent la civilisation; le patriotisme, qui fit la gloire de l'antiquité; la chevalerie, qui fut la religion guerrière de l'Europe; et l'amour de la liberté, dont l'histoire a commencé vers l'époque de la réformation. (Part I, chapter 4. FD II, pp. 11–12)

34. Savent-ils de quel espoir l'on se sent pénétré, quand on croit manifester par le don de l'éloquence une vérité profonde, une vérité qui forme un généreux lien entre nous et toutes les âmes en sympathie avec la notre? (Part IV, chapter 12. FD II, p. 255)

35. Dès que l'homme se divise au dedans de lui-même, il ne sent plus la vie que comme un mal; et si, de tous les sentiments, l'enthousiasme est celui qui rend le plus heureux, c'est qu'il réunit plus qu'aucun autre toutes les forces de l'âme dans le même foyer. (Part IV, chapter 12. FD II, p. 254)

36. Balayé, pp. 41, 167.

37. La différence des langues, les limites naturelles, les souvenirs d'une même histoire, tout contribue à créer parmi les hommes ces grands individus qu'on appelle des nations; de certaines proportions leur sont necessaires. (Preface, FD II, p. 2)

38. Il ne faut chercher dans un peuple, comme dans un homme, que son trait caractéristique: tous les autres sont l'effet de mille hasards différents; celue-là seul constitue son être. (Part I, chapter 11. FD I, p. 253)

39. Chaque caractère est presqu'un monde nouveau pour qui sait observer avec finesse, et je ne connais dans la science du coeur humain aucune idée générale qui s'applique complètement aux exemples particuliers. (Part IV, chapter 6. FD II, p. 241)

40. L'esprit des Allemands et leur caractère paraissent n'avoir aucune communication ensemble: l'un ne peut souffrir de bornes, l'autre se soumet à tous les jougs; l'un est très entreprenant, l'autre très timide. (Part I, chapter 2. FD II, p. 9)

41. (Part I, chapter 16. FD II, pp. 31–34)

42. Si l'Allemagne était réunie à la France, il s'ensuivrait aussi que la France serait réunie à l'Allemagne, et les Français de Hambourg, comme les Français de Rome, altéreraient par degrés le caractère des compatriotes de Henri IV: les vaincus, à la longue, modifieraient les vainqueurs, et tous finiraient par y perdre. (Preface, FD II, p. 2)

43. Le grand avantage donc qu'on peut retirer de l'étude de la littérature allemande, c'est le mouvement d'émulation qu'elle donne; il faut y chercher des forces pour composer soi-même, plutôt que des ouvrages tout faits qu'on puisse transporter ailleurs. (Part II, chapter 29. FD II, p. 154)

44. (Part VIII, chapter 4. FD II, p. 733)

45. Beatrice Le Gall, "Le Paysage chez Madame de Staël," *Revue d'Histoire littéraire de la France* LXVI, no. 1 (January–March, 1966):43.

46. Le Gall, p. 50.

47. Maija Lehtonen, "Le Fleuve du temps et le fleuve de l'enfer: Thèmes et images dans *Corinne* de Madame de Staël," *Neuphilologische Mitteilungen* 69 (1967):107–28.

48. Ibid., (Part II, chapter 2. FD I, p. 665)

49. Il faut de l'harmonie dans les sentiments et de l'opposition dans les caractères, pour que l'amour naisse tout à la fois de la sympathie et de la diversité. (Part XVI, chapter 1. FD I, p. 805)

50. Le talent a besoin d'une indépendance intérieure que l'amour véritable ne permet jamais. (Part XV, chapter 9. FD I, p. 805)

51. Gutwirth, "Du Silence de Corinne et de sa parole," p. 82.

52. Gutwirth, "Forging a Vocation: Germaine de Staël on Fiction, Power, and Passion," p. 250.

53. Quand il y a, comme en Angleterre, de grands intérêts politiques à discuter, les sociétés d'hommes sont toujours animées par un noble intérêt commun: mais dans les pays où il n'y a pas de gouvernement représentatif, la présence des femmes est nécessaire pour maintenir tous les sentiments de délicatesse et de pureté sans lesquels l'amour du beau doit se perdre. L'influence des femmes est plus salutaire aux guerriers qu'aux citoyens; le règne de la loi se passe mieux d'elles que celui de l'honneur. (Part I, chapter 17. FD II, p. 35)

54. Gutwirth points out the influence of Montesquieu, p. 4.

55. Mary Ritter Beard, *Woman as Force in History: A Study in Traditions and Realities* (New York: Macmillan, 1949); Joan Kelly, "Early Feminist Theories and the 'querelle des femmes,' " in *Signs: A Journal of Women in Culture and Society* 8, no. 1 (August, 1982):4–28. The essays of Joan Kelly have recently been reprinted in *Women, History, and Theory: The Essays of Joan Kelly*, edited by Joan Kelly (Chicago: University of Chicago Press, 1984); Regine Pernoud, *La Femme aux temps des cathédrales* (Paris: Stock, 1980).

56. In her journals Staël was making similar statements about the Italians. For example she said, "Romans are like their statues, an arm, a foot which are ancient, and all the rest is modern." (Les Romains ressemblent à leur statue [sic], un bras d'antique, un pied, et tout le reste est moderne.) *Carnets de Voyage*, p. 174.

57. Mais leur empressement gracieux et complaisant pour le pouvoir fait de la peine, surtout quand on les aime, et qu'on les croit les defenseurs speculatifs les plus éclairés de la dignité humaine. (Part III, chapter 13. FD II, p. 209)

58. Ceux qui n'ont plus ni l'ambition, ni la possibilité de jouer un rôle dans le monde. (Part VI, chapter 3. FD I, p. 703)

59. La plus militaire de toutes, la plus jalouse de sa liberté dans les républiques du moyen âge, et, dans le seizième siècle, la plus illustre par les lettres, les sciences et les arts (Part VI, chapter 3. FD I, p. 703)

60. *Carnets de Voyage*, p. 229.

61. Le pays tout entier ressemble au séjour d'un grand peuple, qui depuis longtemps l'a quitté. (I, 1. FD II, p. 5)

62. Laurence Porter, "The Emergence of a Romantic Style: From *De la littérature* to *De l'Allemagne*," pp. 135–36.

63. La multitude et l'étendue des forets indiquent une civilisation encore nouvelle . . . . L'Allemagne offre encore quelques traces d'une nature non habitée . . . . Il semble que le temps marche là plus lentement qu'ailleurs. (Part I, chapter 1. FD II, p. 4)

64. In Madelyn Gutwirth, see especially her pages on "Italy, Art, Woman," pp. 209–15. Marie-Claire Vallois states, "All the Italian descriptions can be read as the development of a metaphorical portrait of Corinne, as an indirect way of talking about the oppressed woman," "Les Voi(es) de la Sibylle," p. 46. In "Madame de Staël, Napoleon, et l'indépendance italienne," *Revue des Sciences Humaines* 34, no. 133 (January–March, 1969), 47–56, Simone Balayé indicates that since unity and independence, in the face of the Napoleonic threat, were issues for Italy, Staël identified with that country.

65. Elles ne tiennent à la vie que par les liens du coeur et lorsqu'elles s'égarent, c'est encore par un sentiment qu'elles sont entraînées. Leur personnalité est toujours à deux. (Part I, chapter 3. FD II, p. 10)

66. La destinée des femmes reste toujours la même, c'est leur âme seule qui la fait, les circonstances politiques n'y influent en rien. (Part I, chapter 3. FD II, p. 10)

67. In *Carnets de Voyage* we read "Italians have the characters of women," p. 238. (Les Italiens ont des caractères de femme.)

68. Les femmes cultivent leur esprit, et le sentiment et la rêverie conservent dans leur âme l'image de tout ce qui est noble et beau. (Part I, chapter 3. FD II, p. 10)

69. Gutwirth, p. 191; Peterson, *The Determined Reader.*

70. Geneviève Gennari, in *Le Premier Voyage de Madame de Staël en Italie et la Genèse de Corinne* (Paris: Boivin, 1947) discusses Staël's defense of Italian literature, pp. 202–22. Franco Simone recounts and assesses Staël's treatment of this subject in his "La Littèrature italienne dans *Corinne*," in *Madame de Staël et l'Europe,* pp. 289–300.

71. In *Carnets de Voyage* Simone Balayé quotes "They are verbose because they have never had permission to say things." (Ils sont verbeux parce qu'il ne leur a jamais été permis de dire des choses.) p. 232.

72. La plupart de vos écrivains en prose, aujourd'hui, ont un langage si déclamatoire, si diffus, si abondant en superlatifs, qu'on dirait qu'ils écrivent tous de commande, avec des phrases reçues, et pour une nature de convention; ils ne se doutent pas qu'écrire c'est exprimer son caractère et sa pensée. (Part VII, chapter 1. FD I, p. 709)

73. Des circonstances malheureuses ayant privé l'Italie de son indépendance, on y a perdu tout intérêt pour la vérité, et souvent même la possibilité de la dire. Il en est résulté l'habitude de se complaire dans les mots, sans oser approcher des idées. Comme l'on était certain de ne pouvoir obtenir par ses écrits aucune influence sur les choses, on n'écrivait que pour montrer de l'esprit, ce qui est le plus sur moyen de finir bientôt par n'avoir pas même de l'esprit; car c'est en dirigeant ses efforts vers un objet noblement utile qu'on rencontre le plus d'idées. Quand les écrivains en prose ne peuvent influer en aucune genre sur le bonheur d'une nation, quand on n'écrit que pour briller, enfin quand c'est la route qui est le but, on se remplie en mille détours, mais l'on n'avance pas. (Part VII, chapter 1. FD I, p. 709)

74. Ce n'est pas que les Italiens n'étudient habilement les hommes avec lesquels ils ont affaire, et ne devinent plus finement que personne les pensées les plus secrètes; mais c'est comme esprit de conduite qu'ils ont ce talent, et ils n'ont point l'habitude d'en faire un usage littéraire. Peut-être même n'aimeraient-ils pas à généraliser leur découvertes, à publier leurs aperçus. Ils ont dans le caractère quelque chose de prudent et de dissimulé, qui leur conseille peut-être de ne pas mettre en dehors, par les comédies, ce qui leur sert à se guider dans les relations particulières, et de ne pas révéler par les fictions de l'esprit, ce qui peut être utile dans les circonstances de la vie réelle. (Part VII, chapter 2. FD I, pp. 711–12)

75. *Du caractère de Monsieur Necker et de sa vie privée.*

76. Nos poètes subtilisent et exagèrent le sentiment, tandis que le véritable caractère de la nature italienne, c'est une impression rapide et profonde, qui s'exprimeraient bien plutôt par des actions silencieuses et passionnées que par un ingénieux langage. En général, notre littérature exprime peu notre caractère et nos moeurs. Nous sommes une nation beaucoup trop modeste, je dirais presque trop humble, pour oser avoir des tragédies à nous, composées avec notre histoire, ou du moins caracterisées d'après nos propres sentiments. (Part VII, chapter 2. FD I, p. 713)

77. Lorsque j'ai commencé l'étude de l'allemand, il m'a semblé que j'entrais dans une sphère nouvelle. (Part II, chapter 31. FD II, p. 158)

78. La littérature de chaque pays découvre . . . une nouvelle sphère d'idées. C'est Charles-Quint lui-même qui a dit qu'un homme qui sait quatre langues vaut quatre hommes. (Part VII, chapter 1. FD I, p. 710)

79. Il est amusant de prononcer des mots étrangers: on s'écoute comme si c'était un autre qui parlât. (Part II, chapter 9. FD II, p. 57)

80. This work, originally published in 1809, can be found in FD II pp. 260–61.

81. Mais ceux qui ne sont pas sous le charme de sa présence analysent comme un auteur celui qu'il faut écouter en le lisant, car les défauts même de son style sont une grâce dans la conversation. Ce qui n'est pas toujours bien clair grammaticalement le devient par l'à propos de la conversation, la finesse du regard, l'inflexion de la voix, tout ce qui donne enfin à l'art de parler mille fois plus de ressources et de charmes qu'à celui d'écrire. (FD II, p. 260)

82. Lucia Omacini, introduction to *Des circonstances actuelles* . . . , p. LXVII.

83. Robert de Luppe quotes this account in his *Les Idées littéraires de Madame de Staël et l'héritage des lumieres, 1795–1800* (Paris: Klincksieck, 1971), 77.

84. Dans toutes les classes, en France, on sent le besoin de causer: la parole n'y est pas seulement, comme ailleurs, un moyen de se communiquer ses idées, ses sentiments et ses affaires, mais c'est un instrument dont on aime à jouer, et qui ranime les esprits, comme la musique chez quelques peuples, et les liqueurs forts chez quelques autres.

Le genre de bien-être que fait éprouver une conversation animée ne consiste pas précisément dans le sujet de cette conversation; les idees ni les connaissances qu'on peut y développer n'en sont pas le principal intérêt; c'est une certaine manière d'agir les uns sur les autres, de se faire plaisir réciproquement et avec rapidité, de parler aussitôt qu'on pense, de jouir à l'instant de soi-même, d'être applaudi sans travail, de manifester son esprit dans toutes les nuances par l'accent, le geste, le regard, enfin de produire à volonté comme une sorte d'électricité qui fait jaillir des étincelles, soulage les uns de l'excès même de leur vivicité, et réveille les autres d'une apathie pénible. (Part I, chapter 11. FD II, p. 22)

85. Ils n'entendent pas un mot sans en tirer une conséquence, et ne conçoivent pas qu'on puisse traiter la parole en art libéral, qui n'a ni but ni résultat si ce n'est le plaisir qu'on y trouve. L'esprit de converstion a quelquefois l'inconvénient d'altérer la sincérité du caractère; ce n'est pas une tromperie combinée, mais improvisée, si l'on peut s'exprimer ainsi. Les Français ont mis dans ce genre une gaieté qui les rend aimables, mais il n'en est pas moins certain que ce qu'il y a de plus sacré dans ce monde a été ébranlé par la grâce, du moins par celle qui n'attache de l'importance à rien, et tourne tout en ridicule. (Part I, chapter 11. FD II, p. 23)

86. Dans un pays où causer a tant d'influence, le bruit des paroles couvre souvent la voix de la conscience. (Part I, chapter 11. FD II, p. 25)

87. De la langue allemande, dans ses rapports avec l'esprit de conversation.

88. Les Allemands trouvent une sorte de charlatanisme dans l'expression brillante, et prennent plutôt l'expression abstraite, parce qu'elle est plus scrupuleuse, et s'approche davantage de l'essence même du vrai.

Sa construction traînante, ses consonnes multipliées, sa grammaire savante, ne lui permettent aucune grâce dans la souplesse; et l'on dirait qu'elle se roidit d'elle-même contre l'intention de celui qui la parle, dès qu'on veut la faire servir à trahir la vérité. (I, 12. FD II, pp. 27–28)

89. See Simone Balayé's article "Fonction romanesque de la musique dans *Corinne*."

90. La musique est un plaisir si passager, on le sent tellement s'échapper à mesure qu'on l'éprouve, qu'une impression mélancolique se mêle à la gaieté qu'elle cause; mais aussi, quand elle exprime la douleur, elle fait encore naître un sentiment doux . . . . Elle a l'heureuse impuissance d'exprimer aucun sentiment bas, aucun artifice, aucun mensonge. Le malheur même, dans le langage de la musique, est sans amertume, sans déchirement, sans irritation. (Part IX, chapter 2. FD I, p. 737)

91. Il n'y a plus de vide, il n'y a plus de silence autour de vous, la vie est remplie, le sang coule rapidement, vous sentez en vous-même le mouvement que donne une existence active, et vous n'avez point à craindre, au dehors de vous, les obstacles qu'elle redoute. (Part IX, chapter 2. FD I, p. 737)

92. Voila de la poésie! ce qui j'aime là dedans, c'est qu'il n'y a pas une idée. (In Necker de Saussure's *Notice*, FD III, pp. 48–49)

93. Aucune parole ne peut exprimer cette impression; car les paroles traînent apres les impressions primitives comme les traducteurs en prose sur les pas des poètes. (Part IX, chapter 2. FD I, p. 737)

94. Sans doute il n'y a pas dans nos poètes cette mélancolie profonde, cette connaissance du coeur humain qui caractérise les vôtres; mais ce genre de supériorité n'appartient-il pas plutôt aux écrivains philosophiques qu'aux

poètes? La mélodie brillante de l'italien convient mieux à l'éclat des objets extérieurs qu'à la méditation. Notre langue serait plus propre à peindre la fureur que la tristesse, parce que les sentiments réfléchis exigent des expressions plus métaphysiques, tandis que le désir de la vengeance anime l'imagination, et tourne la douleur en dehors. Cesarotti a fait la meilleure et la plus élégante traduction d'Ossian qu'il y ait; mais il semble, en le lisant, que les mots ont en eux-mêmes un air de fête qui contraste avec les idées sombres qu'ils rappellent. (Part VII, chapter 1. FD I, pp. 708–709)

95. On se laisse charmer par nos douces paroles, de "ruisseau limpide," de "campagne riante," d' "ombrage frais," comme par le murmure des eaux et la variété des couleurs. (Part VII, chapter 1. FD I, p. 709)

96. La mesure des vers, les rimes harmonieuses, ces terminaisons rapides, . . . imitent quelquefois les pas légers de la danse; quelquefois des tons plus graves rappellent le bruit de l'orage ou l'éclat des armes. (Part VII, chapter 1. FD I, p. 709)

97. Enfin notre poésie est une merveille de l'imagination, il ne faut y chercher que ses plaisirs sous toutes les formes. (Part VII, chapter 1. FD I, p. 709)

98. Gutwirth, pp. 272–78.

99. Je ne veux, à cet egard, ni le blamer ni l'absoudre. (Part XX, chapter 5. FD I, p. 863)

100. Gilbert and Gubar, pp. 539–49.

7. *The Right to Sincerity*

1. Gutwirth, p. 41.

2. J'ai bien envie d'avoir une grande table, il me semble que j'en ai le droit à présent. (FD III, p. 47)

3. For discussions of Staël's theatrical activities, see "Le théâtre de Madame de Staël au Moland," Jean-Daniel Candaux, *Cahiers Staëliens*, n.s., no. 14, (September 1972):19–32, and "Pour un répertoir des rôles et des représentations de Madame de Staël," *Cahiers Staëliens*, n.s., no. 19 (December 1979):79–92. The plays in question are "Le Capitaine Kernadec, ou Sept Années en un jour," "La Signora Fantastici," "Sappho," and "Le Mannequin."

4. Madelyn Gutwirth discusses Staël's plays, pp. 262–66.

5. J'attachais un grand prix à ce livre, que je croyais propre à faire connaître des idées nouvelles en France. In *Dix Années d'Exil.* (Part II, chapter 1. FD III, p. 365)

6. Je m'étais flatté d'un succès honorable. (Part II, chapter 1. FD III, p. 366)

7. Mon existence littéraire, (Part II, chapter 2. FD III, p. 368)

8. *Réflexions sur le suicide.* This work is found out of its chronological order in FD I, pp. 176–96.

9. For treatments of the theme of suicide in Staël, see Jean-Albert Bédé, "Madame de Staël, Rousseau, et le Suicide," *Revue d'Histoire Littéraire de la France* 66, no. 1 (1966):52–70; and Jean Starobinski, "Suicide et mélancolie chez Madame de Staël," in *Madame de Staël et l'Europe*, 242–52. (Paris: Klincksieck, 1970)

10. J'ai loué l'acte du suicide dans mon ouvrage sur *De l'Influence des Passions*, et je me suis toujours repentie depuis de cette parole inconsidérée. (FD I, p. 177)

11. An easily available text of this book is *Dix années d'exil*, with introduction and notes by Simone Balayé, (Paris: Bibliothèque 10/18, 1966). An English translation is *Ten Years of Exile*, translated by Doris Beik, with an introduction by Peter Gay (New York: Saturday Review Press, 1972).

12. Je me consolais de ce grand voyage en pensant à un poème sur Richard Coeur de Lion, que je me propose d'écrire, si ma vie et ma santé y suffisent. (Part II, chapter 9. FD III, p. 390)

13. Les moeurs et la nature de l'Orient. (FD II, p. 390)

14. Une grande époque de l'histoire anglaise, celle où l'enthousiasme des croisades a fait place à l'enthousiasme de la liberté. (FD II, p. 390)

15. Simone Balayé underscores the importance of this work and this trip when she points out that Staël continued to project both as late as 1816, *Carnets de Voyage*, p. 409.

16. Balayé, p. 212.

17. Il y a dans cette manière d'être un peu de rapport avec les sauvages; mais il me semble que maintenant les nations européennes n'ont de vigueur que quand elles sont ou ce qu'elle appelle barbares, c'est à dire non éclairées, ou libres; mais ces nations, qui n'ont appris de la civilisation que l'indifférence pour tel ou tel joug, à condition que leur coin du feu n'en soit pas troublé; ces nations qui n'ont appris de la civilisation que l'art d'expliquer la puissance et de raisonner la servitude, sont faites pour être vaincues. (Part II, chapter 13. FD III, p. 394)

18. Les Russes n'ont pas pris part aux temps de chevalerie; ils ne se sont pas mêlés des croisades . . . . Les Russes, dans les rapports de la société, si nouveaux pour eux, ne se signalent point par l'esprit de chevalerie, tel que les peuples de l'Occident le conçoivent; mais ils se sont toujours montrés terribles contre leurs ennemis. (Part II, chapter 13 FD III, pp. 396–97)

19. The critical edition of this work is *Considérations sur la révolution française*, edited by Jacques Godechot. (Paris: Tallandier, 1984).

20. J'avais d'abord commencé cet ouvrage avec l'intention de le borner à l'examen des actes et des écrits politiques de mon père. Mais, en avancant dans mon travail, j'ai été conduite par le suject même à retracer, d'une part, les principaux événements de la révolution française, et à présenter, de l'autre, le tableau de l'Angleterre, comme une justification de l'opinion de M. Necker, relativement aux institutions politiques de ce pays. Mon plan s'étant

agrandi, il m'a semblé que je devais changer de titre, quoique je n'eusse pas changé d'objet. Avertissement de l'auteur. (FD III, p. 55)

21. For studies of women in the French revolution, see Jane Abray, "Feminism in the French Revolution," *American Historical Review* 80, no. 1 (February 1975):43–62 and related articles in *Becoming Visible: Women in European History*, edited by Renate Bridenthal and Claudia Koontz (Boston: Houghton Mifflin, 1977).

22. John Cleary, "Madame de Staël, Rousseau, and Mary Wollstonecraft," *Romance Notes* 21, no. 3 (Spring 1981):329–33.

23. One may usefully consult Gruffed E. Gwynne, *Madame de Staël et la révolution française* (Paris: Nizet, 1969).

24. Henri Guillemin covers Staël with ridicule for this manner of self-presentation in an excellent example of misogynist history, *Madame de Staël et Napoléon ou Germaine et le Caïd ingrat*, (Bienne, Suisse: Editions du Panorama, 1966).

25. Watson, p. 113.

26. Peut-être des circonstances particulières servent-elles à faire mieux connaître l'esprit et le caractère des temps qu'on veut décrire. (FD III, p. 55)

27. Robert Escarpit, in *L'Angleterre dans l'oeuvre de Madame de Staël* (Paris: Didier, 1954), notes this absence and attempts to reconstruct the *On England* Staël would have written, pp. 13–15.

28. A-t-il eu raison d'effacer, autant qu'il le pouvait, les moeurs orientales du sein de sa nation? Devait-il placer sa capitale au nord et à l'extrémité de son empire? (FD III, 397; part 1, chapter 14)

29. Il y a de la patience et de l'activité dans cette nation, de la gaieté et de la mélancolie. On y voit réunis les contrastes les plus frappants, et c'est ce qui peut en faire présager de grandes choses. (Part II, chapter 11. FD III, p. 391)

30. La nature, aux environs de Petersbourg, a l'air d'un ennemi qui se ressaisit de ses droits dès que l'homme cesse un moment de lutter contre lui. (Part II, chapter 16. FD III, p. 400)

31. Les Russes habitants de Petersbourg ont l'air d'un peuple du Midi condamné à vivre au nord. (Part II, chapter 16. FD III, p. 400)

32. Les gens du peuple . . . transportent les moeurs des Lazzaronis de Naples au soixantième degré latitude. (Part II, chapter 16. FD III, p. 400)

33. On se rappelait Rome en voyant Moscou; non assurément que les monuments y fussent du même style, mais parce que le mélange de la campagne solitaire et des palais magnifiques, la grandeur de la ville et le nombre infini des temples, donnent à la Rome asiatique quelques rapports avec la Rome europeénne. (Part II, chapter 14. FD III, p. 396)

34. Les Russes ont, selon moi, beaucoup plus de rapports avec les peuples du Midi, ou plutôt de l'Orient, qu'avec ceux du Nord. Ce qu'ils ont d'européen tient aux manières de la cour, les mêmes dans tous les pays; mais leur nature est orientale. . . . On se sent, en Russie, à la porte d'une autre

terre, près de cet Orient d'où sont sorties tant de croyances religieuses, et qui renferme encore dans son sein d'incroyables trésors de persévérance et de réflexion. (Part II, chapter 11. FD, p. 392)

35. Tous ces noms de pays étrangers, de nations qui ne sont presque plus européennes, réveillent singulièrement l'imagination. II, 10. FD III, p. 392.

36. La langue esclavonne est singulierement retentissante; je dirais presqu'elle a quelque chose de métallique; on croit entendre frapper l'airain quand les Russes prononcent de certaines lettres de leur langue, tout à fait différentes de celles dont se composent les dialectes de l'Occident. (Part II, chapter 12. FD III, p. 393)

37. Leur nature n'est point changée par la civilisation rapide que Pierre I leur a donnée; elle n'a, jusqu'à présent, formé que leurs manières; heureusement pour eux, ils sont toujours ce que nous appelons barbares, c'est à dire, conduits par un instinct souvent généreux, toujours involontaire, qui n'admet la réflexion que dans le choix des moyens, et non dans l'examen du but: je dis heureusement pour eux, non que je prétende vanter la barbarie mais je désigne par ce nom une certaine énergie primitive qui peut seule remplacer dans les nations la force concentrée de la liberté. (Part II, chapter 14. FD III, p. 398)

38. Ils sont plus capables de superstition que d'émotion: la superstition se rapporte à cette vie, et la religion à l'autre; la superstition se lie à la fatalité, et la religion à la vertu; c'est par la vivacité des désirs terrestres qu'on devient superstitieux, et c'est, au contraire, par le sacrifice de ces mêmes désirs qu'on est religieux. (Part II, chapter 16. FD III, p. 401)

39. Maria Lehtonen's documentation of images of specters and phantoms strongly suggests this superstition, pp. 103–5.

40. On éprouve je ne sais quel effroi superstitieux qui porte à considérer tous les honnêtes gens comme des victimes. (Part II, chapter, 20, FD III, p. 411)

41. La douceur et l'éclat des sons de leur langue se fait remarquer par ceux même qui ne la comprennent pas; elle doit être très propre à la musique et à la poésie . . . Leurs ouvrages, jusqu'à présent, sont composés, pour ainsi dire, du bout des lèvres, et jamais une nation si véhémente ne peut être remuée par de si grêles accords. (Part II, chapter 14. FD III, p. 398)

42. J'avais oublié la guerre dont dépendait le sort de l'Europe, (Part II, chapter 19. FD III, p. 407)

43. On finit par découvrir le vrai; mais l'habitude de se taire est telle parmi les courtisans russes, qu'ils dissimulent la veille ce qui doit être connue le lendemain. (Part II, chapter 19. FD III, p. 407)

44. Les raffinements de la civilisation altèrent en tout pays la sincérité du caractère; mais quand le souverain a le pouvoir illimité d'exiler, d'emprisonner, d'envoyer en Sibérie, etc., etc., sa puissance est quelque chose de trop fort pour la nature humaine. On aurait pu rencontrer des hommes assez fiers

pour dédaigner la faveur, mais il faut de l'héroïsme pour braver la persécution, et l'héroïsme ne peut être une qualité universelle. (Part II, chapter 19, FD III, p. 406)

45. Je ne pouvais pas me dissimuler que je n'étais pas une personne courageuse; j'ai de la hardiesses dans l'imagination mais de la timidité dans le caractère. (Part II, chapter 5. FD III, p. 376)

46. Les Anglais, avec cette admirable droiture qui distingue toutes leurs actions, rendent compte aussi véridiquement de leurs revers que de leurs succès, et l'enthousiasme se soutient, chez eux, par la vérité, quelqu'elle soit. (Part II, chapter 14. FD III, p. 398)

47. Les Anglais donnent dans leurs feuilles publiques le compte le plus exact, homme par homme, des blessés, des prisonniers et des tués dans chaque affaire; noble candeur d'un gouvernement qui est aussi sincère envers la nation qu'envers son monarque. (Part II, chapter 19. FD III, p. 408)

48. Ne trouvez-vous pas que le préfet déclare ses opinions avec beaucoup de franchise? . . . Oui, il dit avec sincérité qu'il est dévoué à l'homme puissant; il dit avec courage qu'il est du parti le plus fort; je ne sens pas bien le mérite d'un tel aveu. (Part II, chapter 5, FD III, p. 375)

49. Le roi fut conduit à Paris, pour adopter à l'Hôtel de Ville la révolution qui venait d'avoir lieu contre son pouvoir. Son calme religieux lui conserva toujours de la dignité personnelle, dans cette circonstance comme dans toutes les suivantes; mais son autorité n'existait plus; . . . Les hommages apparents qu'on rend alors au souverain détrôné révoltent les caractères généreux, et jamais la liberté ne peut s'établir par la fausse situation du monarque ou du peuple: chacun doit être dans ses droits pour être dans sa sincérité. (FD III, p. 109)

50. Lucia Omacini, "Pour une typologie du discours narratif de Madame de Staël," p. 386.

51. *De l'esprit des traductions.* This essay is found in FD II, pp. 294–97.

52. In a letter to Benjamin Constant, quoted by Simone Balayé, *Carnets de Voyage,* p. 412. "Les débris absorbent les ruines." "L'habitude de se taire ou de parler de commande a fait des progrès qui ne laissent rien à qui veut commander."

53. Balayé, *Carnets de Voyage*, p. 432.

8 Conclusion

1. "Madame de Staël et Rousseau," *Preuves* 190 (December 1966):36.

2. See especially Monique Wittig and Sande Zeig, *Brouillon pour un dictionnaire des amantes* (Paris: Grasset, 1976) or in English *Lesbians Peoples: Material for a Dictionary* (New York: Avon, 1979); and Mary Daly, *Pure Lust: Elemental Feminist Philosophy (Boston: Beacon Press, 1984)*.

Bibliography

Works of Germaine de Staël

Considérations sur la révolution française. Présentées et annotées par Jacques Godechot. Paris: Tallandier, 1984.

Corinne, ou l'Italie. Une édition féministe de Claudine Herrmann. Paris: des femmes, 1979.

Corinne, or Italy. Translated and with an introduction by Avriel Goldberger. New Brunswick, NJ: Rutgers University Press, 1987.

Correspondance Générale. Edited by Beatrice W. Jasinski. Paris: Pauvert, 1972–1978.

De la littérature considérée dans ses rapports avec les institutions sociales. Edited by Paul van Tieghem. Geneva: Droz, 1959.

De l'Allemagne. With an introduction by Simone Balayé. Paris: Garnier-Flammarion, 1968.

Delphine. Une édition féministe de Claudine Herrmann. Paris: des femmes, 1981.

Des circonstances actuelles qui peuvent terminer la révolution et des principes qui doivent fonder la république en France. Edited by Lucia Omacini. Geneva: Droz, 1979.

Dix Années d'Exil. With an introduction by Simone Balayé. Paris: Bibliothèque 10/18, 1966.

"La Folle de Sénart," In *Correspondance Littéraire, Philosophique, et Critique par Grimm and Diderot*. Vol 2, pp. 519–24. Paris: Buisson, 1813.

"Mon Journal." In *Occident et Cahiers Staeliëns* 1 no. 3/4, (October 1932). Edited by Simone Balayé in *Cahiers Staeliëns* 28 (1980):55–79.

Oeuvres Complètes de Madame la Baronne de Staël-Holstein. 3 vols. Paris: Firmin Didot, 1861.

Oeuvres Complètes de Madame la Baronne de Staël, publiées par son fils. 20 vols. Paris: Treuttel et Wurtz, 1820–1821.

Ten Years of Exile. Translated by Doris Beik, with an introduction by Peter Gay. New York: Saturday Review Press, 1972.

Secondary Sources

Abel, Elizabeth, ed. *Writing and Sexual Difference*. Chicago: University of Chicago Press, 1982.

Abray, Jane. "Feminism in the French Revolution." *American Historical Review* 80, no. 1 (February, 1975):43–62.

d'Andlau, Beatrix. *La Jeunesse de Madame de Staël, de 1766 à 1789, avec des documents inédits*. Geneva: Droz, 1970.

Balayé, Simone. "Absence, exil, voyages." In *Madame de Staël et l'Europe*, pp. 289–300. Paris: Klincksieck, 1970.

———. "A propos du Préromantisme: Continuité ou Rupture chez Madame de Staël." *Le Préromantisme: Hypothèque ou Hypothése*. Edited by Paul Viallaneix, pp. 153–168. Paris: Klincksieck, 1975.

———. "Corinne et la ville italienne, ou l'espace extérieur et l'impasse intérieur." *Mélanges Offerts à la mémoire de Franco Simone*. (1984):33–50.

———. "Fonction romanesque de la musique et des sons dans *Corinne*." *Romantisme* 3 (1972):23–24.

———. *Les Carnets de Voyage de Madame de Staël, contribution à la genèse de ses oeuvres*. Geneva: Droz, 1971.

———. *Madame de Staël: Lumiéres et Liberté*. Paris: Klincksieck, 1979.

———. "Madame de Staël, Napoléon, et l'indépendance italienne." *Revue des sciences humaines* 34, (January–March 1969):47–56.

Beard, Mary Ritter. *Woman as force in history: A study in traditions and realities*. New York: Macmillan, 1949.

Bédé, Jean-Albert. "Madame de Staël et les mots." In *Madame de Staël et l'Europe*, 317–29. Paris: Klincksieck, 1971.

———. "Madame de Staël, Rousseau, et le Suicide." *Revue d'Histoire Littéraire de la France* 66, (1966):52–70.

Borowitz, Hélène. "The Unconfessed Précieuse: Madame de Staël's Debt to Mademoiselle de Scudéry." *Nineteenth Century French Studies* 1–2 (Fall-Winter, 1982):32–59.

Bowman, Frank Paul. *Le Christ Romantique*. Geneva: Droz, 1973.

Bridental, Renate, and Claudia Koontz, eds. *Becoming Visible: Women in European History*. Boston: Houghton Mifflin, 1977.

Butler, Marilyn, and Christina Colvin. "Maria Edgeworth et *Delphine*." *Cahiers Staeliëns* 26–27 (1979):77–91.

Candaux, Jean-Daniel. "Le théâtre de Madame de Staël au Molard (1805–1806)." *Cahiers Staëliens* 14 (September, 1972):19–32.

Causse, E. *Madame de Staël et l'Education*. Paris, 1930.

Chodorow, Nancy. *The Reproduction of Mothering: Psychoanalysis and the Sociology of Gender*. Berkeley: University of California Press, 1967.

Cleary, John. "Madame de Staël, Rousseau, and Mary Wollstonecraft." *Romance Notes* 21 no. 3 (Spring, 1981):329–33.

Corbaz, André. *Madame Necker: Humble vaudoise et grande dame*. Paris: Payot, 1945.

Diesbach, Ghislain de. *Madame de Staël*. Paris: Librairie Académique Perrin, 1984.

Escarpit, Robert. *L'Angleterre dans l'oeuvre de Madame de Staël*. Paris: Didier, 1954.

Gardiner, Judith Kegan. "On Female Identity and Writing by Women." In *Writing and Sexual Difference* edited by Elizabeth Abel, 177–91. Chicago: University of Chicago Press, 1982.

Gennari, Geneviève. *Le Premier Voyage de Madame de Staël en Italie et la Genèse de Corinne*. Paris: Boivin, 1947.

Gilbert, Sandra, and Susan Gubar. *The Madwoman in the Attic: The Woman Writer and the Nineteenth-Century Imagination*. New Haven and London: Yale University Press, 1979.

Gilligan, Nancy. *In a Different Voice: Psychological Theory and Women's Development*. Cambridge, MA: Harvard University Press, 1982.

Grange, Henri. *Les Idées de Necker*. Paris: Klincksieck. 1894.

Guillemin, Henri. *Madame de Staël et Napoléon ou Germaine et le Caïd Ingrat*. Bienne: Editions du Panorama, 1966.

Gutwirth, Madelyn. "Corinne et l'esthétique du camée." In *Le Préromantisme: Hypothèque ou Hypothèse*. Edited by Paul Viallaneix, 153–68. Paris: Klincksieck, 1979.

———. "La *Delphine* de Madame de Staël: Femme, Révolution, et Mode Epistolaire." *Cahiers Staeliëns* 26–27 (1979):151–65.

———. "Forging a Vocation: Germaine de Staël on Fiction, Power, and Passion." *Bulletin of Research in the Humanities* 86 no. 3 (1983–1985):242–54.

———. *Madame de Staël, Novelist: The Emergence of the Artist as Woman*. Urbana: University of Illinois Press, 1978.

———. "Madame de Staël, Rousseau, and the Woman Question." *Publications of the Modern Language Association* 86, (January 1971):100–109.

Gwynne, Guffred. *Madame de Staël et la révolution française*. Paris: Nizet. 1969.

Hamilton, James F. "Madame de Staël, Partisan of Rousseau or Voltaire." *Studies on Voltaire and the Eighteenth Century* 106 (1973):253–65.

———. "Structural Polarity in Madame de Staël's *De la Littérature*." *French Review* 50 (April 1977):706–712.

Hoffman, Paul. *La Femme dans la Pensée des Lumières*. Paris: 1977.

Huber, Catherine. "Notes sur l'enfance de Mme de Staël," in *Occident et Cahier Staeliëns* 2, no. 1 (June 30, 1933):41–47; 2, no. 2 (March, 1934):140–46.

Jacobus, Mary. "The Question of Language: Men of Maxims and *The Mill on the Floss*." In *Writing and Sexual Difference*. Edited by Elizabeth Abel, 37–52. Chicago: University of Chicago Press, 1982.

Kelly, Joan. "Early Feminist Theory and the 'querelle des femmes.'" *Signs: A Journal of Women in Culture and Society* (August 1982):4–28. Reprinted in *The Essays of Joan Kelly*, ed. Joan Kelly, pp. 65–109 Chicago: University of Chicago Press, 1984.

Kitchen, Joanne. "La littérature et les femmes selon Madame de Staël." In *Benjamin Constant, Madame de Staël, et le Groupe de Coppet*, edited by Etienne Hofman, 401–425. Oxford: The Voltaire Foundation and Lausanne: Institut Benjamin Constant, 1980.

Lanser, Susan Sniader, and Evelyn Torton Beck. "[Why] are there no great women critics and what difference does it make?" In *The Prism of Sex: Essays in the Sociology of Knowledge*, ed. Julia A. Sherman and Evelyn Torton Beck, 79–91. Madison: University of Wisconsin Press, 1979.

Larg, David Glass. *Madame de Staël: La Vie dans l'Oeuvre*. Paris: Champion, 1924.

Le Gall, Béatrice. "Le Paysage chez Madame de Staël." *Revue d'Histoire littéraire de la France* 66, no. 1 (January–March, 1966):38–51.

Lehtonen, Maija. "Le Fleuve du temps et le fleuve de l'enfer: Thèmes et images dans *Corinne* de Madame de Staël." *Neuphilologische Mitteilungen* 69. (1967):107–28.

Man, Paul de. "Madame de Staël et Rousseau." *Preuves* 190 (December 1966):35–41.

Marks, Elaine, and Isabelle de Courtivron. *New French Feminisms*. Amherst: University of Massachusetts Press, 1980.

Miller, Nancy K. "The Text's Heroine: A Feminist Critic and Her Fictions." *Diacritics* 12 no 2 (Summer 1982):49–53.

———. "Emphasis Added: Plots and Plausibilities in Women's Fiction." *Publications of the Modern Language Association* 96, no 1 (January 1981):41–48. Also in *Feminist Criticism: Essays on Women, Literature, and Theory*. Edited by Elaine Showalter, 339–60. New York: Pantheon, 1985.

Moers, Ellen. *Literary Women*. New York: Anchor, 1977.

Moi, Toril. *Sexual/Textual Politics: Feminist Literary Theory*. New York: Methuen, 1985.

Mortier, Roland. "Madame de Staël et l'Héritage des Lumières." In his *Clartés et ombres du siècle des lumières*, pp. 125–33, Geneva: Droz, 1969.

Necker, Suzanne Curchod. *Mélanges extraits des manuscrits de Madame Necker*. Paris: Pougens, 1798.

———. *Nouveaux Mélanges extraits des manuscrits de Madame Necker*. Paris: Pougens, 1801.

———. *Réflexions sur le Divorce*. 1783. Reprint. Lausanne, 1815.

Necker de Saussure, Albertine de. "Notice sur le caractère et les écrits de madame de Staël," in *Oeuvres Complètes*, vol. III, pp. 2–54. Paris: Firmin-Didot, 1861.

Omacini, Lucia. "Pour une typologie du discours staëlien: Les procédés de persuasion." In *Benjamin Constant, Madame de Staël, et le Groupe et Coppet*. Ed. Etienne Hofman, 362–81. Oxford: The Voltaire Foundation; Lausanne: Institut Benjamin Constant, 1982.

Pernoud, Régine. *La Femme aux temps des cathédrales*. Paris: Stock, 1980.

Peterson, Carol. *The Determined Reader: Gender and Culture in the Novel from Napoleon to Victoria*. New Brunswick, NJ: Rutgers University Press, 1985.

Pizzorusso, Arnaldo. "Madame de Staël et *L'Essai sur les Fictions*. In *Madame de Staël et l'Europe*. Paris: Klincksieck, 1971, pp. 273–285.

Porter, Laurence M. "The Emergence of a Romantic Style: From *De la Littérature* to *De l'Allemagne*." In *Authors and Their Centuries*. Edited by Philip Crant, 129–42. French Literature Series, no. 1. Columbia: University of South Carolina Press, 1974.

Poulet, Georges. "*Corinne* et *Adolphe*: Deux roman conjuguées." *Revue d'Histoire Littéraire de la France* 4 (July–August, 1978):586–98.

———. *Etudes sur le temps humain*. 1949. Reprint. Paris: Plon, 1956.

———. "La pensée critique de Madame de Staël." *Preuves* 190 (December 1966):27–35.

Rougemont, Martine de. "L'Activité théâtrale dans le Groupe de Coppet: La dramaturgie et le jeu." In *Le Groupe de Coppet*, edited by Simone Balayé and Jean-Daniel Candaux, 269–79. Paris: Champion; Geneva: Slatkine, 1977.

Showalter, Elaine, ed. *The New Feminist Criticism: Essays on Women, Literature and Theory*. New York: Pantheon, 1985.

Simone, Franco. "La littérature italienne dans *Corinne*." *Madame de Staël et l'Europe*. Paris: Klincksieck, 1970, pp. 289–300.

Starobinski, Jean. "Critique et principe d'autorité (Madame de Staël et Rousseau)," in *Le Préromantisme: Hypothèque ou Hypothèse*. Edited by Paul Viallaneix, 324–43. (Actes et Colloques 18).

———. "Suicide et mélancolie chez Madame de Staël." In *Madame de Staël et l'Europe*, pp. 242–52. Paris: Klincksieck, 1970.

Swallow, Noreen J. "The Weapon of Personality: A Review of Sexist Criticism of Madame de Staël, 1785–1975." *Atlantis* 8, no. 1 (Fall/Autumn 1982):79.

Vallois, Marie Claire. "Les Voi(es) de la Sibylle: Aphasie et discours féminin chez Madame de Staël." *Stanford French Review* 6, no 1 (Spring 1982):38–52.

Watson, Barbara. "On Power and the Literary Text." *Signs: A Journal of Women in Culture and Society* 1 no. 1 (Autumn 1975):111–24.

West, Rebecca., Review of Christopher Herold, *Madame de Staël: Mistress to an Age, Encounter* 18, no. 1 (July 1959):67–70.
Winegarten, Renée. *Madame de Staël.* London: Berg Publishers, 1985.
Woolf, Virginia. *A Room of One's Own.* London: Hogarth Press, 1929. Reprint. New York: Harcourt, Brace, World, 1963.

Index

Charlotte Hogsett has published articles on eighteenth-century French literature in *Studies on Voltaire and the Eighteenth Century* and in *Eighteenth Century Studies*, and on women's studies in *Feminist Visions: Toward a Transformation of the Liberal Arts Curriculum*, edited by Diane L. Fowlkes and Charlotte S. McClure.

DATE DUE
